Y0-DCU-944

THIS ITEM HAS BEEN
DISCARDED BY THE
UNIVERSITY
OF PUGET SOUND
COLLINS MEMORIAL LIBRARY

THE Future
OF Educational
Studies

COUNTERPOINTS

Studies in the
Postmodern Theory of Education

Joe L. Kincheloe and Shirley R. Steinberg
General Editors

Vol. 218

PETER LANG
New York • Washington, D.C./Baltimore • Bern
Frankfurt am Main • Berlin • Brussels • Vienna • Oxford

THE Future OF Educational Studies

EDITED BY
George Noblit and Beth Hatt-Echeverria

PETER LANG
New York • Washington, D.C./Baltimore • Bern
Frankfurt am Main • Berlin • Brussels • Vienna • Oxford

Library of Congress Cataloging-in-Publication Data

The future of educational studies / edited by George Noblit
and Beth Hatt-Echeverria.
p. cm. — (Counterpoints; vol. 218)
Includes bibliographical references.
1. Education—United States—Philosophy. I. Noblit, George W.
II. Hatt-Echeverria, Beth. III. Counterpoints (New York, N.Y.); v. 218.
LB14.7 .F895   370′.973—dc21   2001050632
ISBN 0-8204-5799-X
ISSN 1058-1634

Die Deutsche Bibliothek-CIP-Einheitsaufnahme

The future of educational studies / ed by: George Noblit....
–New York; Washington, D.C./Baltimore; Bern;
Frankfurt am Main; Berlin; Brussels; Vienna; Oxford: Lang.
(Counterpoints; Vol. 218)
ISBN 0-8204-5799-X

√596

Cover photo by Steven Paul Whitsitt Photography, Chapel Hill, North Carolina
Cover design by Lisa Barfield

The paper in this book meets the guidelines for permanence and durability
of the Committee on Production Guidelines for Book Longevity
of the Council of Library Resources.

∞

© 2003 Peter Lang Publishing, Inc., New York
275 Seventh Avenue, 28th Floor, New York, NY 10001
www.peterlangusa.com

All rights reserved.
Reprint or reproduction, even partially, in all forms such as microfilm,
xerography, microfiche, microcard, and offset strictly prohibited.

Printed in the United States of America

Table of Contents

Acknowledgments

This volume is the product of many collaborations. Initially, this book was a product of discussions of the Executive Council of the American Educational Studies Association (AESA). To the Executive Council, it was apparent that scholarship in Educational Studies had changed in dramatic ways in the last decade of the twentieth century. Our scholarship was less centered in the various academic disciplines and more informed by the politics of identity and culture. It was thought to be important to collect this new scholarship in one place since scholarship in Educational Studies is published in many different journals and books. For AESA, this book provides an opportunity to see what these changes look like at this point in time. We hope it will lead both to critiques and to a sense of productive lines of thought. We are indebted to AESA's Executive Council for fostering this idea.

The second collaboration has been with the authors of the chapters. The goal was to have as many authors as possible and to restrict the length of their contributions. This required extensive negotiations. The authors have been responsive and patient in working with us, and we are very grateful.

Finally, the book would not have been possible without the support of colleagues, friends, and family. Completing this book meant that we were absent from many events and interactions. We thank them for tolerating the many absences of presence and/or mind.

Grateful acknowledgment is hereby made to XCP: Cross Cultural Poetics for permission to reprint "Needles and Pins" by Mary E. Weems.

Chapter One

Introduction: The Future of Educational Studies in the United States

George W. Noblit
Beth Hatt-Echeverria

Educational studies in the United States is in the midst of generational and intellectual transformations. The field is becoming younger and is reducing the reverence felt for the academic disciplines that had been central to the field's claim to distinctiveness in education and rigor in the wider academy. The editors of this volume and authors of this chapter reflect these transformations. George is an experienced scholar and a past president of the American Educational Studies Association (AESA). Beth is an advanced Ph.D. student in social foundations and a recent member of, and presenter at, AESA. George was prepared as a specialist in the discipline of sociology. Beth is participating in a more multidisciplinary program, but is of the current generation of women who see their work as part of working out the politics of identity in which the disciplines are seen as problematic tools.

This trajectory of educational studies is especially troubling to those who fought to legitimate the field, which was termed social foundations early in its history and later became educational studies when the foundational metaphor broke down, yet both terms linger, and thus, are used interchangeably in this book. George's generation sees the centering of identity as in some ways a rejection of all they have struggled to accomplish, and this development certainly threatens the status of this generation as the senior scholars they had envisioned for themselves. Beth's generation has come to see the disciplines as a privileging of objectivity and take the term literally. For this generation, the disciplines control who is to be regarded as a scholar and what is to be counted as knowledge. In this postmodern world, the grand narratives of the academic disciplines have imploded while knowledge and understanding are to be established partially and discursively. That is, any claim to knowing must be earned and argued.

This book is an attempt to depict educational studies at this particular point in time. Ironically, the transformations in educational studies are coming of age in a new millennium. This in itself is fortuitous even if the new millennium in itself is of little significance, reflecting primarily how we have constructed time and how we invest meaning into our structured conceptions of time. Yet it is common to ritually invest in temporal beginnings and endings such as the New Year and the new millennium. These moments afford time for reflection on the past and consideration of desired futures. We are appropriating this ritual opportunity to think about a particular field of intellectual and practical endeavor, educational studies in the United States, because its transformations coincide with the end of one century and beginning of a new century.

It is common practice to approach such ritual reconsiderations by commissioning a set of elite scholars to pontificate on their view of the world. Yet educational studies, particularly as embodied in AESA, has had an explicit agenda of providing voice for educational scholars who have been silenced in the educational research dialogue dominated by disciplines, whites, men, and heterosexuals.

AESA was created to promote scholarship that was broadly interdisciplinary and positional. By design, the scholarship in educational studies is normative. Moral concerns about equity and justice drive much of our work. The accomplishments on these fronts are, of course, partial and incomplete. Yet for educational studies, commissioning a panel of regarded scholars is both inappropriate to the norms of our field and misrepresents the field. AESA is now a young and diverse group of intellectuals. It is also no longer dominated by a few scholars, if it ever was. Thus, this millennial volume is different from many.

The Book

As this volume reveals, educational studies now centers identity in new, provocative, and intellectually demanding ways. Centering identity creates several possibilities for the futures of educational studies.

The chapters in this volume are written by a variety of scholars with different experiences, perspectives, generations, and identities. They were selected from papers presented at the American Educational Studies Association's annual meeting in 1999. The themes of this volume were created from the papers submitted. We encouraged a set of papers that embodied these themes and asked the authors to rewrite their papers to be included in this volume. The authors did not rewrite to fit this volume, but rather rewrote to express their ideas as well as they could in very limited space. These papers, in turn, were peer-reviewed by members of AESA. As a result, the papers were written a third time to respond to criticisms.

Since anticipating the future for educational studies has many possibilities, we wished to include a number of chapters. In the end, the nearly 200 presentations at AESA were winnowed to less than 1% of the presentations. This number was necessary to capture the possibilities for the future of educational studies, but it required that the chapters be short and to the point. The future that we see for educational studies in the United States has at least four possibilities and each is represented as a section in this volume.

However, a caveat is in order. The four sections (Redisciplining; Linking Ideas, Practice, and Context; Centering the "Other"; and Troubling Differences) are not fully distinct possibilities. Many chapters could be in more than one section. We encourage the reader to reconsider our classifications and see what others may be suggested. Our view is that the millennial viewpoint does not allow definitive projections of the future of educational studies but rather a lively and argumentative dialogue.

Redisciplining

Educational studies began as a reconsideration of the offerings of the disciplines. Reconsidering the nature of our discourse has become one of the hallmarks of educational studies. This has included both reappraising the disciplines as identities and touchstones while pushing educational studies into the lived experiences of current and prospective teachers. The chapters by Stone, Tozer, Levine, and Brayboy speak only to the disciplines of philosophy, history, and anthropology. Yet all share the view that disciplines may not be about warranted assertions. Instead they are about thoughtful lenses that when reflected upon move beyond disciplinary knowledge and into intellectual lives. A chapter concerning sociology of education was not included due to recent works that speak to similar issues in this volume (See Pallas 2001; Hallinan, 2000).

Brayboy's chapter addresses class (and race) but within the context of how anthropologists of education portray struggle and what this means for conducting "fieldwork" and representing those whom the research is "about." His chapter also addresses the methodology of conducting fieldwork. Levine, in his chapter concerning the history of education, problematizes the ways historians have depicted the development of education over time, especially how schools have been interconnected with class conflict throughout history. Stone discusses philosophy of education as a "guild" and how its membership has changed over time. She also addresses issues concerning the practicality of philosophy within classroom customs. Building on Stone's chapter, Tozer discusses further the practical dimensions of the philosopher-of-education life in the current postmodern era.

Linking Ideas, Practice, and Context

Educational studies has a powerful future in linking educational ideas, practices, and contexts. Each of the chapters in this section pushes educational studies beyond a simple version of improving practice. Educational studies' broader role is to reveal the "nestedness" of practice in ideas, assumptions, and contexts. These chapters serve as a critique of the instrumental rationality behind studies of schooling while pointing to how knowledge is a vehicle to promote substantive rationality (Collins, 1982). Abascal-Hildebrand's chapter challenges social foundation educators to explore cultural relations with their students through critiquing and refiguring language as a means to social justice. Bassey builds upon Abascal-Hildebrand's work by discussing language and its relationship to the identity of students along with the importance of awakening students' consciousness, particularly those marginalized by the system. Collins discusses the national political context, the media, morality, and what this means for children. Pae also looks at the role of the media along with other influences that determine how children view the world and other people, which becomes more and more important as the world becomes "smaller" through technological advances concerning communication and travel. Li, along with Pae, looks at how technological advances, especially virtual communities, impact our lives. Li is particularly concerned with the potential for virtual communities to perpetuate current class and racial structures.

Centering the "Other"

The third future of educational studies is in the new approaches to studying the "other." Instead of the "other" being the definition of deviance, we now understand that the margins are created to enable the definition of the center. One future of educational studies is in revealing what the boundaries teach us about the assumptions within the taken-for-granted aspects of social life.

Aggrey critiques teacher education programs for not preparing white teachers to deal with their racially diverse classrooms. She suggests that a beginning would be to encourage white student teachers to explore their own racial identity. Sears discusses multicultural curricula, especially the importance to learn and share marginalized stories such as that of the Mississippi Freedom Democratic Party. Shore elaborates how issues of femininity and sexuality relate to the educational goals of young women, offering a critique of the social construction of gender. Williams and Xanthopoulos discuss the importance of education in reducing the likelihood incarcerated youth will return to prison. Hatt-Echeverria's chapter relates to Williams and Xanthopoulous' work by discussing the educational histories of incarcerated youth and the implications for public schooling.

Troubling Differences

The fourth future before educational studies is to move beyond what boundaries can teach us to troubling the boundaries themselves. These contributions support social justice but question how we conceive of difference in knowledge, teaching, policy, and people.

Dees questions the boundaries of what it means "to teach" and how the arts can assist us in moving beyond traditional pedagogical paradigms. Piliawsky discusses the state takeover of Detroit's public schools and questions whether the motives were to create positive reform or simply a political game to attract middle-class residents. Weems pushes the boundaries of "traditional scholarly texts" in the hopes of promoting social justice through an alternative form of writing. Carreiro encourages alternative pedagogy that assists student-teachers in enhancing their own research and presentation-giving skills through critical thinking and creative awareness.

What is being offered here is a picture of educational studies "on the ground," as practiced by AESA members. The volume reveals the vibrancy of educational studies, even as it makes generalizing statements difficult to sustain. We believe this volume provides a lens through which we can reflect on the history, present, and possible futures of educational studies. In the final chapter, we explore the shifts that have occurred in educational studies over time and how they have led us to the "millennial contradiction" of identity versus knowledge.

References

Collins, R. (1982). *Sociological insight: An introduction to non-obvious sociology.* New York: Oxford University Press.

Hallinan, M. (2000). Introduction. In M. Hallinan (Ed.), *Handbook of the sociology of education.* New York: Kluwer.

Pallas, A. (Ed.) (2001). Currents of thought: Sociology of education at the dawn of the 21st century. *Sociology of Education*, extra issue, 1.

Part One

Redisciplining

Chapter Two

The History of Anthropology and Future Research: Conducting "Fieldwork"

Bryan McKinley Jones Brayboy

I am a Lumbee-Cheraw from Prospect, North Carolina; I am also an educational anthropologist trained at an Ivy League university. I come from a long line of farmers and agricultural people. My father was born in a house with a dirt floor in Pembroke, North Carolina. My mother's family was not as poor as my father's, but her upbringing in Prospect, North Carolina, revolved around farming and hard work in the fields. Each came from a family of eight and each farmed for parts of their subsistence. This work in the fields to raise crops is quite different than that fieldwork done by anthropologists. This work revolved around cotton, corn, beans, and tobacco rather than people. It provides food for human beings and communities, and is done respectfully with much work being put back into the earth from which food and medicine is taken; it is not exploitive. This work is brutal on the hands and body and can be dangerous; it is not something that happens with a pad and pen or laptop computer and tape recorder. It occurs with mules and tractors, bad backs, and old, worn boots. The fact that I am a product of both a farming community and an Ivy League university serves as the backdrop for this chapter and provides the reader with my own positionality around the ways that field work and work in the fields interact in my daily life as both a Lumbee-Cheraw and an educational anthropologist.

In this chapter, I hope to do at least two things. First, I hope to complicate what educational anthropologists mean by fieldwork. I will contrast anthropological fieldwork to the work done in fields by Indigenous people from my home community and in other communities. Along the way, I will argue that fieldwork—of the anthropological sort—does not have to be exploitive or arrogant; it can be, has been, and must continue to be, at its roots, activist-oriented. By activism, I mean the vigorous and politically minded activities of individuals and groups aimed at correcting or highlighting inequities, problems in societal institutions or communities. Building on this further, I argue that we must be radical activists in our work. An etymological view of the word "radical," as defined in the *Random House Dictionary of the American Language*, reveals that it means "of or going to the root of origin; fundamental." The concept of addressing issues and problems at the root or origin, then, takes on special meaning as I discuss both fieldwork and work done in fields.

Second, I want to make problematic the romanticizing of marginalized and oppressed groups and the work done in fields as well as the poverty often found in communities that "do" this kind of work. Anthropological fieldwork and its resulting academic products and policies have misrepresented Indigenous cultures as "simple" and have led to efforts of exterminating Indigenous people. Unfortunately, Indigenous peoples' field work and the poverty surrounding it has also been construed as natural, normal, or part of their core beings.

Ironically, some faculty and graduate students who are members of traditionally oppressed and marginalized groups have also created and reified boundaries around what constitutes being a "real Indian" or a "real person of color." By drawing from autobiographical sources, I argue that identity issues surrounding certain criteria (such as working in the fields) become romanticized by individuals who have never worked in fields under extremely difficult circumstances.[1] These individuals also do not understand the purposes or philosophies guiding this work done by members of marginalized and oppressed communities. As an "academic" who does fieldwork, my own positioning (and that of other faculty of color) becomes "unreal" or that of a "sellout" when placed in opposition to the labor-intensive work done by members from our communities on and with the land. This opposition leads into a discussion of fieldwork from an educational anthropologist's perspective.

Being in the Field or Working in the Field:
What Is Fieldwork/Field Work?

Anthropologists, in general, and educational anthropologists specifically speak of one aspect of their work as "being in the field." Many of my relatives or community members also speak of "working in the field." Clearly, each group means something different by the way in which the term is used. I believe that both forms of work in the field can be viewed as radical activism and each can serve as a way to inform the other.

For educational anthropologists, fieldwork is often associated with ethnographic research methods. These methods include participant observation, interviews, document analysis, focus groups, and "hanging out with the natives." From this work and through these methods, we endeavor to offer or present a full picture that is filled with "thick description" of how groups of people live and how *they* view the world (Geertz, 1983). Importantly, the participants in our work can be any number of people: students, teachers, administrators, parents, and communities of all colors, shapes, and sizes. More often than not, educational anthropologists find a site where there is a "problem" to be examined so that their research has an intellectual basis. These sites also happen to be communities of color, from lower economic brackets, and rural/urban environments. Of course, the context (or specific place in time) and situation (the specific time, environs, and other intangible indicators and factors) are important. Educational anthropologists' work is often grounded in offering a solution to whatever problem is being studied.

Anthropological fieldwork offers insights into what is happening in a particular place at a specific time, under particular circumstances. Educational anthropologists often can conduct ethnographies that are particularly descriptive and all-encompassing in nature. In this work, the description is rich and thick and details and catalogs the physical and intellectual landscape of the area, people, and/or surrounding structures.[2] After reading this work, other educational researchers may make their own interpretations of what is happening, why, and how. Educational anthropologists also conduct ethnographic work that is at times outwardly political while offering analyses of the societal and structural barriers that exist which make "achievement" or "schooling" easier or more difficult.[3] In the process of being "more political," such anthropologists attempt to offer possible solutions to issues and problems and highlight what kinds of points are missing or needed to better the situation of our research participants. In this way, researchers become more like activists in their work by seeking the root and origin of issues that they study.

As educational anthropologists, we can do more in our research. Inherent in the way that educational anthropologists conduct research is a belief that we are, or can be, "experts" because of the time we spend in the communities in which we work; the privilege associated with our status as "learned" people specifically trained in research methods and theories also heightens the call to "expertness." Certainly, educational researchers who spend considerable time in particular settings do know more than individuals who have not spent time in these settings; however, our status as experts when compared to individuals who have lived in the community for decades is dubious. Our work—as educational anthropologists—is arrogant because we are trained to "see" things, analyze them, and report that we do, in fact, know more about what we see than anyone.[4] This knowledge, of course, includes the people from the communities in which we work. These assumptions are problematic when compared to the knowledge of those who live in the communities, and have all of their lives.[5]

How do we, as educational anthropologists characterize the knowledge of the 87-year-old elder who knows what has happened in the community and lived there her entire life? What about the 59-year-old teacher who was born and raised in the community and has 37 years of institutional memory? What of the 6-year-old who goes to school and experiences it, from a child's perspective, every day and goes home in the afternoon to a "traditional" household?[6] How do we, as educational anthropologists, incorporate these community members' knowledge and vision into the research process to inform our research and analyses? Further, how do we ground these knowledges into the community's beliefs and/or standards? These are questions that push those of us in the field to examine the radical nature of schooling, community, and individual lives and to refocus the concept of "expert" on others who do not have advanced educational degrees, but rich lived experiences. In addressing these questions, educational researchers must root our identities as researchers and scholars in humility and willingness to admit and acknowledge that expertise comes in many different flavors.

To start, educational anthropologists can begin to reorient our groundings, beliefs, ideas, and teachings of what it means to be an expert. Rather than drawing solely on other academics that write of fieldwork and communities of the "Other," educational anthropologists can actively push and tear apart the boundaries of our discipline and the methods tied to it. We can begin to think of how to raise and address concerns as well as report and build on the knowledge and perspectives of the 87-, 59-, and 6-year-olds previously mentioned. Going beyond simply reporting these knowledges and perspectives, however, we can center these knowledges next to the theories of Bourdieu, Erickson, Foucault, Geertz, and other theorists upon whom we rely in our academic work. As educational anthropologists we can learn from work done in a field; this work can inform our methods and fieldwork in unique and important ways.

When my Uncle William McKinley Jones, Jr.—we call him Uncle June (for Junior)—works his fields of tobacco, corn, hay, and beans in Walkhulla, North Carolina, he does so with humility. He believes that arrogance, in thinking one can control the land, crops, weather, or the way that things grow, is unproductive. He listens to the ground and to traditions of farming that have been present in the community, in these fields and the surrounding ones, for at least five hundred years. Building on, and inherently respecting, this knowledge leads to an ability to know what works, under what conditions, and with what crops.

My Uncle June respects and honors the institutional knowledge and lived experiences of those that came before him and draws strength in his technique and problem-solving from our ancestors. This respect and honoring illustrate an ability to learn from the past and to adapt and adjust to present demands, concerns, and callings from the community and society. There is a belief that we need to remember things, ideas, and concepts that we (as Indigenous people) have always known. Based on the cumulative experiences of his work and those that came before, he knows (or remembers) when to plant, where, and under what conditions. His memory—which contains the memories (and remembrances) of our ancestors—and advice from community members allow him to make the best possible decisions. His respect for the process and the humility with which it is addressed allow him to best serve his (and his larger community's) needs by being productive. I do not mean here to discount his skills in reading the land or knowing how to farm; the point is that his skills—which are abundant—are utilized with a form of humility from which educational anthropologists can learn.

For educational anthropologists, there is a sense that we, as researchers, can learn, humbly, from the expert knowledges of the elder, teacher, and student. While these individuals do not have doctorates or formal experience in collecting ethnographic data, they each bring unique sets of experiences and references to the process. The 87-year-old elder may have the knowledge of her 87-year-old mother, who garnered that knowledge from her 91-year-old mother. There is then, in effect, almost 300 years worth of memories, remembrances, and knowledge tied into one individual. From this rich knowledge base, researchers and educational anthropologists can learn much about communities, norms, practices, and what has been tried before in schools. Imagine what the 59-year-old teacher has to offer as a lifelong community member and a 37-year veteran of a school; how could we think that after two years in the community one can be an expert when held up against these individuals? The question might better be asked: How can these individuals inform educational anthropologists' analyses of schools and communities as we search for possibilities to improve school achievement? In this way, educational anthropologists can honor the knowledge of others and build on this knowledge, memories, remembrances, and "expertness" to address the "problem" as defined by our study. Better yet, we can allow these individuals to define these "problems" for us as researchers. In the connection to work done in fields, educational anthropologists' own fieldwork is rooted in listening to the ground and the collective wisdom of community members; the ground in our study is represented by the institutional memories of elders, teachers, custodians, community members, and present-day students. Humility allows educational anthropologists to ask important questions and hear responses to our queries. The responses to our questions may address our preconceived questions or assumptions or lead us to ask different questions; either case benefits our own work and allows us to be activists in addressing the problem.

My Uncle June also knows that humility is important, because even in his best efforts and planning, other factors play into what happens with his crops and the process of planting, harvesting, and completing them. Humility, for him, means that larger forces (anthropologists often call them structural or societal forces) can and do overwhelm or humble the efforts of an individual. In 1996, what some individuals have called the worst hurricane in the history of North Carolina struck the southeastern shores of the state. Hurricane Floyd rolled inland, causing tremendous flooding and leaving many families and businesses without electricity for long periods of time. In the wake of the destruction and resulting chaos, my Uncle June had seven barns full of tobacco. Earlier, the tobacco had been cropped (leaves picked from tobacco stalks), and tied to long sticks, and then placed in a barn to dry and cure. Many individual farmers use fans to expedite and enhance the drying and curing process. The curing process is one of the final stages before taking the bundled tobacco to auction where companies bid on it by the lot and a farmer receives compensation for his work.

Hurricane Floyd's rain and the absence of electricity for drying was devastating for many tobacco farmers who had "hung" their tobacco. Some farmers had access to gas powered generators that allowed them to utilize fans; others did not. My Uncle June found generators for two barns; the other five barns were lost. The yield of crop for the season was less than a third of what had been originally planned. The season for my uncle, in a matter of a week, went from being profitable to unprofitable. In spite of reading all of the signs correctly, picking leaves when necessary and ready, properly fixing the leaves to the hanging rods and placing them in the barns at the appropriate time, Uncle June—and many of our community members—were devastated by the losses. Access to gasoline generators during this time may have helped the situation and led to a different outcome. If the Federal Emergency Management Agency and the electrical companies had been less overwhelmed, perhaps electricity and aid would have been restored and given sooner, and the outcome may have differed. Or if my community were in a "high priority" area, electricity may have found its way to the fans earlier. None of these things occurred, and many individuals, in spite of being capable and competent farmers, lost money and crops.

Much like Hurricane Floyd, there are structural processes that may arise and be more severe than originally thought, or that may not be outwardly visible in the work of educational anthropologists. These unexpected barriers or processes serve as points of humility. In many cases, structures and policies overwhelm individual agency. Although much of our work places an emphasis on providing agency for individual students, teachers, parents, and administrators, we cannot move away from the fact that structure can and does overwhelm individual efforts. For example, the standards movement along with a heavy emphasis on testing may limit a teacher's ability to be fully antiracist or to use creative teaching methods in her or his classroom. A teacher and her students may do all they can to prepare for standardized exams, and the exams are culturally biased so that the students "fail" the tests. In spite of a teacher's and her students' hard work, preparation, and devotion, all the participants appear to be a failure after the test scores are returned. As educational anthropologists, we may be prepared for research activities and analyses, only to gather "flawed" data or be misled in our analyses and "get it wrong." Both of these brief examples illustrate similar devastating effects on the lives of the individuals involved. In each case, participants could go from being profitable to being "broke" by factors out of our control.

Community poverty or institutional racism are the Hurricane Floyds of many of the communities in which we work. Listening to and valuing institutional memory and those who experience schools and the schooling process are valuable tools as educational anthropologists move toward being more active. My Uncle June now has generators for all of his barns, and he and many others have contingency plans for hurricanes and other natural disasters. These precautions and plans will become embedded in the memories of young people who will be our future farmers. Building on the knowledge of prior generations, these young people will be better equipped to address the issues that confront them. They are being prepared to see, address, and attempt to solve the problems that arise from natural wonders and other uncontrollable events. Our work, as educational anthropologists, can occur in conjunction with local communities and schools to address poverty and racism and see the connections between the two. Finally, senior educational anthropologists can proactively prepare junior scholars in this work. The work of Deyhle (1995, 1998), Foley (1990, 1995), Foster (1994), Macias (1987), McCarty (2001), and Villenas (2001) are perfect examples of educational anthropologists doing proactive work.

As educational anthropologists, we should begin to address the following questions in our work and methods: How can we, as educational anthropologists, create methods, behaviors, beliefs, ideas, and concepts, as well as the ways we report data, to be more proactive and directly combative of these issues? How can we ensure that those scholars with whom we work and train adequately learn and enact these behaviors, methods, ideas, and concepts for the benefit of the community in which we work? This is a serious challenge for scholars, as educational anthropologists, in the coming years. Our work must also be in our classrooms and undergraduate and graduate programs to recruit and train (as well as be trained by) students who come from the communities in which we work. In the process of educating students and in thinking about the people with whom we study, educational anthropologists must face the issue of romanticization and essentializing the people with whom we work or the very groups in whom we count membership. It is to these points that I now turn.

Be for Real: Fieldwork Versus Work in the Field for Faculty and Students from Traditionally Marginalized and Oppressed Groups

The work that individuals do in fields has recently become a point of contention in conversations of which I have been a part. The conversations have created an interesting form of an exotic "Other" even though the othering has been done by members of the same group as those working in the field. This exotic or romantic other is problematic when addressing the issues of anthropological fieldwork versus work done in fields because in conversations this has been discussed in a binary manner. These field workers, who often toil 16 hours a day in difficult conditions and sleep in the very fields in which they work, have become markers of all that is "good" and "right" among particular ethnic groups. While I do not and cannot deny the celebration of the hard work that is done in fields, particularly in terms of the sacrifices, pain, and agony that accompany work dedicated to creating a better situation for home communities and families, I question the fact that field work is romanticized as "authentic."[7] In articulating that tomato pickers or tobacco farmers are "real Indians" because of their land-based work, an unfortunate and problematic situation is created. At the heart of this is more than claims of authenticity; this field work is seen as the norm and expectation of what "Indians" or "Mexicanos" are *supposed* to be doing. This is a dangerous path that can lead to a stance that reifies racist ideologies. The argument that this work is "real" and "authentic" underscores important issues around what individuals from these groups should be doing. Because this romanticization normalizes this work, or situates it as real, members of these groups must do manual labor in order to be authentic.

If those who do work in fields are the authentic ones, it naturally follows that the expectation for realness is located in work that benefits others and places Indigenous people at the bottom end of the economic structure. So the work and the resulting poverty, or the poverty that leads to individuals engaging in this kind of work, becomes the norm and marker for what is "real." Following this logic, the individuals in graduate school and the faculty who note these markers of realness romanticize poverty while also denigrating the work of academics.

My tribal community is made up of farmers. We have worked in fields and grown crops that feed the community for centuries, using the local river for irrigation and taking advantage of the fertile, black soil found in Robeson County, North Carolina. My parents grew up poor and worked in fields every day. It was not uncommon for them, or others in the community, to rise early enough in the morning to work in the fields before going to school and returning home to work in the fields after school. This is important in addressing the dichotomy between academic work and work done outside with the land, because they simultaneously valued schooling and farm work. Both sets of my grandparents valued schooling and formal education as a way to better enhance not just their children's lives, but those of all of the members in our community. So, my parents and their many siblings eventually left the fields and went to school. In school, they learned to read and write and to think of how formal education might be used to assist our community in rising out of poverty and moving toward self-determination. Schooling was not viewed as "better than" field work; it was simply viewed as something that needed to be done in the same way that picking cotton in the morning was something that had to be done. One was not more "real" because she worked in the fields, just as an individual was not more "real" because she went to school. She did both and understood what the purposes for each were.

Both of my parents finished high school, graduated from college, and later earned doctorates.[8] While stressing the importance of education, they also stressed the need for humility and for honoring their agricultural roots and the life choices of other community members. They also said that they wanted their children to have opportunities and choices in what we did with our lives. My parents made us aware of the importance of activeness in our community and the importance of being Indigenous and Lumbee-Cheraw people. I knew that, for me, being an activist involved doing things made possible by my academic credentials that would assist both my family and community; I chose to do it through anthropological fieldwork and by pursuing an education that could be used to fight larger societal and governmental structures and policies. To engage in the devaluing of education, then, would be to devalue my parents, grandparents, aunts, uncles, and extended family and community. To romanticize poverty—when I knew what it was like to not have indoor plumbing and a savings account or know where the next meal would come from—was to disrespect my relatives who had to encounter a society that was harsh and unforgiving. At the root of the issue of my education is a sense of responsibility to give back to my community and to honor them through my fieldwork and writings.

In romanticizing the poverty and the work done on farms by people who have been considered the exotic "Other" by mainstream American society, graduate students and faculty of color serve to distance themselves from their communities, defining those who do field work as "real," in comparison to those who do academic work. In one educational department, a group of graduate students got together socially and began discussing the faculty of color in the department. Based on where the faculty lived, the language they used in class, the theorists they taught, and what their perceived backgrounds were, the students determined that these faculty were not authentic. In the process, they distanced themselves from the academic process and aligned themselves with those who pick tomatoes and farm tobacco. Missing from this discussion and articulations of authenticity was not only a lack of recognition that they were engaging in behavior that exoticizes poverty and reifies notions of a romantic noble savage, but also a critical examination of what it means to do both anthropological fieldwork and work in agricultural communities. Many members of my community are poor; as far as I know, none of them wants to be poor. My community members recognize their poverty and they work hard so that their children may have different choices and options or be better equipped to address larger societal structures that limit Indigenous peoples' choice sets.

Academics, and educational anthropologists, in particular, can learn something from these examples as they relate to the work they do among people skilled and experienced in doing work out in fields with their bodies. Those of us that come from communities where farm work is used as a way to help later generations have other options understand that individuals make sacrifices by doing such work. There is great humility in this field work; there are also expectations. There are expectations that those who choose more academic paths value this work done by their elders by taking on activist roles through anthropological fieldwork in order to highlight the problems and issues that are at their core. We are expected to be activists through our work and to give back to our communities in ways that are different than farm workers. As educational anthropologists, we can offer different ways of examining "problems" and issues as they arise and attack taken-for-granted notions that some communities do manual farm work because they are "better at it" or because it is their place in society. In this process, educational anthropologists can draw on lessons of humility to see that the roots are much more deeply embedded than originally considered or to name the issues for our colleagues who do not see them. Drawing on the experiences of communities and honoring their beliefs provides an entrée for educational anthropologists to rethink traditional fieldwork methods.

Educational anthropologists can also show graduate students and faculty how problematic it is to normalize and romanticize field work for discussions of identity and authenticity for some communities. Anthropological fieldwork can be active in exposing and destroying this hegemony. In so doing, educational anthropologists may begin to move closer to recognizing that work done in fields can and must inform our anthropological fieldwork.

The Final Harvest: Conclusions

In this chapter, I have attempted to offer ways that work in fields and anthropological fieldwork can inform each other and the ways that they also detract from one another. Our fieldwork as educational anthropologists does not have to exploit the Other; it can be radically activist in nature. It can be born from humility, rather than arrogance, and it can be life-serving for the communities that we study. We can give back to these places in ways that inform our own practice and study; we can also offer different ways of seeing issues that will later inform practice.

Deyhle's (1995) ethnographic fieldwork offers a model for what we can and must be doing in our own work. In examining the schooling experiences of Navajo students, she recognized that there were structural factors and issues that directly confronted these students on a daily basis. In the process, she listened to communities, having spent 18 years in the community, and served as a source of re-examining possible ways to disrupt these systems. Her work offers humility in that it is driven by the community and community members and paints the research participants as experts in their own lives. Importantly, it is also radical, because it exposes and seeks to destroy the racist practices at work in this community. Rather than taking from the community, she has given back to it in myriad ways. Her work led to an investigation of educational practices and she is currently an expert witness in a federal trial in the community. Her "expertness" comes from her humble approach to understanding the community and the community's experts. Her educational credentials allow her to be a credible witness and to serve the community. The credentials, along with her humility, place her in a position of having done fieldwork and being seen as an activist and an ally in the community. Much of that "realness" is located in honoring community voices and being active through educational research. This notion of "realness" complicates those raised in the earlier example. We can do fieldwork and be "real"; we can also do fieldwork that is activist-oriented, humble, and rigorous.

While Deyhle's work is one example of several that can be offered, it provides educational anthropologists with an explicit example of what humble, rigorous, activist-oriented research looks like.[9] It serves as a model for beginning and new researchers and highlights the connections between field work and fieldwork. In the roots of our communities lie the keys to doing fieldwork that will best serve their interests and our research agendas. I believe that as educational anthropologists, we must continue to focus on the issues that are important to communities and on the ways that our work can be mutually beneficial to us as researchers and to the communities in which we work.

Notes

1. Interestingly, many of these individuals come from middle-class backgrounds. While they are members of the ethnic or racial groups, their experiences differ dramatically from those of the people whom they emulate. My opinion is that there is a certain panache in being viewed as poor or working class within the "academy." This is complicated among marginalized and oppressed groups as well.

2. I do not mean here to imply that our descriptions and that which we see are objective or apolitical. Clearly our lenses through which we see and view the world are politically oriented. The point is that our analysis occurs through that which we report and describe. There are no overt analyses of occurrences, structures or actions. In this way, anthropologists have argued that their work is objective. This chapter is not the place in which to address this issue; the problems with the argument have been addressed elsewhere (e.g. see Ladson-Billings, 2000; Rosaldo, 1989).

3. Following Giddens (1984), I believe that structures can be, and are, both constraining and enabling in nature. Our work as educational anthropologists has shown that the overarching structures benefit some and hinder others (e.g. see Deyhle, 1995; Gonzalez, 2001).

4. I include myself in this characterization. I am not calling individuals, generally or specifically, arrogant. Rather, I am calling our work arrogant when we take on characteristics of knowing more than others. Ironically, this arrogant stance is rewarded in many circles within academe. I understand the tensions here, but also believe that as educational anthropologist, we must find a way to be "expert" in our disciplinary fields and recognize that those with whom we work in our research communities will always know more about the communities than we. Recently, Ray McDermott told a group of young educational anthropologists that our work lacked humility. Professor McDermott called for more humility and grace in the way we present our findings. In fact, we must be humble in order to recognize that, at worst, we may get some/most/all of our interpretations "wrong," or at best, we offer one interpretation or set of interpretations of data.

5. I recognize the argument that an outsider brings fresh eyes to a new context and that many cultural norms and mores are invisible to those who are a part of groups. These arguments certainly have some merit; however, seeing differences and noting interesting actions does not connote expert status in the ways of being "Lumbee," for example.

6. I put quotation marks around the use of "traditional" for two reasons. First, we cannot assume that I mean a traditional family in the sense that it is one with a mother who stays at home, a father who works, and other siblings. Clearly, what we mean by family and household varies from home to home. Second, there is an inherent assumption in the use of this work that tradition refers to a particular way of living. In

this assumption is a static view of culture and an essentialized view what it means to be "real" or "traditional."

7. Clearly, the list of those who benefit from this work is long and numbered. In the United States we enjoy cheap produce and other products coming from the livestock, farm, and construction industries because individuals and groups of individuals are being taken advantage of and unfairly treated by individuals with power and money. Ultimately, produce companies, livestock and farming companies, and home builders and developers benefit financially from these injustices. Communities in different parts of the United States and Mexico suffer because men leave to work while women stay in the communities to hold them together and maintain their operations. I do not mean here to diminish what these individuals do or the tremendous costs incurred by them, their communities, and families; rather, the point is that I question issues of authenticity as they relate to these individuals who are privileged academics.

8. Interestingly, my father earned a doctorate before he was awarded his high school diploma. When he was a senior in high school, a teacher failed him for misbehaving in a course. He did not go to summer school; instead he attended college on a baseball scholarship and somehow the official high school transcript was never an issue. I was 11 years old when my father finally walked in his high school graduation.

9. The work of Villenas (2001) is another example of humility and activism done by an educational anthropologist. My own work (Brayboy, 1999, 2000) also begins to address issues of humility and in listening to the wisdom of community elders and the individuals with whom I have worked. Deyhle's (1995) work is one of the best examples of a long-term commitment to hearing what the community wants and needs.

References

Brayboy, B. (1999). Climbing the ivy: Examining the experiences of academically successful Native American Indians at two ivy league institutions. Unpublished doctoral dissertation. University of Pennsylvania.

Brayboy, B. (2000). The Indian and the researcher: Tales from the field. *International Journal of Qualitative Studies in Education,* 13(4), 415–426.

Deyhle, D. (1995). Navajo youth and Anglo racism: Cultural integrity and resistance. *Harvard Educational Review*, 65(3), 403–444.

Deyhle, D. (1998). From breakdancing to heavy metal: Navajo youth, resistance, and identity. *Youth & Society*, 30(1), 3–31.

Foley, D. (1990). *Learning capitalist culture: Deep in the heart of Texas*. Philadelphia: University of Pennsylvania Press.

Foley, D. (1995). *The heartland chronicles*. Philadelphia: University of Pennsylvania Press.

Foster, M. (1994). The power to know one thing is never the power to know all things: Methodological notes on two studies of black American teachers. In A. Gitlin (Ed.), *Power and method: Political activism and educational research* (pp. 129–146). New York: Routledge.

Geertz, C. (1983). *Local knowledge*. New York: Basic Books.

Giddens, A. (1984). *The constitution of society*. Berkeley: University of California Press.

Gonzalez, N. (2001). *I am my language: Discourses of women and children in the borderlands*. Tucson: University of Arizona Press.

Ladson-Billings, G. (2000). Racialized discourses and ethnic epistemologies. In N.K. Denzin & Y.S. Lincoln (Eds.), *Handbook of qualitative research* (2nd Edition) (pp. 257–277). Thousand Oaks: Sage.

Macias, J. (1987). The hidden curriculum of Papago teachers: American Indian strategies for mitigating cultural discontinuity in early schooling. In G. Spindler & L. Spindler (Eds.), *Interpretive ethnography of education at home and abroad* (pp. 365–380). Hilsdale, NJ: Erlbaum.

McCarty, T.L. (2001). *A place to be Navajo: The struggle for self-determination in indigenous schooling*. Mahwah, NJ: Lawrence Erlbaum Associates.

Rosaldo, R. (1989). *Culture and truth: The remaking of social analysis*. Boston: Beacon Press.

Villenas, S. (2001). Latina mothers and small town racisms: Creating narratives of dignity and moral education in North Carolina. *Anthropology and Education Quarterly*, 32(1), 3–28.

Chapter Three

Reform and Conflict in U.S. Urban Education During the Early Twentieth Century: Reflections on the Interpretive Struggle

David Levine

Prior to the 1960s, most educational historians presented the development of American education as the struggle of enlightened reformers against benighted foes of progress. They also tended to focus narrowly on institutional history and neglect the interplay between schooling and social and intellectual developments within the larger society. Their accounts uncritically presented U.S. schools as "thoroughly democratic in spirit and thoroughly representative of the best in our American development..." (Cubberley, 1919). During the last four decades, this celebratory perspective has been sharply challenged. Historians have devoted increased scrutiny to both primary documents and uncritical presumptions about the goals and impact of schools. As scholars have worked toward more nuanced understandings of our educational past, many have focused on crucial changes within urban education between 1890 and 1930. During those years, the number of youngsters attending school mushroomed, and city schools experienced profound changes in governance, organization, personnel, and scope of responsibilities. This transformation produced many of the institutional patterns and cultural expectations that shape today's schools. Study of these changes has brewed conflicting interpretations that will continue to color discussion among educational historians during the coming decades. This essay offers a review and assessment of how different scholars have tried to understand the evolution of urban education during this critical period, particularly in regard to issues of institutional power and control.

Lawrence Cremin's influential *The Transformation of the School* (1964), a general analysis of educational progressivism, marks a decisive advance over prior, one-dimensional accounts of U.S. schools. Cremin shows how the impulse toward educational innovation grew out of a broader progressive movement, and explains how Darwinism, the mania for "social efficiency," and new work in educational psychology shaped school people's intellectual framework. He also suggests the liberating potential of student-centered innovation by painting lively portraits of such educational experiments as John Dewey's Laboratory School at the University of Chicago and the Lincoln School at Teachers College.

For Cremin, educational progressivism was a largely beneficent trend pushed on by reformers eager to enlarge the role of schools in improving the health, moral development, and vocational opportunities of young people. Sharply diverging from this perspective, "revisionist" educational historians published a number of influential books during 1960s and 1970s (Bowles & Gintis, 1976; Callahan, 1962; Karier, 1975; Karier, Violas, & Spring, 1973; Lazerson, 1971; Spring, 1972; Tyack 1974). These scholars did not have a monolithic perspective, but did share common themes. Puncturing the self-congratulatory rhetoric which characterized much of the literature on American education, they argued that schools have often helped perpetuate an unjust social order. Much of their work focuses on how businessmen and their allies constructed bureaucracies designed to provide the emerging corporate economy with a compliant and well-trained working class.

This trend enlivened debate among educational historians, sparking responses which fall into two general categories. Some scholars tend to agree with the anticapitalist critique of the revisionists, but also emphasize working-class resistance to elite social control. These "struggle-ists" (to coin an awkward term) have focused on grassroots initiatives to humanize schooling and the shifting alliance and contention through which school politics unfolded (Cohen & Mohl, 1979; Hogan, 1985; Katznelson & Weir, 1985; Reese, 1986; Wrigley, 1982). Another tendency definitively rejects the revisionist project, contending that it is flawed by economic determinism and exaggerates the power of the upper class to control education. These researchers (who I will dub "pluralists") contend that educational battles have demonstrated the vitality of American democracy because the contending forces have all been strong enough to ensure that no one consistently dominates the field. They argue that coalition and compromise govern the evolution of schools, allowing new groups to enter the arena and influence educational policy (Peterson, 1985; Ravitch, 1978; Troen, 1975).

From the 1960s on, a crucial aspect of debate among educational historians focused on the issue of how to define the "progressive education movement." Cremin provides a helpful orientation by asserting it was "the educational phase of American Progressivism writ large" (1964, p. viii), which correctly places school reform in the context of a more general impulse to remedy the problems spawned by the maturing of industrial capitalism. Unfortunately, this formulation also reflects a tendency to treat progressive education, and Progressivism itself, as a unified movement. Cremin explicitly denies such an intent, and his book clearly delineates contradictory trends within progressive education. But this does not prevent him from constructing an analysis colored by sunny generalizations. For Cremin, Progressivism was "part of a vast humanitarian effort to apply the promise of American life—the ideal of government by, of, and for the people—to the puzzling new urban-industrial civilization," an effort whose "spiritual nub" was the "radical faith that culture could be democratized without being vulgarized" (pp. viii–ix).

During the past three decades, social historians have produced substantial investigations of education during the Progressive Era which demonstrate the limitations of Cremin's approach. They have shown that Progressivism was a massive umbrella which included both people who readily endorsed all the lofty goals he ascribes to the progressive education movement and others who considered government of and by the people to be the problem, not the solution. Although Cremin masterfully captures the spirit and nuances of many reformers and trends, he conveys an inaccurate picture of American educational history from the 1890s on as a benign and steady march toward more humane and democratic schools. He fundamentally downplays the divisions and conflicts within educational politics, and the powerful role of policymakers who believed that working-class people needed to be managed rather than empowered.

Reflecting on the efforts of historians since 1960 to define progressive education, Herbert Kliebard (1995) offers a useful corrective to Cremin's undiscriminating framework. He suggests that the term "progressive education movement" is too broad to be accurate or useful and contends that educational politics in reality involved the interplay of several "movements." Kliebard defines a movement as "a broad category of persons who share certain fundamental beliefs and who, over a sustained period of time, self-consciously act to gain public acceptance of those beliefs" (p. 244). These movements engaged in conflicts and alliances with other groups around specific issues. Coalitions were temporary, often bringing together people with different values and different visions of the end result promised by the reform they were fighting for.

I believe that Kliebard's notion of shifting coalitions approximates reality much more accurately than the idea of a unified progressive education movement. It allows us to reformulate important generalizations made by Cremin in a way which captures their validity and notes their limitations. Cremin correctly identifies beliefs shared by most progressive educators. They considered nineteenth century patterns of education hopelessly unsuited for the demands of the new industrial age. They were likely to agree that schools needed to address the health, vocational, and community needs of students and their families; that research from psychology and the social sciences should be applied to classroom practices; and that teaching needed to adjust to the more diverse population flooding into the schools. But these common premises were general enough to be shared by people with very different values. They encompass John Dewey, the philosopher who wanted to democratize schools, and David Snedden, the Massachusetts Commissioner of Education who wanted schools to sort and train youngsters to the specifications of the corporate elite. In contrast to educational traditionalists, both men were eager to embrace rather than flee the twentieth century. But they had very different ideas about what they wanted that century to look like.

Although Cremin offers trenchant descriptions of educational pioneers and experiments, he only sketches in the most general terms their impact on how schools were run and children were taught. In contrast, David Tyack's revisionist overview of urban education, *The One Best System* (1974), effectively focuses on the actual policies and practices of city school systems. His work marks an important advance from Cremin because he is able to explore how the general impulse toward reform which characterized the Progressive Era held within it a multitude of conflicting ideologies and social forces whose interactions included uneasy alliance and frequent conflict. By looking at the way reforms played out on the ground, Tyack is able to examine how the trend toward social efficiency and elite control dominated most city school systems. He chronicles the efforts of a group he calls "administrative progressives." These mostly WASP superintendents and college professors, strongly supported by prominent businessmen and civic groups, forged effective professional networks and passionately lobbied for innovations. They refashioned school governance to reflect a corporate model, implemented extensive standardized testing and tracking along class, ethnic, and racial lines, and built up school bureaucracies. The administrative progressives tended to believe that schools suffered from an excess of democracy, and the centralized systems they constructed often diminished the roles of teachers and less prosperous citizens in running schools. Although Tyack includes perceptive accounts of the some administrators and teacher union leaders who fought for more humane and democratic visions of schooling, he concludes that that the administrative progressives were largely successful in shaping the basic contours of modern American urban education.

In terms of urban classroom practice, the inspiring experimental schools described by Cremin remained privileged sanctuaries beyond the reach of working-class children. While some administrative progressives wanted to reform the rote-bound teaching methods of the nineteenth century, their hierarchical orientation compromised their capacity to promote deep innovation. Thus they were often sympathetic to educational experts who seemed to promote dramatic change, but actually offered little challenge to the emerging bureaucracies. As Tyack explains:

> These 'pedagogical progressives' spoke about the 'project method,' the 'activity curriculum,' and other ways to 'meet individual needs' of children by subverting the hegemony of established school subjects. The curricular reformers who advanced such ideas normally took the hierarchical structure of differentiated schooling as a given and concentrated on inspiring the teacher to change

her philosophy, her curriculum, and her methods in the classroom. In the horta-
tory, individualistic style of these pedagogical progressives there was little
threat to the established power of the school managers; indeed, as David Swift
has said, by promoting more subtle techniques of teaching students and less
overt control of teachers, the 'new education' probably made both more tracta-
ble. (1974, p. 197)

When I looked at a campaign to implement the project method in
Milwaukee during the 1920s I found powerful confirmation of the pattern described above. Milwaukee Public Schools Superintendent Milton
Potter waxed eloquent in favor of the democratic classroom and project
instruction. However, the reality experienced by Milwaukee elementary
teachers—45 students, little chance to collaborate or plan with colleagues, limited or no training in innovative pedagogy, a rigid, fact-based
curriculum—was inhospitable to classroom practices which embodied
the most promising educational trends. Potter had a shallow understanding of the potential of a Deweyan approach, and little interest in providing the structural changes and resources it would need (Levine, 2001).

But the attempt to popularize project teaching in Milwaukee also
suggests that while Tyack is fundamentally correct in his assessment that
the pedagogical progressives posed little threat to the hierarchical systems being built by administrative progressives, he may underplay the
extent to which classroom practices were influenced by new ideas about
teaching. In 1922, the Milwaukee Public Schools published an anthology
in which 38 teachers described how they used projects and games in their
teaching. These accounts don't give us the means to gauge how popular
project teaching was among Milwaukee's teachers. But they do indicate
that some of them employed techniques that were a distinct improvement
over the mechanical regimentation characteristic of many schools around
the turn of the century (Rice, 1893). As Tyack suggests, these "more subtle techniques" of teaching may have enhanced administrators' control of
teachers and students. Even so, the new approaches were oriented toward
linking formal knowledge to student experience and giving children
more active and absorbing roles in learning. In the hands of capable
teachers the new methods could deepen student learning and enjoyment
of school. It has proven notoriously difficult to measure how many stu-

dents were affected by "the new education." But Larry Cuban's careful 1984 study of teaching practices indicates that many teachers, schools, and even entire school systems tried to introduce "a core of progressive teaching practices," particularly at the elementary level. In classrooms around the country, observers found small group work, project activities, varied grouping of students, curriculum integration, field trips, and more student freedom of movement.

Cuban's research suggests that *The One Best System* may convey too bleak a picture of what went on in urban classrooms. But this evidence does not overturn Tyack's documentation of the negative effects of hierarchy and top-down management. Few urban districts have shown much interest in developing the collaborative relationships and experimental ethos conducive to excellent teaching. Even in districts trying to promote innovative pedagogy, Cuban believes that not more than one fourth of the teachers were affected. In districts where student-centered teaching was not particularly encouraged, he estimates that between one in five and one in ten classrooms were affected by the new approaches (1974, pp. 135–138).

Even when progressive teaching methods were favored, the class background of the students was likely to have a large impact on implementation. In a handful of pioneering experiments, such as Dewey's Laboratory School or the Lincoln School at Teachers College, middle-class children benefited from favorable teacher-student ratios and highly dedicated staffs who were encouraged to consult and coordinate their instruction (De Lima, 1969; Mayhew & Edwards, 1936). Few city schools enjoyed such resources or working relationships. Pervasive class bias meant that an "activity curriculum" did not necessarily promote equal education. In Buffalo, working-class children judged "maladjusted" were segregated in an "Opportunity School" with a hands-on vocational program (Thomas, 1986, pp.16–20). Even identical activities could be shaped by differing expectations. Thomas and Moran found that when teachers took higher-status children on field trips to an art museum the goal was to teach them to appreciate high culture. When lower-status students went, the emphasis was on teaching them proper behavior in public places (1988, pp. 78–79).

Widespread patterns of ethnic, race, and class discrimination which Thomas and Moran found in Buffalo schools are consistent with the picture of urban education offered by other revisionists. Though sharply challenged since the early 1970s, much of the work of these scholars has proven durable. They succeeded in documenting the intent of administrative progressives to build school systems designed to inculcate loyalty to the social order and train young people for vocational futures determined by their class origins. Such goals harmonized with widespread sentiment among the prosperous that strong social controls were needed to enforce proper behavior among the lower classes. Although they probably would have used less frank language, many would have agreed with David Snedden's mentor, sociologist Edward Ross, when he approvingly classified schools as "an economic system of police" (Spring, 1972, p. 75). The influential 1918 Cardinal Principles Report of the National Education Association endorsed the comprehensive high school as the best way to sort students for training in workplace skills while still allowing them to mingle enough in sports and homeroom to create social cohesion. In *Education and the Rise of the Corporate State*, Joel Spring accurately describes school-based initiatives in social control as part of a larger movement to promote a welfare capitalism which would defuse class conflict. By 1901 Rockefeller's Colorado Fuel and Iron Company (later made infamous by the 1912 Ludlow Massacre) had established a Sociology Company in charge of recreation, sanitation, education, and the company magazine. In a more recent work, historian Lizabeth Cohen (1990) demonstrates that during the 1920s, corporate liberals were mounting sophisticated plans to win workers' loyalty through company unions, social secretaries, social services, benefits, and athletic associations.

In some revisionist accounts, however, the portrayal of the drive for social engineering fails to fully capture the attitudes and impact of diverse pedagogical reformers. Spring's version implies that those who advocated child-centered instruction were mostly interested in finding sophisticated ways to get children to internalize social controls. He reduces educators who seriously explored ways to make learning more joyful and authentic to thought-police analogues of social efficiency enthusiasts such as Franklin Bobbitt and David Snedden. This picture does not account for the role of such figures as William Heard Kilpatrick and other proponents of the project method. These educators were hardly flaming radicals, but their suggestions for cooperative classroom activities did not represent a plot to snuff out subversive behavior. John Dewey's educational ideas are an outright contradiction to a social control schema, which is probably why Spring skips lightly over his role to focus on Colin Scott, a more obscure figure he alleges used cooperative learning for coercive ends.

Some scholars have faulted revisionists for focusing so much on the role of elite advocates of social control that they neglect the impact of other groups. This generalization is not entirely accurate. For example, Lazerson, McLaughlin, McPherson, and Bailey (1985) note that parents and communities have a long history of struggling with educators over the content and goals of schooling, and Tyack chronicles neighborhood resistance to centralization and the powerful role of teachers and organized labor in Chicago school controversies. But even if we factor in such exceptions, the work of some of the revisionists does tend to underplay the involvement of middle- and working-class groups. Post revisionist efforts to remedy this deficit have demonstrated that many teachers, middle-class reformers, and working-class parents viewed schools as important means to building equal opportunity and community. They initiated or supported such programs as supervised playgrounds, school lunches, and medical inspections. And when the agendas of school officials and communities came into conflict, ordinary citizens were not necessarily passive. Plans to implement a vocational school system in Chicago and platoon schools in New York City were brought to grief by working-class wrath (Wrigley, 1982; Cohen and Mohl, 1979). Administrative progressives rarely had the luxury of imposing their plans at will. School systems were more likely to be contested terrain in which complex patterns of alliance and conflict shaped policy.

Pluralist historians have articulated a perspective which sharply differs from the views of both revisionists and struggle-ists. Though hardly comprising a monolithic perspective, strong commonalties draw them together into a distinct trend. They tend to see the growth of educational bureaucracy as a politically neutral response to the logistical difficulty of managing growing numbers of students. They argue that the more elaborate structures created often brought reduced corruption and popular new programs. Though not oblivious to class bias, they contend that middle-class educational reformers emerged as a group with plenty of clout and a different agenda than business leaders. Since schools remained subject to popular electoral control, they believe that urban education failed to come under the domination of corporate leaders. Rather, the essentially democratic nature of the system was enhanced as new ethnic groups gained increasing representation on school boards and in classrooms. While acknowledging that in some cities this process was characterized by sharp class conflict, they cite other instances which indicate that school change could happen in a relatively harmonious fashion (Mirel, 1993; Peterson, 1985; Ravitch, 1978; Troen, 1975).

It is difficult to make valid generalizations about the impact of growing centralization and bureaucratization on corruption and inefficiency in urban schools. Troen (1975, pp. 224–226) believes that graft and mismanagement were sharply reduced in Saint Louis after reforms in school governance. Tyack cites countervailing evidence that in some cities corruption merely continued on a more centralized basis and enhanced bureaucracy was no guarantee of increased efficiency (1974, pp. 167–176). There are no multicity studies which systematically compare the amount of fraud and waste before and after centralization. The local boards common before the triumph of the administrative progressives seem to have been filled with members who ranged from the clean and conscientious to the slipshod, crooked, or both. It is doubtful, however, that the decentralized governance of the late nineteenth century meant a stronger role for the working class. Both Tyack (1974) and Reese (1986) indicate that middle-class businessmen and professionals dominated ward boards.

Although the growth of educational bureaucracy brought some positive changes, the pluralist scenario ignores how this trend intimately bound together valid organizational imperatives with elitist preferences. Since school systems now entailed larger budgets, more varied expenditures, accelerated building programs, and larger staffs, changes which added efficiency to managing the logistical dimension of schools undoubtedly were justified. Callahan and later critics of bureaucracy have no quarrel with the use of business accounting for this sort of system building. Their critiques have focused on how business ideology began to shape the purposes, governance, and classroom practices of urban schools in ways which were profoundly hostile to democratic notions of what schools should be about. William H. McAndrew, Chicago Superintendent of Schools during the 1920s, epitomized this viewpoint. For McAndrew, education was best conceived as a technical endeavor aimed at efficiently producing "a human, social unit, trained in accordance with his capabilities to the nearest approach to complete social efficiency possible in the time allotted" (quoted in Wrigley, 1982, p. 157). This rather mechanical process was best achieved, he believed, if experts like himself were allowed to proceed with little interference from school board members or teachers councils.

Regarding the differences among revisionists, struggle-ists, and pluralists, I would affirm David Tyack's 1974 assertion that the administrative progressives were largely successful in imposing their vision on city schools, while cautioning that we give full weight to the impact of less influential groups. Between 1890 and 1930 city schools were most powerfully shaped by policies set in motion by elite actors and aimed at constructing systems which emulated and served the corporate sector of society. At the same time, traditional expectations that schools should reflect the desire of the citizenry allowed people with diverse perspectives to either ally with or oppose administrative progressives. School politics cannot be reduced to a conflict between an upper class and a restive working class it wants to control. As David Labaree (1988) illustrates in his history of Philadelphia's Central High School, middle-class parents formed an important constituency whose demands could help shape an entire school system. As the old rote-bound and rudimentary curricula of the nineteenth century gave way to more expansive conceptions, children were pulled in contradictory directions—toward stratification or "child-centered" instruction, narrow vocationalism or an enriched curriculum, political indoctrination or more informal, supportive relationships with teachers. As is true today, there was great variety among classrooms, schools, and school systems. If a substantial number avoided the most dismal images of education for "social efficiency," it is also true that very few came near to realizing the liberatory potential evident in a handful of suburban or private experimental schools.

According to Paul Peterson, Progressive Era educational developments were "not an imposition of reform from the top down, but an unprecedented give and take" (1985, pp. 170–171):

> Conflicts over school policy did not have predictable outcomes....The winners in one political contest were the losers in the next. No one social group held sufficient economic and political power to dictate the course of school policy....The ultimate winners in such an uncertain contest were, of course, the schools themselves. As organizations, they could only prosper from contests and conflicts among competing groups. (pp. 22–23)

I think this analysis is fairly representative of the key premises held by educational historians with a pluralist perspective. In this model, the engine of progress is interest-group competition in which most of the players have substantial influence. Acknowledging the more negative experience of racial minorities, the schema suggests that with a bit of jostling, previously excluded newcomers such as immigrants, Catholics, and union members were able to grab power through electoral mobilization, lobbying, and gaining jobs in education. The result was a rough parity among the players which produced a democratic give-and-take which "satisfies most of the participants and crushes none" (Ravitch, 1978, p.17). Although it does not always result in the best decisions, pluralists believe that this clash of contending interests generally produces the best of all possible educational worlds. This perspective gives us two choices. We can throw in our lot with the revisionists, an unattractive alternative if we accept Ravitch's estimate that they are afflicted by a penchant for economic determinism and crude social control theories. Or we can opt for the pluralist outlook, which implies that though not always pretty, school politics vindicated American democracy.

This analysis contains a fragment of truth. Since schools are public institutions formally under democratic control, they have been influenced by diverse constituencies. But some constituencies are more equal than others. Although pluralist accounts often describe the interplay of different social strata, they generally fail to accurately portray the decisive impact of class and social inequality on education. My concluding remarks focus on this failure. I believe that the pluralists minimize the capacity which upper-class Americans and their allies in the educational arena had during this time period to frame debates over educational policy and influence public opinion.

Although schools have their own peculiar dynamics, they generally reflect the larger social world. The behavior of teachers, students, and administrators is shaped by their experiences beyond the schoolhouse door. Educators are expected to inculcate skills, beliefs, and values, and censured if part of the public is offended by how they carry out these responsibilities. For Ravitch, this interconnection between schools and society confirms the democratic nature of schools, since the electorate can control school policy (1978, p.16). But if antidemocratic ideology and practices cast a long shadow over civil society, schools will hardly be immune from their influence. Although victories which enhanced democracy in the United States were won between 1890 and 1930, that time period also witnessed the increasing domination of industrial capitalism and those captains of industry and finance who controlled growing economic empires. Their explicit intervention into school policy battles had a significant impact, but represents only part of their impact on education. Without digressing too far into a review of American politics during these forty years I want to at least point out that it hardly constituted a level playing field. On one end we have the 1896 McKinley campaign outspending Bryan by perhaps twenty to one (Wiebe, 1967, p. 104), on the other we have that hostility of the great majority of newspapers to Roosevelt and the New Deal. When teachers and administrators pondered what values and behaviors they were responsible for passing on to the new generation, their conclusions were influenced by both widespread social practice and public opinion. Hierarchy, competition, and class stratification were not simply ideas, they were palpable realities of everyday life. Teacher-rebels challenged the status quo, but they were pulling against a powerful current. Regarding the impact of the political climate on schools during the 1920s, teacher Leonard Covello wrote:

> [O]n our public-school system the heavy hand of conformity descended. Freedom to teach became to a great extent a mockery, and such slogans as "Democracy in Education and Education for Democracy" that we had adopted in our Teachers Union seemed a far off Utopia.

In fact, to express one's political opinions was sure to result in reprisals. Obedience to authority—'unquestioning obedience'—was expressed by some as one of the goals of American education. (1958, p. 164)

The atmosphere which Covello described was a product not only of school-based policies, but of the ideological hegemony of an increasingly cohesive group of corporate leaders. It rested upon faith in capitalism embraced by broad elements of the middle and working classes, and was buttressed by the capacity of elite citizens to dominate the media and define what range of opinion would be considered respectable. It provided a congenial context for administrative progressives to launch their ambitious plans to transform the nation's schools.

The view that upper class and upper middle-class citizens exercised a predominant role in policy debates is antithetical to pluralist interpretations of both American politics in general and the specific dynamics of school reform. In regard to education, pluralists assume that access to the vote was a guarantee of access to equal power and participation. Teachers, administrators, unions, businessmen, civic organizations, and ethnic groups become players of equal weight, acting in fluid coalition and winning and losing in roughly equal proportion. In this scenario, middle-class professionals provide a balancing influence which makes schools more democratic. Their ambition was balanced by genuine commitment to public service. Since their self-interest was "readily distinguishable from the class interests of corporate elites," they were just as likely "to cooperate with trade union leaders and working-class groups" (Peterson, 1985, p. 207).

But the effects of electoral participation during the Progressive Era and the 1920s offer frail support for the democratic picture presented by pluralists. Nationally, the growing number of school boards elected through at-large elections increased the dominant role of "a better class of men" and decreased neighborhood clout. In 1916, Scott Nearing reported that over three fifths of city school board members were doctors, lawyers, merchants, real estate men, bankers, brokers, and manufacturers (Tyack, 1974, p. 141). In his 1927 study of Chicago, George Counts describes how the Chamber of Commerce was able to have an impact on school programs far beyond that achieved by organized labor or other citizen groups. He concludes that through "relying on its social prestige, intellectual resources, and economic power," the Chamber "has succeeded in maintaining an intimate and even advisory relationship with the board of education" (pp. 163–164). In San Francisco, the Chamber of Commerce, Merchant's Association, and other elite groups played a decisive role in the triumph of the corporate model of school governance, including the 1920 charter amendment which abolished the elective school superintendency (Katznelson & Weir, 1985, pp. 95–96). It is difficult to find examples of cities in which the trade union movement or middle-class civic organizations achieved comparable influence over school policy.

Peterson criticizes Tyack for typecasting reform-oriented administrators and exaggerating their power. He also argues that they shared the desire of middle-class reformers to expand school services and promote expertise, science, and professionalization within school systems, priorities which did not tie them to any one social group. He implies that they were just as likely to come into conflict with conservative elites, politicians, and business leaders as trade unionists and school employees. "Reform superintendents were neither heroes nor devils, but they had an agenda that placed them at odds with a diversity of opponents that changed according to the issue at stake and the political context in which it was raised" (p. 155).

It is true that top school officials had to juggle the interests of varied groups. But to portray them as independent arbiters, lifted above the fray by an Olympian commitment to their own priorities, is a substantial mischaracterization. Despite frequent claims that their neutral expertise put them "above politics," reform-oriented top school administrators were usually highly political actors whose agendas carried plenty of ideological freight. Some superintendents, like Alfred Roncovieri of San Francisco and Ella Flagg Young of Chicago, tried to implement genuinely democratic conceptions of how schools should function. But these figures offer a stark contrast to most school leaders. As Carl Kaestle suggests (Reese, 1986, p. xvi), the multitude of school battles during the early twentieth century reflected a war between democracy and efficiency. As a group, administrative progressives enthusiastically attempted to mobilize their school systems under the banner of efficiency.

Their dominance contradicts the pluralist perspective. Firmly ensconced on the "commanding heights" of school management, they were able to implement "scientific" testing to enshrine tracking, "expert" management which subordinated teachers, "Americanization" of immigrant children into knee-jerk patriotism and ethnocentric ideals, vocational education which aimed working-class kids at working-class futures, and "expansion of school services" which featured "adjustment" schools for poor, immigrant, and minority youth. Administrative progressives also supported more beneficent reforms, but these goals constitute the heart of their agenda. Despite the arguments of Ravitch, Peterson, and other fans of a pluralist interpretation, the evidence suggests they left us a durable legacy.

As educational historians work toward deeper understandings of this period, they should try to develop insights into the multiple meanings of "democracy" in the context of educational policy battles. Grassroots resistance to the centralizers was often motivated by the idea that schools be under popular control, but there is little evidence that the old ward system promoted enlightened pedagogy. Democracy was championed by local politicians jealous to preserve their power base, businessmen anxious to protect a reliable source of boodle, and parents whose image of a proper education fastened on the rote rituals of their own childhood. For the administrative progressives, democracy often meant efficiently training young people for genetically appropriate occupations in the corporate economy. But democracy could also mean Milwaukee Socialist school board member Meta Berger's support of teacher councils which would empower teachers to pursue child-centered pedagogy, or Margaret Haley's conviction that the Chicago Federation of Teachers was the best hope of ensuring a decent livelihood for educators and small enough classes to give the city's children a decent education (Levine, 1995). Usually on the defensive, those who saw democracy as part of a comprehensive struggle for social justice often failed to articulate a clear vision or work through the challenge of forging viable structures for participatory decision making. By exploring the conflicting meanings of democratic schooling that have swirled around schools, historians might help us discuss more intelligently our contemporary disagreements about what schools should provide for our children.

References

Bowles, S., & Gintis, H. (1976). *Schooling in capitalist America: Educational reform and the contradictions of economic life.* New York: Basic Books.

Callahan, R. (1962). *Education and the cult of efficiency.* Chicago: The University of Chicago Press.

Cohen, L. (1990). *Making a new deal: Industrial workers in Chicago, 1919–1939.* Cambridge, England: Cambridge University Press.

Cohen, R., & Mohl, R. (1979). *The paradox of progressive education: The Gary plan and urban schooling.* New York: Kennikat Press.

Counts, G.S. (1927). *The social composition of boards of education: A study in the social control of public education.* Chicago: The University of Chicago Press.

Covello, L. (1958). *The heart is the teacher.* New York: McGraw-Hill.

Cremin, L.A. (1964). *The transformation of the school: progressivism in American education, 1876–1957.* New York: Random House.

Cuban, L. (1984). *How teachers taught: Constancy and change in American classrooms, 1890–1980.* New York: Longman.

Cubberley, E. (1919). *Public education in the United States. A study and interpretation of American educational history: An introductory textbook dealing with the larger problems of present-day education in the light of their historical development.* Boston: Houghton Mifflin Company.

De Lima, A. (1969). *Our enemy, the child.* New York: Arno Press.

Hogan, D. (1985). *Class and reform: School and society in Chicago, 1880–1930.* Philadelphia: University of Pennsylvania Press.

Karier, C. (1975). *Shaping the American educational state: 1900 to the present.* New York: Free Press.

Karier, C., Violas, P., & Spring, J. (1973). *Roots of crisis: American education in the twentieth century.* Chicago: Rand McNally

Katznelson, I., & Weir, M. (1985). *Schooling for all: Class, race, and the decline of the democratic ideal.* New York: Basic Books.

Kliebard, H. (1995). *The struggle for the American curriculum, 1893–1958.* New York: Routledge.

Labaree, D.F. (1988). *The making of an American high school: The credentials market and the central high school of Philadelphia, 1838–1939.* New Haven: Yale University Press.

Lazerson, M. (1971). *Origins of the urban school: Public education in Massachusetts, 1870–1915.* Cambridge: Harvard University Press.

Lazerson, M., McLaughlin, J., McPherson, B., & Bailey, S. (1985). *An Education of Value: The purposes and practices of schools.* New York: Cambridge University Press.

Levine, D. (1995). *Milwaukee socialists and the struggle for democratic schools, 1916–1930.* Masters Thesis, University of Wisconsin-Madison.

————. (2001). The project method and the stubborn grammar of schooling: A Milwaukee story. *Educational Foundations*, Winter.

Mayhew, K.C., & Edwards, A.C. (1936). *The Dewey school: The laboratory school of the University of Chicago, 1896–1903.* New York: Appleton-Century.

Mirel, J. (1993). *The rise and fall of an urban school system: Detroit, 1907–81.* Ann Arbor: University of Michigan Press.

Peterson, P.E. (1985). *The politics of school reform, 1870–1940.* Chicago: University of Chicago Press.

Ravitch, D. (1978). *The revisionists revised: A critique of the radical attack on the schools.* New York: Basic Books.

Reese, W. (1986). *Power and the promise of school reform: Grassroots movements during the progressive era.* Boston: Routledge and Kegan Paul.

Rice, J.M. (1893). *The public-school system of the United States.* New York: The Century Publishing Company.

Spring, J. (1972). *Education and the rise of the corporate state.* Boston: Beacon.

Thomas, W.B. (1986). Mental testing and tracking for the social adjustment of an urban underclass, 1920–1930. *Journal of Education*, 168 (2), 9–30.

Thomas, W.B., & Moran, K.J. (1988). Social stratification of school knowledge in character training programs of south Buffalo, New York, 1918–1932. *Journal of Education*, 170 (1), 77–94.

Troen, S. (1975). *The public and the schools: Shaping the St. Louis system, 1838–1920.* Columbia, Missouri: University of Missouri Press.

Tyack, D. (1974). *The one best system: A history of American education.* Cambridge, MA: Harvard University Press.

Wiebe, R.H. (1967). *The search for order, 1877–1920.* New York: Hill and Wang.

Wrigley, J. (1982). *Class politics and public schools: Chicago 1900–1950.* New Brunswick, NJ: Rutgers University Press.

Chapter Four

Philosophy of Education as Guild Work

Lynda Stone

Alle ye bretheren & sisteren of yis gilde shul comen togeder to ye paroche chirche.

-cited in Brentano, 1870, Renard, 1919

Introduction

It is perhaps ironic that a field of education scholars whose historic and present purpose is change and reform, given the derivative and normative meanings of education, is itself organized as a medieval institution. Philosophy of education, conceptualized largely around associations of scholars, is best characterized as a *guild*.[1] The purpose of the chapter is to describe this guild organization but to suggest that it has a contemporary form (a postmodern one?) with a decided distinction from an earlier formulation of tradition and resistance to change. In the view of this author, it is characterized today—at least in some respects—by difference of membership, interest and practice rather than by sameness of convention. Indeed within a somewhat "singular" form of organization, diversity flourishes.

Guild

Scholars disagree somewhat on the historical roots of guilds; some claim beginnings in family associations of Germanic warriors in Scandinavia while others refer to communal groups from the Roman Empire and early Christendom. According to German scholar Lujo Brentano in an English language introduction to a new edition of the 1389 text above, the oldest existing guild statutes establish three such associations in England in the eleventh century.[2] Disagreement too—again only minimally—exists over the derivation of the term "guild," "gild," or "guilde." From Teutonic origin, it means payment, compensation, offering, and collective tribute. Other roots are to feast or sacrifice—the latter from similar terms in Dutch, Gaelic, and Welsh. All point to the meaning that has survived: As Brentano writes, "Guilds appear to be the brotherly banding together into close unions of man and man, sometimes even established on and fortified by oath, for the purpose of mutual help and support" (Brentano, 1870, p. 3).

For better or worse, and no value judgment is offered herein, philosophy of education organizationally shares today many features of a guild. Among similarities are association in which "standing members" are admitted by vote of peers; in which at an annual meeting, craft-work, judged by peers, is presented; and in which a compilation of that representative work is published. It follows from the organization that this "brotherhood" is at once inclusive and exclusive, is controlled by elders who exercise some influence over those who follow in their footsteps but who all together receive some advantage through their joining (see *Oxford English Dictionary*, 1989, p. 933).

In the chapter that follows, the guild that comprises contemporary philosophy of education from the perspective of one U.S. member is described. Given the backdrop of guild-characterization, the claim is yet made that today's association allows for difference in background and in "doing the work" by its members. As will be revealed, this is a relatively recent development—at least in the guild of North America, the Philosophy of Education Society.[3] Following a bit of general situating, the chapter has two parts. The first characterizes the guild and the second illustrates one "approach" from multiple sources for doing contemporary philosophy of education.

Situating

Philosophy of education is a field, actually, with an ancient and continuing history since at least from the Greeks onward philosophers have written about education. Traditions in education practice, for instance, still can trace roots to ideas from Plato and Rousseau. Moreover, Kant, Locke, and others wrote about education before the twentieth century, while more recently Dewey, James, Whitehead, and Montessori wrote, often concentrating, on the topic as well. This chapter takes up the history of the field approximately across the twentieth century: it is a 'catching up' with the guild today. Other historic resources with a similar purpose are worth noting at the outset: *Modern Philosophies and Education*, the fifty-fourth yearbook of the National Society for the Study of Education, edited by Nelson B. Henry (1955), *Philosophy and Education*, the eightieth yearbook of NSSE edited by Jonas Soltis (1981), and a recent textbook, *Philosophy of Education*, authored by Nel Noddings (1995).

As histories attest, the professional organization of the Philosophy of Education Society (PES) is about sixty years old. At the outset some general relations require attention: Its members, who largely identify themselves with education interests, have at the least an ambiguous relationship both with those who people the parent discipline, philosophy, and those who are educational practitioners. On the one hand, only a relative few conventional philosophers "do" education; this applied topic has less value (in my view) than traditional topics or than in other applied professional fields such as business or medicine.[4] One notes that there are a few social scientists who study education today—and as well, some interest in American studies, cultural studies, and women's studies and feminist pedagogy. On the other hand, a tradition of practitioner engagement in philosophy of education as part of a past history of American letters is also largely absent. For example, the kind of discussion club of local school people and university faculty with which Dewey took part is almost nonexistent today.[5]

The upshot of these ambiguous relationships is that philosophers of education face a double problem of status; they are not "proficient enough" for the parent discipline and "too technical" for the arena of practice. However, one place where individual philosophers of education have made visible contributions and are well-respected is within the education research community: Soltis and Noddings from above, as well as Maxine Greene, Thomas Green, Jane Roland Martin, Denis Phillips,

Kenneth Strike, James Garrison, and Nicholas Burbules are noted philosophers in educational research who come to mind. Moreover, in the initial group just described, as mainstream philosophers interested in education, Israel Scheffler and his students, Harvey Siegel, Dwight Boyd, and Jane Martin also deserve significant mention.

Guild Characterization

Identity

As in any academic specialty, philosophy of education and its practitioners self-identify and are identified as members by others. One is a "a philosopher of education." In the United States, this identification arises primarily because of graduate school training and background, although at any career point through study and practice one can become a guild member. Across the second half of the preceding century, identity was tied to specific doctoral graduate institutions and lineages. In the recent past (and into the present), among key institutions have been Illinois, Stanford, Teachers College Columbia, Ohio State, Florida State, Syracuse, and Harvard. A key institution develops both because it has an identified "star," and usually more than one philosopher of education on the faculty. Some few persons have named positions on education faculties as "philosophers." Faculty teach the field, publish widely, and establish professorial traditions of students who come after them. Today there are members of second and third generations; thus philosophers of education are found at Cornell, Wisconsin, Utah, Indiana, North Carolina, Nebraska, and numerous other colleges and universities. Except at institutions with several practicing philosophers who have core groups of students, the prevalent pattern is a single doctoral advisor having a student or two every few years. Upon graduation, many of these students seek positions as philosophers of education (and some desire positions in philosophy departments). However, since named positions each year are very few (perhaps as low as one per year), many philosophy of education specialists seek and hold professorships in general foundations and in teacher education.

Guild membership in the United States is not very large, say a couple of hundred active people. Outside of the United States, the field is well entrenched in Great Britain, Canada, Australia, and New Zealand. Increasingly there is international contact through the International Network of Philosophers of Education (INPE). This group meets every other summer and has membership from all over the Western world—and in Japan, South Africa, and Turkey among places of strong interest. At meetings of the North American and British guilds, there is an increasing international presence from these places and especially from Scandinavia and parts of Western Europe.

History

Various stories are told about the history of the professional field, philosophy of education, as it developed in the United States and elsewhere. In a recent text, James Kaminsky presents an intellectual history of the field in the United States, Great Britain, and Australia. For the United States, his thesis is that the field has general roots in American progressivism and in the establishment of social science out of the university tradition of a basic "capstone course" in "moral philosophy." From general moral interests, as Kaminsky relates, "[social] science, education, and therein, educational philosophy were understood by...[a significant] group of Progressive intellectuals to be instrumental elements of social reform" (1993, p. 14). Thus as schools of education were formed in leading universities, philosophy of education was a "foundational element" that distinguished these institutions from high schools and normal schools. At college, as the twentieth century entered its middle decades, it thus became important to study John Dewey, George Counts, and Harold Rugg, among others. Kaminsky also sets the initiation of the professional field with the founding of the John Dewey Society in 1935, followed in short order by the formal founding of the Philosophy of Education Society in 1941. In 1951 another professional landmark was the initiation of the U.S. guild's journal, *Educational Theory*, at the University of Illinois. By this time, as both Kaminsky and fellow commentator Tony Johnson declare, the field was not only "professional" (read guild-like) in organization but also more concerned with the doing of philosophy itself than with "philosophizing" about education reform (Johnson, 1995).

The details of the perspective of Kaminsky and Johnson on the technical turn of the field are debatable (and still debated); it is from mid-century, however, that an informal lore of the field also has its roots. Stories concern subsequent "traditions" in the field, in pragmatism, in the "isms" approach to educational practice, and then in British-inspired analytic philosophy.[6] What an older generation knows "about" and even remembers is the successive domination of PES meetings by like-minded groups of philosophers of education—those who were "in" who controlled the program, and those who were "out" who met in hotel rooms. One hears about groups of Deweyans surviving, of existentialists and phenomenologists having conversations, of analytics "critiquing" papers. The lore focuses on (now in a relatively fuzzy form) the acrimony between groups distinctive in philosophical tradition and in kinds of attention to education.

Today, there is undoubtedly disagreement over this point, the field exhibits a healthy diversity—at least as indicated from programs of the past several years at PES and contributions to *Educational Theory* during the preceding decade.[7] This diversity is discussed in more detail subsequently: for we now know that in PES, Deweyans and other pragmatists are prominent, analytical philosophers continue to have an important presence, and feminists themselves diverse are well established. Moreover, growing out of an earlier strand of work in phenomenology and existentialism, with Marxist and other infusions, philosophers of education utilizing various Continental traditions are also writing, presenting, and publishing. In addition, groups focus on various sources for doing philosophy such as literature and on several subtopics in education such as teacher education or classroom pedagogy.

Also, the John Dewey Society continues its influence today, with membership that extends well beyond philosophers and with continued interest in the reform of educational practice. One of its sources of strength, for instance, is the national Association for Supervision and Curriculum Development. In addition, the field of "curriculum studies" relates to philosophy of education in a kind of parallel development. With early origins the same, a historical divergence of interest in "curriculum" coincided with philosophy of education's turn to analytical philosophy. A 1999 meeting of noted curriculum theorists and philosophers of education interested in "social theory" and issues for education signals affinity between the two groups and at the least, some intellectual confluence (Philosophy of Education and the Internationalization of Curriculum, March 1999). Finally, many who theorize in educational research read philosophy—such as educational research methods theorists—and they too have affinity with the field of philosophy of education.

Participation

As indicated above, a philosopher of education identifies with the field and practices within it; from participation she or he is then identified by others as a member. Importantly within the field one must "make a name," and above all, one must "pay one's dues" in commitment over time of continuing scholarship and service. Making a name and paying dues are undertaken simultaneously and those who are most respected by their peers indeed do both. Regarding scholarship, what generally counts is passing through principal "gatekeeping vehicles," of publishing books, articles, critiques, and commentaries. One can be active in the professional organization, attending meetings, and getting on and contributing to committees, but without publication, respect is limited. At all stages of a career, a philosopher of education continuously earns respect and reputation—and primarily from "doing the work," of writing.

The mention of gatekeeping requires elaboration. Although again there is some disagreement, there seems widespread acknowledgment that gatekeeping is not as narrowly construed today as in past years when each succeeding dominant tradition often blocked participation by others. Moreover, clearly no philosopher of education, even the best ones, are expert in all subparts of the field, but the most respected leaders know enough in general to truly attempt to be fair when judging peers.[8] Contemporary diversification of background training also has meant that anyone who persists in participation can earn recognition—but again there seems no instantaneous recognition. Some chafe at the time this process takes but there is no mistaking the hard work that it takes. For the guild, the "crowning" symbol of peer respect is election as PES President!

Individual Careers

In naming noted persons above, implied is the influence that individual philosophers of education have on the profession, its research, its theory, its conception. An important point for understanding member participation is the specifics of interaction of each person with guild structures. Each person naming herself as a philosopher of education—just like any other professional—establishes a career path. Influencing that path, of course, is a set of connections, a network out of which opportunities arise. These are begun with graduate school background but they develop well beyond for most. Thus as an individual progresses, one is offered invitations to write and to speak, and, as well, one builds opportunities himself—and offers them to others. One develops subspecialties that along with an "approach" determines what one writes about and with whom. It should be obvious that this "with whom" matters, because through participation and the building of reputation people who do similar work reinforce the careers of each other. This is an important part of being an initiate, a peer, and a mentor in the guild. But, even with the influence of "the who," overall within the guild those who are most respected, again to emphasize, earn status from the sustained quality of the writing.

Methods

Philosophers of education variously utilize the basic methods of the parent discipline—and of extended academic disciplines today. Given the diversity of the field, doing philosophy of education can look very different in style. Styles range from work that looks a lot like intellectual history to work that offers traditional argument to work very narrative or literary in form. Arguably, the identifying marks of practice are two: the use of analysis and of specific textual reference. Central analytical tasks concern attention to syntactical usage and semantic meaning in definition, clarification and elaboration, extensive discussion and application, and the raising of objections. "Philosophic texts" rely both on their own "ordinary language" views and on meanings developed by others. Most often, but not always, a philosophic text is recognizable by citation of specific textual references: in an era when academic citation is very numerous but loose (with names and dates only), quotes are provided since the philosophical project is to present very specific language use and take it apart.

Like their siblings in philosophy, philosophers of education practice analysis broadly defined. Analysis itself various from the presentation of strong or formal argument—with a syllogistic form—to a weaker and more informal "argumentation." A positive characterization of analysis is that in the "taking apart,"clarification and clarity emerges. Less positive characterizations point to the pedantry and terseness of some writing: indeed text is often dense and detailed necessarily in order to attend to the complexities of language and meaning. Viewing their skills as basic to academic work, philosophers of education point out that analysis is used by virtually everyone who sets out definition and premises, summarizes the literature, and reports findings from data. The key difference then for philosophers is that they analyze but (almost always) do not use systematically gathered empirical data.

Something more at this point should be said about distinctions between philosophy of education and philosophy: by the way, some disagreement within the field does arise whether one sees oneself as doing philosophy of education. A key point is that any formulation of philosophy of education begins and ends with a normative premise since its purpose is positive change in the lives of persons. This premise arises of course from the meaning of "education" itself. Given the premise, the traditional distinction between "is" and "ought" statements is blurred, if indeed it remains sacrosanct anywhere. The work of philosophers of education is never merely descriptive.

Returning to methods, as indicated above, increasingly philosophers of education have extended interests in and attention to orientations and processes from disciplines beyond those currently conceived as traditional philosophy. Several examples suffice for the moment: One, from above, is the undertaking of empirical study that then suggests philosophical treatment or vice versa. A second is the use of narrative, itself in various forms that range from incorporation and analyzing narrative texts to the construction of autobiographical accounts for philosophical import. Another example is a turn to specific, bounded textual discussion in the manner of "literary criticism." Still others tie philosophy of education to other disciplines or disciplinary orientations. Here are three: one is doing a form of intellectual history, another is undertaking "cultural studies," and a last is discussion of studies for educational implication that looks a lot like summarizing in the social sciences. Finally, feminist theory, too, is strongly represented in the field. With much of this cross- or interdisciplinary work, the boundaries between philosophy of education and other forms of inquiry in education (and in the larger academy) are themselves blurred. This blurring too, as a final note, concerns matters of voice and position. While most retain a kind of "distancing" of voice in attention to the topic of investigation, some do write in a more personal tone and form. Choices about methods, of course, are individual: persons may write exclusively in one, change these over time, or mix methods with different educational purposes.

Stance toward education is one last methodological characterization. At issue here is not only style and purpose but also audience. Some members of the guild primarily envision themselves as professional philosophers, others hold positions as foundations professors, still others are teacher educators—and of course some (perhaps many) write for multiple audiences. As indicated, training and occupational position, among other factors, contribute to one's view and treatment of education, of schooling, of teaching, of the lives of teachers and students and the like. Moreover attention to the application of the subdisciplines of philosophy and of other disciplinary fields also occurs, as writings are about epistemology, ethics, politics, identity and development, aesthetics, rhetoric, curriculum, pedagogy, and numerous other topical areas. Education, after all, is an applied field wherein theory and practice meet.

Guild-Work

What do philosophers of education do? It is hoped that the central idea from the previous section continues: Within a guildlike organization, difference is today evident and appreciated as each philosopher of education does her or his own work. As just indicated, this combination of training and background, and interests in philosophy and education plays out in what one writes about and how one writes. In the writing there is a combination of one's focus (or foci) and one's style that equals an "approach." Approach may change—be experimented with over time—but often in well-known philosophers of education an approach becomes recognizable.[9]

The idea that individual approaches are extant and identifiable arises, in part, from the preoccupation with language in the twentieth century in philosophy—as it does among most disciplines. What resulted across the century were a number of "subturns" to the more general linguistic turn. Put another way, the writing within disciplines was no longer taken for granted; it became "rhetorical" interpretive, critical. Moreover, not only has language itself become of prime importance, but also its own theoretical and historical contextualization receives significant attention. Particular terms are employed in particular intellectual traditions—and there is more. An approach within philosophy of education thus has the following attributes: connection to and distinction from specific roots and forebears, relations to disciplinary traditions and subtraditions, principal topics of interest, intentions of language usage, styles of writing, and specific employments of textual references. But for all of the individual differences in approaches, there are also some confluent, general approaches. Among these, referred to above, are conceptual analysis, intellectual history, and broad discussion and criticism in social theory, as applied to education. This last approach reminds that there is one other central commonality of the field: this is connection to liberal, democratic aims. Requiring further attention not provided here, one result of the blurring of the fact-value distinction across the intellectual disciplines has meant that the doing of philosophy of education is somehow always understood today as entailing politics and ethics. It is, in the language of a preceding generation of scholars, always normative.[10]

One Approach

Even given personal approaches, arguably a more or less general approach to doing the work is manifest: here follows a three-part illustration of typical guild-work. Its approach combines intellectual history and analysis as focuses textual explication; its approach is not a demonstration of the avant-garde, except for the turn to Continental theory that currently is influential. The topic also has been of perennial interest in the field, that is, aims of education. This account is based on the writings respectively of Richard S. Peters, John Dewey, and Michel Foucault. Their own "explications" of aims appeared across the recent century and, importantly, are suggestive for today: In a present era of schooling accountability and high stakes testing, there seems little discussion of larger aims; they are assumed somehow.[11] But at the least, a return to earlier philosophical considerations posits one central idea. By implication, any simply functional view of educational aims—as in learning simple basic skills or narrowly defined content—is ill-conceived. Again for emphasis, the approach to philosophy of education here is standard and explicative, a demonstration of the "common rhetoric" of the field.

Peters on Aims

Taken out of chronological order (since Dewey dies before Peters becomes prominent), relevant text from British analytical philosopher of education, Richard Peters, is a pertinent place to start. This is because of the dominance of the analytical tradition in the field, at least in the middle decades of the recent century, and also because for philosophers "conception" is often a logical beginning. Conceptual questions are everywhere, as premises, as theses, as parts of analyses, as foci for critique. In the analytical context the larger question concerns the meaning of terms used. Herein "meaning" emerges from a set of papers written over approximately a decade beginning in the early sixties as part of Peters's general project on the concept "education."

The classic paper on aims of education was occasioned by a seminar in 1965 and published along with a set of objections and rebuttals in 1973. Analysis therein demonstrates the doing of analytical philosophy as much more than a technical exercise. To begin, for Peters, philosophy is "not a sort of super-science of good and evil" (Peters, 1963/1968, p. 89).[12] He explains, "I don't take the philosophical analyst's job, with a concept like 'education,' to formulate hard and fast, necessary and sufficient conditions which must always be satisfied if the word is to be used correctly" (Peters, 1965/1973a, p. 44). Rather one explores typical ways of talking in order to determine distinctions between meanings. The result of analysis, moreover, is to become clearer about "the contours of concepts" that are not "purely *de facto* connections" (1973a, p. 45).

Turning to aims of education, Peters starts with the nature of education, in which "some state of mind is presupposed which is regarded as commendable, and some particular experiences are regarded as leading to or contributing to it" (Peters, 1968, p. 90). Distinctions then follow that separate education from other professions and that identify three standard forms (especially as the concept "education" has been connected to schooling since the nineteenth century). These three are liberal, technical, and vocational. Across all forms, aims and procedures of education are differentiated. Of the first, aims is distinct from ideals, purposes, and intentions: "Aim," it is generally suggested, refers to attention and directed action, as Peters puts this, "rather like the question 'What are you trying to do'?" (1973a, p. 13) Furthermore entailed in the term is the idea of an "objective" that is not too close nor too far away and that might or might not be reached. Procedures then connect aim to education through a fusion of content and process. Importantly, Peters wants to disavow a common means-end model since such a model misses the meaning of "education" itself. Writes Peters,

> [The central fact is] that education consists essentially in the initiation of others in to a public world picked out by the language and concepts of a people and structured by rules governing their purposes and interactions with each other...[Herein] the teacher...acts as a guide in helping the children] explore and *share*...[a] public world. (1973a, p. 26, emphasis in original)

As part of this public world, education refers to a larger ideal of "the educated man" and, as indicated, within the institution, "education" takes on meaning as "initiation" into forms of knowledge and understanding. Aims then relate specifically to principles "immanent to procedures" that direct what teachers and students are to do. In this pedagogical process, Peters concludes, "[arguments,] of course, would have to be produced for emphasizing some desirable qualities...[of, and conditions for particular distinct forms of knowledge and understanding] rather than others" (1973a, p. 57).

Elsewhere the arguments Peters alludes to are presented, notably detailed in his text, *Ethics and Education* (Peters, 1966), and in a paper, "The Justification of Education" (Peters 1970/1973b). In the latter, meanings of knowledge and understanding are considered through a dichotomy of instrumental and noninstrumental values. Within instrumental values for education (and an attitude that supports them) are interests of both the individual and the community wherein the importance of survival is based on what is taken to be true along with a greater degree of predictability. These last, Peters writes, "[are] essential to the survival of a civilized community in which process of communication are important" (1973b, p. 243). But, he continues, a problem is posed: instrumental justifications are incomplete because they do not detail the further values of use, in what is done. His answer to this problem is to turn to noninstrumental or intrinsic values for education and to consider this central matter: "[whether and how] knowledge and understanding have strong claims to be included as one of the goods which are constitutive of a worth-while level of life" (p. 247). In an interesting logical development, Peters's tact is to assert constitutive value in the posing of the question itself. To ask "What is the point of life?" in general already demonstrates possession of a noninstrumentalist attitude. As Peters puts this, it means that he who asks is already dissatisfied with an unexamined life, a dissatisfaction that entails several significant values of its own. To conclude, here is Peters on values held by the educated person—he who asks the question:

> He will, first of all, enjoy performing well according to the standards required. He will have an attitude of care in other words. But this care will be related to the point of the activity. He will feel humility towards the givenness of the features of the activity, towards the demands of its standards. And he will have a sense of its connection with other things in life, a wary consciousness of the past and the future and of the place of what is being done in the passage through the present. (p. 264)

For Peters, putting these values into activity (one that benefits the individual and the community) thus fulfills the overall aim of education as acquiring knowledge and understanding.

Dewey on Aims

In his analysis, Peters refers to and distinguishes his view from the earlier philosophical approach to aims of education from Dewey (Peters, 1973a, p. 12). In contrast to the analytical tradition of Peters, Dewey is 'one of the last great speculative philosophers.' His work remains (and today rejoins *us* to) what contemporary philosopher of education, Nel Noddings, names as "the immortal conversation" that connects philosophy of life, wisdom, and the like (Noddings, 1995, p. 1). Dewey is also arguably the spokesperson for classical American pragmatism, the nearly "indigenous" philosophical movement begun around the turn of the last century and enjoying a renaissance today. Having both connections that are made with contemporary Continental theories and with postmodernism, its adherents generally believe in philosophy as antifoundational and truth as realized in consequences. This general view underlies what Dewey believes about education and about aims; specific discussion of aims appears as a central topic in his classic, *Democracy and Education* (1916). The text is easier to read than many of his writings because it was commissioned as a textbook and demonstrates clearly Dewey's own approach to "doing" philosophy of education.[13]

In comparison with Peters, one common element of the two is the provision of criteria for desirable conditions of education. Two other aspects contrast: one is Dewey's attention to background from "the history of ideas," and the other is his stipulation of uncommon definition. (Peters allows for quaintness, inconsistency and idiosyncrasy, but he does not start with the last [See Peters, 1973a, p. 48]). One other contrast, too, is Dewey's strategy of placing "aims" within a larger conceptual wholeness: this becomes clear in what follows.[14]

Dewey's conception of education begins with an avowed democratic premise with experience as its starting point. Democracy is the ideal form of human association, based in two criteria. Here is his summing:

> The two points selected by which to measure the worth of a form of social life are the extent in which the interests of a group are shared by all its members, and the fullness and freedom with which...[any group] interacts with other groups. An undesirable society, in other words, is one which internally and ex-

ternally sets up barriers to free intercourse and communication of experience. (Dewey, 1916, 1985, p. 105)

This stipulated definition of democracy is then substantiated in typical Dewey fashion by historical reference to three contrasting social orders in which the two criteria are not met. These are first, Platonic from the classical era, second what he terms "individualistic" from the eighteenth century—primarily from Rousseau—and third, that in which "education is national and social" based in the nineteenth century German thought of Kant, Fichte, and Hegel.[15]

In addition to a democratic premise, aims also arise from a basic conception of education as growth. The centrality of growth indicates many components of Dewey's general philosophy: it naturalism, its root-edness in evolution, its ideal of progress. Growth is to foster further growth for Dewey, something that reads a bit strangely unless one sees growth as analogous to life (Noddings, 1995, p. 26). Growth also has criteria or conditions. One begins with immaturity, as Dewey puts this, "a force positively present—the ability to develop" (Dewey, 1985, p. 26). Growth is something the immature *do* (emphasis added), given natural traits. These are seen positively as dependence and plasticity. Again one sees that Dewey uses terms in new ways; dependence becomes social as interdependence and plasticity becomes the ability to learn from experience (see pp. 48–50). Dewey writes:

One net conclusion is that life is development, and developing growth is life. Translated into educational equivalents, this means…that the educational process has no end beyond itself; it is its own end; and that…the educational process is one of continued reorganizating, reconstructing, transforming. (1985, p. 54)

Now to aims specifically, the concept that for Dewey ties together democracy and education. Here he starts with the nature of aim as falling within an activity as one "which completes or fulfills what went before it" (p. 107).[16] From intrinsic continuity, aim provides direction, direction connected to conditions for realization. One condition of aim is particularly noteworthy: since activity is undertaken, this is that determination and realization of aims means acting intelligently. For Dewey this is to have a mind. He explains that "[mind] is capacity to refer to present conditions to future results, and future consequences to present conditions....[It] is to have a plan that takes account of resources and difficulties" (1985, p. 110). Several criteria then follow for "good aims," with one especially significant for education. This is that aim is an "end-in-view," representative of a "freeing of activities" (p. 112). Relating back to growth, aims direct activities to further, expansive activities. As Dewey makes connection to education, he elaborates,

> [Education as an abstract idea] has no aims. Only persons, parents, teachers, etc., have aims....And consequently their purposes are indefinitely varied....[Furthermore even] the most valid aims which can be put into words will...do more harm than good unless one recognizes that they are...suggestions to educators as to how to observe, how to look ahead, how to choose in liberating and directing the energies of concrete situations. (1985, p. 114)

What this means in practice, Dewey concludes, is that aims must be intrinsic to the needs of the individual being educated, suggest the environment and methods of organizing capacities for activity, and while expansive, be both particular and tangible.

Foucault on Aims

Again one starts with differentiation, of Foucault from Dewey and Peters: to do this is a bit strange theoretically. From within the French intellectual tradition, Foucault does not himself seek comparison or contrast with either American pragmatism or Anglo-American analytical philosophy. Rather his work is response to what he calls "the human sciences" (somewhat different from the social and behavioral sciences in the United States), and concerns what he names as humanist and structuralist traditions. For present purposes, both Dewey and Peters fall within the humanist grouping, even as Dewey, as Foucault, critiques Kantian preoccupations in philosophy. Structuralist forebears to Foucault, one notes, are primarily but not exclusively French from linguistics and anthropology. Foucault's "counter-tradition" is philosophical but also heavily literary. By Anglo-American standards he is ambiguously a philosopher and likely thought of as a historian.

One other distinguishing mark is Foucault's positioning as a "postmodern." Here in another chronological reversal, Peters is modern in his participation in the first part of the linguistic turn (at least in the earliest work) and Dewey, interestingly, does not participate in the turn but for other antifoundational reasons may be said to "sit on the cusp" of postmodernism.[17] In the philosophy of education text cited above, Noddings "situates" Foucault well. She explains:

> Postmodernists believe that the search for an all-encompassing description of knowledge is hopeless. Instead they emphasize...how knowledge and power are connected, how domains of expertise evolve, who profits from and who is hurt by various claims to knowledge, and what sort of language develops in communities of knowers. (Noddings, 1995, p. 72)

Several of these themes are reflected in the three theoretical shifts in philosophical orientation or historical methodologies undertaken by the late Foucault, these accompanied by particular methods of inquiry.[18] The three, emphasizing different vectors of relational "games of truth" (Foucault, [1984] 1985, p. 6) are archaeology, genealogy, and ethics.[19] The first focuses on knowledge relations among discursive practices set in nondiscursive environments, the second poses technologies and strategies in which disciplined micropower relations are "produced," and the third takes up the relation of the self to the self as the first two relations become internalized and "the subject" (persons) comes to be constituted. For present purposes, Foucault's now famous genealogical inquiry into a "history" of discipline demonstrates what might be taken as his vision of "aims"—a term he never used. It is its own form of doing philosophy of education.

Before turning to discipline, indication of what Foucault means by his philosophical work provides additional implicit comparison to Peters and Dewey. In an illuminating (and now oft-quoted) introduction to his ethics, the second volume of *The History of Sexuality* (*The Use of Pleasure*) (cited above), Foucault writes:

> The studies...are of 'history' by reasons of the domain they deal with and the references they appeal to; but they are not the work of a 'historian'.... [They were] a philosophical exercise. The object was to learn to what extent the effort

to think one's own history can free thought from what it silently thinks, and so enable it to think differently. (1985, p. 9)

The result, Foucault concludes, is to attempt to see what one has done from a new vantage point, to serve as bases for problematizations. One general way to do this is to study—as Foucault did—the "margins" and the "marginalized" of society in madness, illness, and criminality.

Criminality is the topic of a now-famous genealogical study, *Discipline and Punish: The Birth of the Prison* (Foucault [1975] 1979). Therein discipline takes on new meaning from its earlier treatment as knowledge in archaeological study;[20] the different focus is on the body and how individual bodies become objects of power relations. Foucault shows that during the seventeenth and eighteenth centuries, control over the body moves from a giving up of torture to an establishment of surveillance. Likewise definitions of criminality change as within the institutions of prison, the military barracks, and the school various technologies operate to produce "disciplined" bodies—those correctly trained and docile.

Discipline, Foucault reveals, functions as hierarchical observation and normalizing judgment organized in specific procedures of examination. Historically a significant aspect was design of buildings, as in schools where at one and the same time individual students were separated from each other in small cells or latrines yet seen at once through cell placement, half-windows and specific lighting. Another aspect was pedagogical practice, and a third, and most important, was the examination itself. Pedagogical practices included creation of differentiated "teaching" roles arranged hierarchically to help the teacher. Foucault writes that "selected from among the best pupils...[were] a whole series of 'officers'—intendants, observers, monitors, tutors, receivers of prayer, writing officers, receivers of ink, almoners, and visitors" (Foucault, 1979, p. 175). Among them all, only the tutors undertook pedagogical tasks. Lastly, in the examination, processes of the "positive production of power" were strengthened and normalized. For example in one French school in 1775, sixteen different examinations were given each year. Foucault explains that "the examination in the school was a constant exchanger or knowledge: it guaranteed the movement of knowledge from the teacher to the pupil, but it extracted from the pupil a knowledge destined and reserved for the teacher (1979, p. 187). Thus, through specific building design, pedagogical organization and examination function as disciple and form the aims of schooling. Most importantly, these aims become scientific; and in Foucault's words, they create reality, "[producing] domains of objects and rituals to truth...[about hierarchically differentiated 'individuals']" (p. 194).

Conclusion

This chapter has undertaken two related purposes, first to characterize the guildlike professional organization of philosophy of education (primarily in its North American/U.S. form) and second, to offer an illustration of guild-work. There is an intentional irony in the chapter overall as its subthesis has been to posit that a singular structure has nonetheless fostered a contemporary diversity of background, interest, and approach to doing the work. The irony is furthered in presentation of a relatively conventional illustration. But the chapter does suggest diversity in many characterizing assertions and in its own example.

To conclude, *I* remind readers that this has been one guild member's analysis of the field. My approach has had two parts, one a historical analysis developed categorically and based primarily in my acquaintance and participation. In part one, except for some general citation, there is almost no reference to authoritative sources. In contrast, in the second part turns to the three traditions, reorganizes them in time, and while presenting them in one-vocal form, does include diverse viewpoints on a singular topic. Given close textual focus of much writing in the field, a multitradition look has been seldom done except for encyclopedia entries.[21]

In this textual analysis a limitation of the chapter requires mention. While implicit I think, Dewey, Peters, and Foucault have specific approaches that play out in the style of their own writings. These perhaps do not emerge sufficiently in what has been extrapolated: a directed criticism of their respective "writing styles" would be more demonstrative.

One last comment situates this chapter in the present volume of "futures" of the various educational studies—I cannot resist. The health of the guild and its work receives mixed reviews. On the one hand, there does seem "something for everyone" in the present diversity within the guild—and a period of some acrimony seems past. Interestingly this diversity does not demonstrate the trend of past history of a new tradition coming to dominate a predecessor. Pluralism—whether all members see each other as "doing philosophy" or not—reigns. On the other hand, debate continues about the purposes and success of the field. Questions continue about the relation of philosophy of education to philosophy and (now more so than in the past) to other disciplines. And questions continue about the influence of philosophy of education on educational thought and practice. With regard to this last, first it does seem to me that now as ever before, educational theorists of all interests and traditions are reading philosophy and thus the field can claim a value. However, the connection between the reading and valuing of philosophy in general to *philosophers of education* seems to lag behind. It is debatable too if educators beyond the theorists appropriately recognize the texts, the individual contributions, and the relevance of the field for more practical work. For both, I believe, recognition in the future of the multifaceted diversity of the field as this chapter has described—of extension beyond doing philosophy in a strictly technical sense—can add support for the guild's reputation of meritorious contributions to education.[22]

Notes

1. An earlier and substantively different version of this chapter entitled "Diversity Is Thy Name: U.S. Philosophy of Education Today" was delivered as part of an invited symposium at the annual meeting of the American Educational Studies Association, Detroit, October 1999. Thanks to George Noblit for the invitation, to Steve Tozer for the reference to "guild," and to other session participants, Nick Burbules, Jim Garrison, and Wendy Kohli. See also an earlier reference to guild from the late Harry Broudy (1981).

2. See "Notice to the Publisher" for the occasion of an introduction to publication from the Early English Text Society in Brentano (1870).

3. The characterization of the guild of the Philosophy of Education Society (PES) is mine alone; I apologize for any misrepresentation of like associations in Great Britain, Australia, and Asia among others. While Canada has its own regional association and its own history of philosophy of education, its vital participating in PES makes it a North American association today.

4. See Curren (2000) for a more positive spin on the relationship to the parent discipline.

5. There are some extant Dewey reading groups and a project devoted to educational practice, the John Dewey Project on Progressive Education at the University of Vermont, directed by Kathleen Kesson. [Contact is uvm.edu/~dewey/].

6. Still found in foundations textbooks, the "isms" are philosophies of education by which practitioners can identify their premises; examples of "isms" range from realism and idealism to existentialism and Marxism.

7. Yearbooks (of refereed meeting proceedings) over at least the past five years demonstrate relatively equal participation by men and women, and scholarly representation of many interests and subtraditions. See Stone (2001) for a recent assessment and other volumes of Philosophy of Education.

8. As PES members earn their "names," they are selected to be national reviewers for the program—and yearbook publication—and they are elected to the nominations committee to select the president and to standing bodies, the executive committee and the commission on professional affairs.

9. Three examples of philosophers of education with distinctive approaches are Maxine Greene, Denis Phillips, and Walter Feinberg.

10. I believe Soltis took this significant position in his very influential text on conceptual analysis; see Soltis (1978).

11. Thanks to Nel Noddings and Stephen Thornton for discussion on aims of education.

12. Note the difference in writing style in this second part.

13. See references in Stone (1999) on using Democracy and Education for teaching.

14. The difference here may be one of emphasis, but Peters's conceptual analyses do not seem as "holistic" as do Dewey's.

15. This is found in Dewey's chapter, "The democratic conception of education," pp. 87–106, just prior to the chapter on aims.
16. Note that Peters emphasizes activity but his is largely focused as intellectual.
17. Dewey's philosophy is nonrepresentational and antifoundational, with truth relying neither on correspondences to reality nor to objective a priori frameworks. See Richard Rorty's (1982) several important essays on Dewey.
18. One commentator usefully suggests a fourth Foucault; see Vincent Descombes (1987) and more generally the collection of commentaries on Foucault from David Hoy (1986).
19. Note the dating of the French edition in brackets.
20. See Foucault's *The Order of Things* ([1966] 1970).
21. Several good examples are from Phillips (1985), Chambliss (1996) and Curren (1998).
22. Thanks to Amy Anderson for editing assistance on the first version.

References

Brentano, L. (1870). *On the history and development of guilds and the origin of trade-unions*. London: Trubner & Co., Ludgate Hill.

Broudy, H. (1981). Between the yearbooks. In J. Soltis (Ed.), *Philosophy and education: Eightieth yearbook of the National Society for the Study of Education (Part I)*. Chicago: The University of Chicago Press.

Chambliss, J. (1996). *Philosophy of education: An encyclopedia*. New York: Garland.

Curren, R. (1998). Education, history of philosophy of. In E. Craig (Ed.), *Encyclopedia of philosophy*. London: Routledge.

———. (2000). Introduction: Philosophy of education at the millennium. *Philosophy of education: 1999*. Urbana, IL: Philosophy of Education Society and the University of Illinois at Urbana-Champaign.

Descombes, V. (1987, March 5). Je m'en Foucault. *London Review of Books*, pp. 20-21.

Dewey, J. (1916, 1985). Democracy and education. In J. Boydston (Ed.), *The middle works of John Dewey, 1899–1924 (Vol. 9)*. Carbondale, IL: Southern Illinois University Press.

Foucault, M. (1979). *Discipline and punish: The birth of the prison*. (A. Sheridan, Trans.). New York: Vintage. (Original work published 1975).

————. (1985). *The Use of pleasure (The history of sexuality, Volume 2)*. (R. Hurley, Trans.). New York: Vintage. (Original work published 1984).

Henry, N. (1955). *Modern philosophies of education: The Fifty-fourth yearbook of the National Society for the Study of Education*. Chicago: The University of Chicago Press.

Hoy, D. (Ed.). (1986). *Foucault: A critical reader*. Oxford: Basil Blackwell.

Johnson, T. (1995). *Discipleship or pilgrimage? The educator's quest for philosophy*. Albany: State University of New York Press.

Kaminsky, J. (1993). *A new history of educational philosophy*. Westport, CT: Greenwood Press.

Noddings, N. (1995). *Philosophy of education*. Boulder, CO: Westview.

Peters, R. (1963, 1968). Must an educator have an aim? In C. Macmillan and T. Nelson (Eds.), *Concepts of teaching: Philosophical essays*. Chicago: Rand McNally.

————. (1966). *Ethics and education*. Atlanta: Scott-Foresman.

————. (1965, 1973a). Aims of education—A conceptual inquiry (Including further thoughts on the concept of education). In *Philosophy of education*. Oxford: Oxford University Press. (This also includes commentary by J.Woods and W. Dray).

————. (1970, 1973b). The justification of education. In *Philosophy of education*. Oxford: Oxford University Press.

Phillips, D. (1985). *Philosophy of education. International encyclopedia of education: Research and studies*. Oxford: Pergamon.

Pinar, W., & Doll, W. (conference leaders), (March 1999). Philosophy of Education and the Internationalization of Curriculum, conference at Louisiana State University.

Renard, G. (1919). Guilds in the middle ages. (D. Terry, Trans.). London: G. Bell and Sons, Ltd.

Rorty, R. (1982). *Consequences of pragmatism: Essays, 1972–1980.* Minneapolis: University of Minnesota Press.

Soltis, J. (1978). *An introduction to the analysis of educational concepts.* Reading, MA: Addison-Wesley.

———. (Ed.). (1981). *Philosophy of education: Eightieth yearbook of the National Society for the Study of Education (Part I).* Chicago: The University of Chicago Press.

Stone, L. (1999, April). *Misunderstanding? Or what Dewey doesn't tell me about teaching.* Symposium paper at the annual meeting of the American Educational Research Association, SIG John Dewey Society, Montreal.

———. (2001). *Post-Millennial PES—Introduction to Philosophy of Education: 2000.* Philosophy of Education: 2000. Urbana, IL: Philosophy of Education Society and the University of Illinois. Urbana-Champaign.

Chapter Five

Making the Philosophical Practical

Steve Tozer

Overview

The thesis of this chapter is that the field of philosophy of education can and should have a greater impact on educational practices than it does, particularly in practices of schooling, but that this may require expanding how we do philosophy of education.[1] The argument begins with the premise that it is reasonable to expect that philosophers of education, whatever else they might legitimately do, should seek to influence the practices of schooling—at least collectively, if not on each individual's part—because educational philosophy is a form of inquiry into the practices of an applied field, and considerable social and economic resources are invested into this branch of inquiry. However, there is reason to believe that the return on this investment is not adequate, and that it suffers in comparison to other areas of educational inquiry. Part of the reason for this is that philosophy of education is considered good and valuable if it is judged to represent good philosophy—if it makes a contribution to the conversation among philosophers of education, rather than a contribution to improving schooling practices. Put differently, the guild values its craftspersons' work primarily on philosophical criteria independent of consequences for schooling practice. There are multiple ways that philosophy of education *can* make a difference to educational practice, but these are not regarded nor practiced as part of the central craft of the guild. For these other kinds of activities to gain currency would require widening our conception of what counts as doing philosophy of education. Such broadening can be of considerable benefit to the educational

and social justice causes that many philosophers of education embrace—
and may be important to the future of philosophy of education.

A Disclaimer Rooted in Postmodern Doubt

As Lynda Stone reminds us in the preceding chapter, the field of philosophy of education has changed over time, and is changing now. In the past few decades, we have seen the profile of the membership and annual programs of the Philosophy of Education Society (PES) change as philosophy of education has been influenced by successive waves of new interests among scholars, and there is no reason to suppose that we will become static in our current configuration. The postmodern move away from a dominant narrative or methodological approach is still evolving. Two years ago, for example, we saw for the first time at PES a small but critical mass of scholars pursuing *Africana* philosophy of education, and we are continuing to see new discussions in gender theory and queer theory. The changes in what qualifies as philosophy of education are readily apparent in the PES program over the past several years. Stone seems reasonable in her view that considerable strength resides in the diversity within philosophy of education and in PES, its primary guild.

The undeniable influence of the "postmodern" on contemporary philosophy of education brings to mind a point Patti Lather (1991) made in *Educational Theory* over a decade ago: that postmodernism is not a new paradigm but a disruptive and a disintegrating impulse in the prevailing one. Lather's observation is one way to interpret familiar remarks about the postmodern challenge to dualisms, to certainty, to grand narratives, and so on. The postmodern challenge to certainty cautions against a too-ready tendency to announce a new epoch in intellectual life. I want to embrace that tentativeness as I pursue this inquiry, for it may appear to be presented with considerably more certainty that I experience as I present it.

A Shared Disquietude

I have approached this paper with disquietude that familiar to philosophers of education. It is that the field in which we are trained does not seem well suited, as it is practiced, to address in effective ways the practical concerns about social justice that brought many of us to education.[2] I would add that when we most effectively address those concerns in our activist practices, we find ourselves standing outside the ordinary practices and discourse of the field. As Lynda Stone has observed, professional rewards in the field of philosophy of education are closely tied to one's production of scholarly philosophical publications. Such publications do not appear, on their face, to have much impact on the conduct of schooling in the United States, as I will discuss.

I believe I am similar to other philosophers of education in that I respect the field and what it has contributed to my ability to think about education and its relations to social justice, issues that led me to philosophy of education in the first place. This respect for the field and its effects on me might be taken as counter evidence to my view that the influences of philosophy of education are insufficient. The contradiction here is that when I am most demonstrably influencing educational practice through work with schools and school districts, I am not doing philosophy of education as it is generally recognized; and when I am doing professional philosophy of education, I am doing very little that I could demonstrate achieves educational change. I would like to engage in a recognizable practice of a philosophy of education that attempts to resolve this contraction, one that more clearly and effectively engages the social justice dimensions of educational practice.

The contradiction causing my disquietude has been framed a number of different ways by philosophers of education, from Dewey (1916) to Broudy (1981) to Renee Arcilla's (2002) recent article, "Why Aren't Philosophers and Educators Speaking to Each Other?" These treatments generally address the putative dual disciplinary parentage and dual audience for philosophy of education, viz., the fields of philosophy and education, and the possible obligations for the field to speak effectively to both audiences. Other recent treatments include Burbules (1990) on "The Dilemma of 'Relevance' in the Philosophy of Education," and Susan Laird (1998) asking, "Can This Marriage be Saved?" Not all of these treatments express my disquietude; some question the validity of the assumptions underlying this well-known concern itself.

Does Philosophy of Education Have an Inadequate Effect on Schooling Practices?

To answer this question affirmatively requires plausible support for at least two premises: first, that it is reasonable to expect philosophy of education to have an impact on schooling practices, and second, that the field is having less impact than we might reasonably expect.

It is reasonable to expect that philosophers of education, whatever else they might legitimately do, should seek to influence the practices of schooling—at least collectively, if not on each individual's part—because educational philosophy is a form of inquiry into the practices of an applied field. Considerable social and economic resources are invested into the assumption that the inquiry will have consequences for application. In an intellectual domain that is committed to thinking about thinking, perhaps it is not surprising that we philosophers would have limited impact on practice. But if philosophy of education, unlike philosophy more broadly, is expected to address an applied field of practice, it resembles research into medical practice, another applied field. If we were to learn that medical research had no consequences for medical practice, we would be reluctant to support it—we would find it difficult to justify society's considerable economic and institutional investment into such inquiry. Philosophy of education is much less expensive, but if we are not able to show that it has consequences for educational practice, it becomes difficult to justify in competition for scarce resources in schools and colleges of education.

A related illustration, concerning the teaching of philosophy of education, might be this: if it could be shown in some compelling way that coursework in medical ethics had no impact on the practice of medicine, the medical field might be tempted to jettison those courses from the curriculum. Instead, it could be countered, we should try to understand what an effective course in medical ethics might be, and how to document its consequences in practice. It is one thing to be unable to demonstrate a field's consequences for practice, and another thing to demonstrate compellingly that is has negligible consequences. Because resources are limited, however, that distinction is easily overlooked by those deciding whether to invest university resources in, say, additional literacy research and teaching vs. philosophy of education research and teaching.

Such an example might be assailed as just so much conservative accountability rhetoric, but it comes from a different intellectual and ethical location. It comes from a belief that it is important to protect and preserve philosophical inquiry in education, and from the conviction that at least some significant body of our work should serve the interests of those who are least well served by contemporary schools. I further believe there is a probable instrumental relationship between those two beliefs: that if we do not do better achieving the latter, it will be more difficult to achieve the former.

Beyond the social investment argument, then, lies the social justice expectation. Philosophers of education have long been concerned about the extent to which schooling practices do or do not serve democratic ideals, as evidenced by the prominence of democratic values in our writing. One's historical review might include such illustrations as Dewey's *Democracy and Education*; the 1930s and 1940s-era social reconstructionist journal *The Social Frontier*; Broudy, Smith and Burnett's *Democracy and Excellence in American Secondary Education* (1964), the emergence of feminist philosophy of education, and recent postmodern analyses of the interconstitutive nature of power, knowledge, and oppression. Your list of illustrations might look entirely different and still make the same point: any comprehensive survey of the history and current practice of philosophy of education would identify the enduring concern philosophers of education have had for the extent to which educational practices, including schooling, embody antidemocratic social processes and the possibilities for a more democratic practice. It is simply unreasonable to suppose that these authors would rest easy believing that their work had no effect on these antidemocratic impulses in American public schooling. While Burbules (1990) pointed out correctly that not all philosophy of education must be evidently "relevant" to educational practice, neither did he argue that position that none of it need be. Not only is that stance untenable if we expect our field to be supported by public and private resources, but it is ethically untenable if we want our work to have consequences beyond the securing of our own tenure in privileged positions.

There is further reason to believe that the return on our social investment in philosophy of education is not adequate, and that we who
value social justice should not take comfort in the achievements of our
field. If philosophy of education were having an impact on educational
practices in schools over time, for example, what might count as evidence of this? One kind of evidence might be the contributions of philosophy of education to the successive waves of reform that have washed
over schooling for the past sixty years, from the life adjustment curriculum of the 1940s to the comprehensive high school movement beginning
in the 1950s to desegregation and busing in the 1960s to the behaviorism
and competency based teacher education of the 1970s to the *Nation at
Risk* reforms of the 1980s to the multiculturalism and standards-based
movements in learning and teacher preparation of the 1990s. Again, pick
your own list of major schooling movements. An analysis I conducted
for the 50th anniversary of the Philosophy of Education Society indicated
that in the pages of the proceedings of the Philosophy of Education Society annual meetings, there has been very little evidence of philosophers
even addressing these movements, let alone influencing them (1991). Although I tempered my criticism with the recognition that PES articles are
not all that philosophers of education produce, Maxine Greene remarked
at the time that it is as if philosophers of education had been sitting for
fifty years in windowless rooms (1991).

But the history of major school reform movements is not the only
place where the impact or non-impact of philosophy of education might
be demonstrated; that history tends to be influenced by social, political,
and economic forces larger than research and the voices of academics.
One might look to the conduct of contemporary schooling, however, and
the debates that are shaping it to see where philosophers of education and
other scholars have contributed. Today's schools are marked by an accountability and standardized achievement testing movement that is antithetical to most of what philosophers of education since Dewey have
argued. We see the rise of a conservative, market-based movement in
school choice, charters, and vouchers that most philosophers have opposed, when they have addressed it at all. At the same time, the small-
schools movement is prominent in many major cities, a movement to
which philosophers have contributed very little in their writing (an ex-

ception to these last two points is former PES President Mary Anne Raywid, who has promoted both schools of choice and small schools in her activism and writing). Teacher education is increasingly standards-based and outcome-measures driven, a movement that owes essentially nothing to discourse in philosophy of education. We see teachers and school systems seeking to embrace constructivist approaches to teaching and learning that have been influenced far more by the field of educational psychology than philosophy, though the concepts are not new to philosophy and are discussed in our writing. Today's schools incorporate far more small-group activity than they did twenty years ago, a movement influenced by educational psychology and that bears no identifiable marks of professional philosophy of education, though most philosophers of education would welcome it. A literacy movement emphasizing particular approaches to the teaching of reading and writing, owing much to federally sponsored literacy research and virtually nothing to philosophy of education, is influencing teaching and teacher preparation across the nation.

In mathematics instruction in schools, the National Council on Teaching of Mathematics has driven major changes in the past decade, with the sources of their agenda locatable in cognition research and mathematics learning research rather than in philosophy of education. The multicultural education, sex education, and character education curricula now prominent in public schooling have taken a character and shape on which no philosophers of education with whom I am familiar would want to claim an influence. And contemporary debates over school funding, the central importance of school leadership, how to re-shape the profession of teaching, and the like are being conducted with little or no visible input from the field of philosophy of education.

This list of characteristics of contemporary schooling is merely illustrative, not comprehensive. If the characterization above is more accurate and fair than not, a plausible explanation for the relative marginality of philosophers of education may lie in the relatively recent history of the professional guild of philosophy of education in the U.S., largely a late twentieth century phenomenon. As the guild has shaped its identity, it has valued its craftspersons' work based on philosophical criteria independent of consequences for schooling practice. Philosophy of education is considered good and valuable if it is good philosophy—if it makes a contribution to the conversation among philosophers of education. There may be multiple ways that philosophy of education could make a difference to educational practice, but these are not typically regarded as the central craft of the guild. Yet, they could be.

It should be noticed that it has *not* been demonstrated here that philosophy of education has no consequences for practice. It might have impact, for example, in shaping the consciousness and understanding of the many thousands of teacher and school administration candidates and practitioners who take courses from philosophers of education, and similarly in affecting the hundreds of non-philosopher faculty in schools of education who might be reading our books and our articles in professional journals.

What is curious about this position, however, is that in a field that highly values knowledge and what counts as knowledge, we don't know—even in a superficial sense—that our work is having either of these effects. If anything, the evidence at hand should cause us to believe otherwise, as the next section suggests. What would count as evidence that our work is having a salutary impact on schooling practices? This question leads, I believe, to a discussion of how philosophy of education might look different in the future

Envisioning New Projects in Philosophy of Education

What this discussion has lacked is a well-developed theory of influence. While I have suggested some ways of assessing the relative influence of philosophy of education on contemporary schooling, there has been no attempt to work out a good theoretical account of what would count as evidence of influence and what would not. Such an account is a necessary step, it seems to me, in going forward with the project I am outlining here, but that task is beyond the scope of this essay. In the interim, a number of examples can serve to illustrate what such a theory of scholarly influence on practice might illuminate: instances of philosophy of education that engage our discourse more adequately with attempts to influence practices in schooling. Each of these examples takes advantage of activities in which philosophers of education are already engaged.

The first example is the scholarship necessary to document and analyze the consequences, if any, of our teaching school practitioners—teacher and administrator candidates and practitioners. As indicated earlier, for us to believe that our teaching and our textbook writing influences teachers and administrators in practice is largely a matter of faith, not evidence or knowledge. It would be an important undertaking to show what counts as influence of our teaching on practice, and to be able to test that theory empirically. Surely no one believes that all kinds of teaching of philosophy of education are equally effective at shaping the understandings and practices of teachers-to-be, for example. But which approaches are more effective than others, and what counts as effective? Such scholarship would have the potential to teach us something we simply don't know about philosophy of education and would likely guide the future teaching practices of our field. Imagine a paper presenting such scholarship, carefully conducted in theory and in empirical analysis, at the Philosophy of Education Society or American Educational Research Association. The resulting discussion could be both philosophically and educationally important.

A second philosophical project could involve developing a theory of educational change that is grounded in active, collaborative school improvement efforts with practitioners, documented in ways that engage the guild in philosophical discourse about change theory, influence theory, and their evidence in practice. Perhaps the greatest change theorist to come out of our field, greater than Dewey in this domain, was former PES president and charter member Kenneth D. Benne. Benne teamed with Warren Bennis and Robert Chin to co-edit and author *The Planning of Change*, an influential book that has remained in print for forty years (1961). Bennis, who thereafter became a high-profile leader in the organizational change and development field, wrote an "intellectual memoir" in 2001 that recalled *The Planning of Change* as "an attempt to encompass in one volume the most seminal and original essays in the yet unborn field of organizational change" (2001). Bennis credits Benne with coining the phrase "change agent" in that volume. The point here is twofold: one is that philosophers of education have something to contribute to change theory in the whole enterprise of school improvement, and the second is that genuine engagement with practitioners is likely to be necessary for the generation of any theory that is sufficiently grounded in the lived experience of practitioners to have credibility, specificity, and likelihood of application in practice. Benne knew this, and his experimental work in group dynamics with the Bethel, Maine, group is now part of the history of organizational change. He last addressed the implications of this topic for professors of education in his final book, *The Task of Post-Contemporary Education* (1990).

A third kind of project involves participating in educational policy formation that affects practice, and documenting this in ways that engage the guild in philosophical policy discourse. Former PES President Mary Anne Raywid is a recent and relatively exceptional example of a philosopher whose policy activism, in her case in the schools-of-choice movement, became material for discourse with her PES colleagues. Her presidential address in 1988 provided an analysis of the extent to which schools of choice could create learning communities involving parents, students, and teachers, and she thereby subjected the premises and values of her policy activism to the critical commentary of her peers (1989). Other philosophers of education also engage themselves in policy activism in their institutions and in wider policy making contexts. Engaging the members of the guild in the philosophical issues raised by these, including the important issue of how philosophy can effect policy change, would be a step toward a mutual influence of the school policy environment on philosophy of education and vice versa.

A final project that would look different from what we ordinarily do in the guild is to interrogate the assumptions of efficacy that underlie our philosophical writing. Do philosophers of education, theorists in an applied field, write with no intention of having any impact on practice, or do they hope and intend to have such impact? What theoretical perspective, what theory of change or of impact, would lead us to believe that writing journal articles, books, and conference presentations would be likely to have any impact at all on the conduct of schooling in the U.S.? One can provide a theory of change for how mathematical learning research, organized and disseminated by the National Council on Teaching of Mathematics through state and local districts, might and does have an impact on school practices. What would such a theoretical account look like for philosophy of education? Absent such a theory of efficacy for our written work, it does not even seem reasonable to believe that it *could* have any impact.

The four examples presented here are grounded in the teaching, writing, and activism that philosophers of education already do. What is different is the focus and kind of inquiry suggested. This is not to suggest that no philosophers of education do this kind of work. I have mentioned some already, and others may come to mind (Susan Laird's work with Girl Scouts, for example, or Bob Floden's work in teacher certification). What is argued here is that not nearly enough of this kind of work is done for philosophy of education to have a visible impact on schooling practice, and that the conventions of the guild actively and mainly reward work that has no discernible effect.

Making (Recovering) the Practical in Philosophy of Education

Widening our conception of what counts as doing philosophy of education in the above ways can be of considerable benefit to the education and social justice causes that many philosophers of education embrace. This wider conception would involve a new philosophical /educational praxis that engages philosophers in theorizing and testing the practical applications of their own work in teaching, collaborating with practitioners, engaging in policy formation, and interrogating the efficacy of their own scholarship. It theorizes practical influence and it tests the theory in practice.

More than making the philosophical practical, however, I am concerned about *making the practical philosophical*. I want to continue to explore what counts as philosophy of education in ways that take the current evolution of the guild further into the practices of schooling. When I was trained in philosophy of education, conceptual analysis dominated, and Dewey and the social reconstructionists were barely of historical interest. However, social philosophy made a resurgence in the 1980s, led by feminist, neo-Marxist, critical, identity, postcolonial and generally postmodern theorizing that has left at least some of our more "analytic" colleagues wondering what happened to philosophy. But very few would challenge the assertion that all of these postmodern modes of discourse are themselves analytic; the term has had to re-expand its meaning away from the narrowly, guild-defined meaning it had taken on for twenty years. Similarly, I expect to join with others in exploring a way to make the practical work we do as individuals—the change-oriented, power-challenging work in professional education programs, schools, school districts, state legislatures, and national agencies—speak to philosophy of education as a field. Given the work of some of our forebears such as Mary Anne Raywid, Harry Broudy, and Kenneth Benne, perhaps what I am calling for is the recovery of the practical in philosophy of education.

One way we may do so is by maintaining a steady posture of listening to the lived experiences of those who are least privileged in this culture, and recognizing that we in our guild are among the most privileged, and then asking how our work can be most valuable to others, rather than primarily to our guild and ourselves. Our work could thus be more clearly motivated by taking seriously the power relations and power differentials of philosophers of education and children in terrible schools, using our resources to do something about them, and then making public the philosophical dimensions of that work to colleagues who may wish to engage in that dialogue.

Finally, to return to the postmodern attitude of doubt and uncertainty: I could be wrong about all of this. I could be wrong that the activist work I and others do in schools is helping anyone at all; that philosophical training ought to be or can be made relevant to schooling practices in documentable ways; or that it matters whether the guild recognizes such work as valuable. But these are the questions that are of most interest to me in my position of privilege in the guild and the larger society that are the context of my work.

Notes

1. An earlier and substantially different version of this paper was presented as a response to papers presented by Nick Burbules and Lynda Stone at a symposium at the annual meeting of the American Educational Studies Association, Detroit, October 1999.

2. For purposes of this discussion, "social justice" concerns might be characterized as those concerns arising from the recognition that formal education is an important social good that contributes to the quality of life and life opportunities and is inequitably distributed in contemporary culture. Further, these concerns include the intention to formulate and implement actions at multiple levels of the educational delivery system—in classrooms, schools, communities, and states, for example—that can alter the inequities and potentially lead to a society more consistent with its professed democratic ideals. More simply, social justice concerns in education have to do with understanding and improving the educational conditions that serve some members of society better than others. See the insightful discussions of these concerns and their consequences for education in what might otherwise be considered the naïvely titled *Teaching to Change the World* (1999) by Jeannie Oakes and Martin Lipton. New York: McGraw-Hill.

References

Arcillla, R. (2002). Why aren't philosophers and educators speaking to each other? *Educational Theory, 5*(4).

Benne, K. (1990). *The task of post-contemporary education: Essays in behalf of a human future.* New York: Teachers College Press.

Bennis, W., Spreitzer, G., & Cummings, T. (Eds.) (2001) *The future of leadership.* San Francisco: Jossey Bass.

Bennis, W., Benne, K., & Chin, R. (1984). *The planning of change.* (4th edition). New York: Holt, Rinehart and Winston.

Broudy, H. (1981). Between the yearbooks. In J. Soltis (Ed.), *Philosophy and education: Eightieth yearbook of the National Society for the Study of Education* (Part I). Chicago: The University of Chicago Press.

Broudy, H. S., Smith, B., & Burnett, J. (1964). *Democracy and excellence in American Secondary Education.* Chicago: Rand McNally.

Burbules, N.C. (1990). The dilemma of 'relevance' in the philosophy of education. In Ralph Page (Ed.), *Philosophy of Education 1989* (pp. 187-196). Normal, IL: Philosophy of Education Society.

Dewey, J. (1916, 1985). *Democracy and education. The middle works of John Dewey, 1899–1924* (Vol. 9). J. Boydston (Ed.), Carbondale, IL: Southern Illinois University Press.

Greene, M. (1991). A Response to Beck, Giarelli and Chambliss, Leach, Tozer, and Macmillan *Educational Theory*, 41(4), 321.

Laird, S. (1998). *Teaching and educational theory: Can this marriage be saved?* Paper presented at American Association of Colleges of Teacher Education, New Orleans, Louisiana.

Lather, P. (1991). Deconstructing/deconstructive inquiry: The politics of knowing and being known. *Educational Theory*, 41(2), 153–173.

Raywid, M.A. (1989). Prolegomenon on community. In James Giarelli, (Ed.), *Philosophy of education: 1988* (pp. 16–23). Normal, IL: Philosophy of Education Society.

Tozer, S. (1991). The Philosophy of Education Society and school reform. *Educational Theory*, 41(4), 301–310.

Stone, L. (In press). Philosophy of education as guild work. In G. Noblit & B. Hatt-Echeverria (Eds.), *The future of educational studies*. New York: Peter Lang.

Part Two

Linking Ideas, Practice, and Context

Chapter Six

Community as Text: Applying Ricoeurean Conceptions of Metaphor in Understanding Cultural Relations

Mary Abascal-Hildebrand

Current attitudes provide for exalting difference as the basis for multiculturalism. The result is a separatist, superficial stance toward cultural relations. However, I propose here a refigured multiculturalism, one that depends instead on difference and commonality as aspects of each other, because I contend refiguring multiculturalism is both an intellectual pursuit and a practical pursuit—such refiguring considers community as a textual set of social arrangements and not as a either a collection of separatist entities or a monolithic framework. The point is that a textual orientation is more unifying and constitutive because a textual orientation enables a more comprehensible narrative to emerge, one that is made of metaphoric juxtaposing of differences to preserve their origins in commonality, while also protecting uniquenesses among differences. Thus metaphor, and the narrative that conveys metaphor, depends on and promotes the coherence of text, just as a community depends on a coherent set of social relations.

At the same time, metaphor and its narrative associations also depend on critique for an expanded sense of difference because critique broadens the interpretation possible within a narrative construction. Critique can unify ideas at the same time it signals the importance of interpreting competing claims and preserving those competing claims that serve the community's vitality. Likewise, communities depend on critique to illuminate the problems they hope to resolve. Interpretation is vital to critique, whether at the level of a narrative or at the level of community relations, because interpretation enables coherent narrative connections among the way parts relate, in configuring and refiguring a whole, while also preserving idiosyncrasies and uniquenesses so as to avoid monolithic tendencies.

Since Paul Ricoeur's theory of language turns on interpretation and critique, because of the metaphoric and narrative relations that critique provides, his theory is offered here as the ground for teaching the philosophical foundations of multicultural education, as a more illuminated, intellectual approach to socially constitutive arrangements.

The basis of this essay is that difficulty with cultural relations emerges in large part from the distinction made between explanation and understanding, and the way we apply the distinction to social life, because we have inherited an Enlightenment belief that explanation is separate from understanding. We believe explanation alone is sufficient for describing the world in which we live; we believe understanding can be achieved apart from what we need to describe our complex social worlds, to find practical prescriptions. Therefore, we distinguish description from prescription—what I refer to in this essay as the intellectual from the practical. We believe describing our social worlds is separate from the process we undertake in prescribing an ethics framework that might better guide how we live within those worlds. A separatist orientation predisposes us against forming coherence through narrative and its metaphor possibilities, and through critical interpretation.

Therefore, my purpose is to urge those who teach in the foundations of education to consider the significance of a critical, interpretive conception of cultural relations, to learn the metaphorical and narrative capacity of a critical interpretive theory of language for community formation, in order to avoid a prolonging separatist, superficial, fixed view of social relations that misconstrues the origins of difference.

To accomplish my purpose, I offer Ricoeur's ideas about explanation and understanding and description and prescription, so I can establish how an intellectual theory of cultural life provides for practical applications. I address his ideas about metaphor and narrative for the purpose of relating them to explanation and understanding—to point out that metaphor enables us to plot together ideas and events from what might otherwise have appeared as unconnected, while narrative enables us to re-explain and re-understand how a set of ideas can be connected. Thus, Ricoeur's intellectual theory urges a philosophy of language orientation as the means for a more intelligible, ethical, and practical anthropology—an intellectual and practical multiculturalism.

Difference and Fixed Worlds

The separation of description from prescription (the intellectual from the practical) poses the world as fixed in time and space. A fixed world cannot accommodate a social world, made of numerous dynamic cultures that emerge from particular concrete historical communities, because a social world turns on the way the members of its communities continuously view and *re-view* their experiences as they move through time and space together. At the same time, they root their experiences within their traditions, all within this larger, interdependent world—a lifeworld.

Fixed worlds require fixed expectations—including fixed expectations about difference. In a fixed world, difference is seen as separate from commonality because an interdependent world is ignored as having no relevance for what might appear as smaller, particular worlds. As such, the relationships between difference and commonality, just as with explanation and understanding, description and prescription, or the intellectual and practical, become self-referential. Differences are acknowledged without much attention to whether they "make sense"; or whether they are useful for making social alignments or for choosing appropriate, *joint* courses of action. Accordingly, difference becomes its own hallmark, artificially separated from commonality.

A focus on difference makes it difficult for many to grasp the concept of difference as an aspect of commonality, even though young children with whom I have addressed these topics can "get it." A five-year-old once said to me gleefully, when we were talking about one another's faces, "We have different noses because we all have noses, and we have different hair because we all have hair—well most of us have hair, except my Uncle Brad," he explained. But then he displayed his deft understanding of an even weightier point, as he added gleefully, "But, he *used* to have hair!"

A tendency to focus on difference has deep historical and intellectual roots in the U.S. social consciousness. Robert N. Bellah, in his landmark piece, *The Broken Covenant* (1963, 1992), explains the polarity in our Calvinist traditions whereby the "saved" and the "sinner" are *called* to separate themselves from one another, to make the sinners the social outcast in order to protect the saved—according to the way John Calvin envisioned the Divine plan. Furthermore, there is no possibility of redemption for Calvin's sinners, and hence there is no obligation on the part of the saved to fold sinners into their midst. Calvin's sinners cannot be tolerated, they must be cast out.

Bellah explains that this Calvinistic polarity has allowed another polarity—in effect doubling the effect of the associated sanctions against outcasts, as Calvinism confronted perceived needs for survival by invoking slavery and indigenous genocide. Hence, John Winthrop and his congregation broke the covenant they made with one another to live by the biblical exhortation to be a community, of one body, even though they made this covenant as a hallmark of thanksgiving for their having made the Atlantic crossing safely. In order to accomplish political settlements and economic development, and respond to the waves of immigration that followed their own, the Calvinistic settlement made new demarcations around their "body," to save themselves from new "sinners." Hence, this double polarity provides for the culturally "different" to be accorded the same rank as that of the sinner—to be cast out of society to protect the society from the sinner's "taint." Likewise, whatever is deemed culturally aligned is accorded social protection or membership within the group, and creates an elite.

As with Calvinism, a cultural polarity does not allow for those who are different to "save" themselves from that condition, such that they can never, even by taking on the cultural hallmarks of the elite group, actually become "cleansed" enough of their earlier attributes to be of one body with the elite. This affords the elite an artificial belief that they have the right to claim sole ownership of the hallmarks of social membership. These double polarities are thus deeply rooted. Because Enlightenment claims developed during the same time as the origins of these double polarities, Enlightenment distinctions added wider legitimacy to Calvinist thinking and its related cultural separatism, in effect cementing an enduring pluralism that challenges the sort of refigured multiculturalism this writing proposes. Altogether, the acceptance of these polarities as fixed polarities, and our Enlightenment adherence to polarizing explanation and understanding, description and prescription, the intellectual from the practical, and also difference and commonality, combine as powerful sets of conditions to overcome. Their power influences us to imagine too readily that it is an artificial pursuit to challenge this fixed world by claiming that these sets of polarizations are and ought to be considered not as distinctive from but as aspects of each other.

Because of these deep roots, refiguring social relations on the basis for what we hold in common is going to require a major shift in social thought, possible only, I believe, through a reeducation—an intellectual refiguring—about difference and commonality. Such refiguring is possible, however, if we learn about and work to appropriate our language capacities, to lay those capacities alongside restrictive and outmoded polarities, in order to point out the potential available to us to critique polarized conditions. This posture on critique can give us confidence that it is possible to reframe such sets of polarities and expose them as superficial, separatist attempts that interfere with deeper, more authentic, and constitutive cultural relations and recognize life as a set of shared conditions.

Language and Shared Worlds

While a focus on difference may be less challenging when there are few problems among social or cultural groups, and there are sufficient resources for everyone, such a focus makes it difficult to seek mutual recognition or form alliances along shared conditions in order to solve more complex problems. We are less likely to believe we have mutual interests and needs which unite us, and are more likely to frame our interests as personal self-interest or as group self-interest in the form of identity politics.

However, if we were to develop a textual and intellectual critique of the Enlightenment distinction we make between explanation and understanding, description and prescription, or between difference and commonality, by making the case that such bifurcation creates problems for cultural relations, we could claim first that cultural relations are not fixed *in* time and space. We could claim then that cultural relations are built *over* time and space, and that apparent polarities actually have shared origins—they each emerge from shared language capacities, the ability we each have to use language to reframe our world.

In practical terms, we could learn, too, that language forms cultural relations because it enables us to explain our experiences to one another, so we might understand better, and so we could learn more about one another's experiences. A more conscious attention to language-use forms cultural relations intellectually as well as practically because our descriptions about cultural life generate into our prescriptions about how we ought to live in the world. By extension, we could learn that language forms our ideas about both difference and commonality. Thus, explanation and understanding share the world of our experience, description and prescription share that world, too, and difference and commonality also share that same world.

Since language is what all these sets of concepts share, then language is the basis for whatever else communities of persons share. These are the intellectual terms by which language forms cultural relations: not only does language enable us to shape explanation and understanding *together*, and prescription and description *together*, language also enables us to shape difference and commonality *together*. But language does so because it provides us with ways to speak of things as we would wish—language is not lodged in a fixed world. Language enables us to generate ideas in novel ways; language enables us to constitute new plots or to refigure new alignments whenever we refigure something we had posed earlier.

Instead of an artificial pursuit, then, a language-conscious examination of the interdependence of explanation and understanding, description or prescription, or difference and commonality would be both an intellectual and a practical pursuit because reframing them would focus on shared social relations. When we base our associations on what bind us, we are more able to imagine ways to sustain our communities during those difficult times that confront all people in finding mutually acceptable solutions.

Imagination As Text

I point to Ricoeur's ideas that imagination provides the means for believing that what we might want to do is possible. Imagination "enables motivation (and) allows us to put conditions on what we might do...reflecting on complex political, economic, and social contexts, and the ethics implicated in them" (Abascal-Hildebrand, 1999a, p. 271). Imagination opens our vistas on how aspects of a situation are bound up in other aspects.

Ricoeur writes that imagination becomes the textual ground from which we discern relationships among conditions that appear different, and portray ourselves as agents with the capacity to discern and to act on our discernments. Imagination is where we "evaluate motives as diverse as desires and ethical obligations, themselves as disparate as professional rules, social customs, or intensely personal values...(and where) I try out my power to act" (1997, pp. 177-178). Imagination puts us closer to engaging our capacities for moving in the directions we seek.

I apply Ricoeur's ideas about language *as text,* to his conceptions of community *as text*, especially his conceptions of the relation between and among explanation and understanding, and metaphor and narrative, by way of imagination. Throughout much of his work he claims that language is primordial, "it is *language* (emphasis in the original) that is the primary condition of all human experience" (Ricoeur 1997, p. 16). We are born into traditions of ideas all of which share a language schema—we are born into a world that already constituted out of language. We engage in language for both thought and action, as thought and action as aspects of each other. Ricoeur writes of this inseparability of thought and action, "...reinscription of the theory of texts within the theory of action (shows that) discourses are themselves actions...(and) this is why the mimetic bond—in the most active sense of the term *mimetic* (emphasis in original)—between the act of saying...and effective action is never completely severed (1997e, p. xiv).

Drawing on Ricouer's notion of mimesis (1987) to relate thought to action, I propose that a textual community forms intelligible cultural relations, because a textual community is able to engage language to reflect on itself, and translate reflections into action. A textual community is made of its past and its future, brought together, given Ricouer's conception of mimesis as a unifier into a refigured present. A textually oriented community seeks to analyze the array of complex conditions that define it, and the relationship those conditions have with other conditions. A textual community is a referenced set of agreements about how we ought to act. Such a community ties together explanation and understanding, description and prescription, and difference and commonality, "It is this world of the text that intervenes in the world of action in order to give it a new configuration, or as we might say, in order to transfigure it" (Ricoeur 1997, p. 10).

A textual world shapes the world of action, in that it provides the motivation for carrying out *refigured* notions of itself. Thus, a textual world remakes itself. If we acknowledge the social world as a textual world, we may be more likely to consider more consciously what we might do to change circumstances we find limiting. Text is made up of words and sentences, drawn from implicit questions made more distinct on reflection about how they are rooted in a context. But, text also reflects the world that enabled the words and the sentences, to form into a text in the first place.

Ricoeur, a theologian and philosopher, claims that it is an Enlightenment mistake to separate explanation from understanding, or to privilege explanation over understanding as some might privilege a giver over a receiver, because he says one explains in order that one understands (1992, pp. 153–163). Furthermore, as Ricoeur reorders explanation, "explanation is not primary but secondary in relation to understanding," (1992, p. 10), because in order to explain in the first place we have to be able to understand what we seek to explain.

This Ricoeurean reordering of explanation and understanding provides a renewed perspective on the significance of reordering difference as commonality as commonality and difference, whereby commonality is the condition out of which difference can be characterized. *It is on this point that this chapter pivots.*

Ricoeur's point is to argue for a withdrawal from Enlightenment bifurcations, for a "less dichotomous and more dialectical sense" of explanation and understanding (1997, p. xv). My point is that difference and commonality ought not to be bifurcated either, but made more dialectical. Effecting a dialectic sense among members of a community of speakers requires a community's willingness to engage in more conscious language exchanges, so members can experience a greater sense of relevance (Bernstein, 1983, p. 3) as they present ideas, find alignments as well as disjunctions, argue competing claims, and test their arguments against norms they establish together as they interpret nuances.

Metaphoric Juxtaposition and Narrative

Accordingly, Ricoeur draws a theory of language that poses critique is interdependent with interpretation. Hermeneutics provides a theory of interpretation, originally attentive to sacred text, but revised by Ricoeur for discernment of general texts, both social and literary.

A critical hermeneutic language theory orients dialectical pursuits, because discernment is necessary in drawing even apparently incommensurate ideas together. Such discernment depends on an interpretative attention to detail. Metaphoric arrangements showcase and juxtapose conditions so they reverberate meanings against one another, meanings that would otherwise never be connected without such interpretation. Therefore, narrative—the enactment of a plotted set of events made understandable by interpreting the words and sentences that form a text—underlies the interdependence of explanation and understanding, because "explanation and understanding would be considered as relative moments in a complex process that could be termed interpretation" (Ricoeur 1997, p. 126).

Ricoeur's interpretive stance foregrounds critique of events in a plot as a precondition for lively interpretation so we can understand also the large scheme in which events fit together—or do not fit together—to achieve "critical distance in all the operations of thought belonging to interpretation" (1997, p. xiv). He gives us the sense that interpretation is "a particular province of understanding" (1997, p. 110), and therefore a particular province of explanation and understanding, or description and prescription, and therefore, a particular province of the intellectual and practical relationship between difference and commonality.

Metaphor is an operation of thought and a mode of language that references two sets of ideas so that together they expand the meaning of each, even and especially when ideas appear different from each other. Our use of metaphor depends on our ability to imagine novel ways that things relate, and thereby metaphor encourages imagination and innovation. Attention to metaphor has classic roots: Aristotle poses, "a good metaphor implies an intuitive perception of the similarity in dissimilars" (1459, pp. 5–9).

Accordingly, a metaphoric approach to cultural understanding can enable us to draw references from what first appear as differences between or among various cultural systems, to establish a common basis for resolving problems we may have considered intractable problems. Cultural systems create lively narratives as they provide a metaphorical mode of reference for each other, since "the theory of metaphor conspires with the theory of narrative in the elucidation of the problem of reference" (Ricoeur, 1997, p. 10). Referenced sets of ideas form narratives; narratives prompt fruitful action among a system's members because members then can understand the meanings they hold in common, and then recognize the value of finding common ground for discerning which actions would be more fruitful for communities.

Reflexively, narrative is the *means* by which we organize referenced sets of events into action plots. Together, sets of events say more about each event than they would without the plot that binds them together. Hence, we can *interpret* the parts of a whole better, through their relatedness, and we can understand the whole better, via the language relatedness between and among the text itself and its parts. Just as we can make new meanings out of juxtaposing two words or utterances alongside one another in a metaphoric arrangement, to signal the commonality the words or utterances hold for one another, we are able to make new cultural meanings by drawing together cultural *systems* which may appear merely to have differences, to find and uphold their commonality—and to delve even deeper into other juxtaposed conditions to uncover other meaning systems. The following example illustrates the value of a metaphoric associations of difference and commonality, given modesty and religion as veil:

> Attempts at juxtaposing Islamic cultures' requirement for wearing various forms of veiling—to cover the hair, or the face, the entire body and the hands and ankles as well—with, say, Latin expressions of Catholicism which ask that women cover their arms and legs in churches, suggest there is a common bond associated with attention to women's garments, as if both traditions both call for modesty in relation to religious devotion. This first-level assumption develops when observers interpret Islamic societies as made of a single orientation to the Islam religion, and that Latin societies are made of a single orientation to Roman Catholicism. The assumed commonality is a static, religious principle.
>
> However, another level of juxtaposition is necessary: one that requires greater attention to the traditions under study. Islam has no religious requirements for women's dress. An historical exploration unveils the veil: restrictions on women's dress are political, even though they have origins to the 8th century, since the restrictions enable a whole society to merge religion with politics and thereby control at least one half of itself through harsh punishments for transgressions of the dress code. In some forms of Latin Catholicism, there is also an element of social control aligned with religious claims, whereby women who show physical modesty reflect Mary, the mother of Jesus, but also are keeping social codes that families recognize, for the purpose of protecting their women from events that would burden families, such as pregnancy, or less desirable marriages.

Hence, the commonality is political control, not religious adherence. So, while the juxtaposing enables two first-level similarities, it also enables a deeper level, political commonality via what appeared to have different conditions via different religions and the variations among the ways they are viewed and practiced. The juxtaposing also enabled a deeper analysis of variations even within the commonality.

What can knowing about language relatedness between and among metaphor, narrative, explanation, and understanding provide for those of us who believe that the current, superficial sense of multiculturalism is vacuous for critiquing and reconstituting a fragmented social world? What can this language relatedness provide for those of us who seek to act as public intellectuals, through culturally cohesive, yet critical social and political action (Abascal-Hildebrand, 1999a)?

However well-intentioned we are in serving social purposes through our work in the foundations of education, we are served pitifully by thinly formed precepts about language that do not regard language as the deep structure of social or political life. We are left with artificial distinctions, and therefore with a culturally fragmented world, one that constrains dialectical arrangements among persons and proposes there is only one use for language—to deliver preconceived, polarized, fixed formulations. Fragmentation is not only an intellectual problem and a practical problem, because a culturally fragmented world not only limits our appreciation of our language capacities, but such a world limits persons' ability to engage in language to form new worlds of understanding, to reflect on and participate in those worlds, and thus reform the way we live together in those worlds (Abascal-Hildebrand, 1999a, 1999b).

Relatedly, Ricoeur relishes the exuberant variations of the ways we could use language, since he is concerned with "preserving the fullness, the diversity, and the irreducibility of the various *uses* (emphasis in the original) of language" (1997, p. 2). I draw on his thinking to make a point along with his that exalting only a few language uses, or promoting a singular language points to a kind of reductionism that ossifies language (or culture) into formalized, expressions, which "ramify into increasingly well-determined literary (or social) genres...by virtue of the major dichotomy that divides the narrative field" (1997, p. 2). Such claims for imagined purity set off reactionary positioning over which narrative modes might otherwise offer truth claims, such as historical narratives, other so-called descriptive forms, literary forms, or, as Ricoeur also suggests, narratives that use other media such as visual media, and so on.

My point is that formalized, ossified expressions shape distinctions between and among contexts and prompt claims for even more fixed conditions, thereby exalting an artificial purity in cultural relations. The problem, we can see by now, is that we are often only willing to explore cultural meanings superficially, so that we can avoid having to rethink our fixed universe of understandings. Such superficial thought enables the most profound strains of cultural antagonism, as well as the more innocent-appearing brands of relativism.

In a parallel way, a singular or even a relativistic conception of culture that appears generous toward various cultural meaning systems still ossifies social life, and limits our conception of myriad metaphorical arrangements of a culture's social text—its social relations and its meaning systems—and the social action members of a community might otherwise be able to take on behalf of one another. Ricoeur's philosophical project is to argue for the unity between text and action. He explains that it is through a textual theory of social life that we can count on our language to propel us to admit the limitations of pluralistic, separatist thinking, and to learn to act in ways we know we ought to act. In particular, his project enables us to argue that a textual approach to cultural meaning systems enables us to portray those systems' coherence in other settings for other purposes, to refigure ways of posing cultural narratives metaphorically, to extend understanding, and to avoid dichotomous forms of social life. He contends that discourse is a form of action, because it creates a "mimetic bond" because saying and the action prompted by what is said is "effective action that is never completely severed" (1997, p. xiv).

The mimetic quality of language for drawing the past, the present, and the future together is not so much an imitation of an earlier view of life that enables us to work out a future sense from our past experience. Rather, the mimetic quality of language provides the means for us to move *among* explanations and understandings—from holding an idea, to acting on an idea; to moving from a reflective state of being to an engaged state of being.

Limitations of Semiology for Explanation, Understanding, and Interpretation

As noted earlier, explanation and understanding are each aspects of interpretation, "relative moments in a complex process that could be termed interpretation" (Ricoeur, 1997, p. 126). The Enlightenment treatment of explanation claimed legitimacy by virtue of its contention that explanation portrays that which is made of stable connections, concrete and fixed, whereas understanding is considered a mode of being of the mind, thus not fixed.

Even though semiology offers a newer set of ideas about the connection between explanation and understanding, and even though semiology offers a model that refers to both linguistic and nonlinguistic signs, the semiological model still does not rescue the Enlightenment separation of explanation from understanding. Semiology models "are more often structural rather than genetic,...based on stable correlations between discrete units rather than on regular sequences between events, stages, or phases" (Ricoeur, 1997, p. 128).

Ricoeur explains that instead of a semiological study of explanation and understanding, we ought to study explanation and understanding through an interpretive orientation to text. He points out that an interpretative orientation enables an application of the concept of text to the study of cultural relations, in his preference for anthropology as *"philosophical anthropology"* (emphasis in original, 1997, p. 128). He points out that an anthropological study of text enables the philosophical study of explanation and understanding in relation to action, and the way in which concrete historical experience is implicated in both culture and language. He posits, "It is indeed through this threefold theoretical articulation of the anthropological field that the flexible dialectic of understanding and explanation unfolds."

One way to relate explanation and understanding as an anthropological problem such as cultural relations pose, is to align the three-part unity of the world of the text with the three-part unity of the lifeworld. The world of the text is made up of its words, its sentences, and the world within which the words, the sentences, and the text reside—the context. Words, sentences, and ideas take on coherence as text, but a text of ideas is both explained and understood in a larger sphere—a *context*, a lifeworld.

I contend that a lifeworld, too, displays a three-part unity. The lifeworld is made up of its persons, their communities, and the histories of those communities within which members make connected or disconnected claims. Persons live as members of communities which provide them with capacities to explain their experience of a lifeworld to one another. But it is in exchanging the experience of a "concrete historical community" (Ricoeur, 1997, p. 326) that *explanations and understandings* of experience enable *shared explanations and shared understandings*. Explanation and understanding emerge in narrative because narrative assumes the process by which a lifeworld forms within a text and a context—a larger sphere that shape the plots of narratives.

Therefore, explanation and understanding can be seen not as merely relating, but as interpenetrating; that is, each provides for the other (Ricoeur, 1997, p. 129). When understanding becomes difficult, it becomes necessary to pose questions for the purpose of verifying whatever it is we provide for ourselves or others, or attempting to explain—to clarify what we sense we or others do not understand. Each of us brings outside codes into the question-posing, from earlier horizons of experience (Gadamer, 1975), as part of mediating understanding with explanation (Ricoeur, 1997, p. 130).

Accordingly, "there is no explanation that does not reach its completion in understanding" (Ricoeur, 1997, p. 130). Ricoeur explains that even when we break down an idea into its constituent parts, we are no less persuaded by the whole, since it is the whole that enables us to ask questions about constituent parts. He writes, "The narrative in question has in a sense been made virtual...(whereby we see) one segment on an interpretive arc extending from naive understanding to informed understanding through explanations" (1997, p. 130).

Metaphor and Reference

Ricoeur illustrates his appreciation for the referential quality of metaphor in terms of its ability to show resemblance not only between words, but also between contexts, and to produce understanding out of explanation. He explains how understandings emerge, as "the sudden insight—inherent in discourse itself, which brings about the change in logical distance, the bringing-closer-together itself' (1997, p. 9). He points out that this referential quality "prepares the way for a comparison between the theory of narrative and the theory of metaphor" (1997, p. 8). Addressing metaphor as reference for one level of understanding, then narrative as plotting references for another level of understanding, points to language applications as the ethical means for re-visioning communities as text, for the most elevated level of understandings.

Metaphor enables imagination and innovation because metaphor enables understanding. It provides for a renewed sense of the familiar, in that its referential quality allows for terms or contexts that were seen as different to take on a commonality, constituting a revised relationship, "a new congruence [in the] functioning of the productive imagination..., by way of a continual interchange...[and] a production of new plots in the interplay between conformity and deviance" (Ricoeur, 1997, p. 8).

In applying the referential quality of metaphor to explaining and understanding cultural relations, we can go beyond the surface quality of cultural attributes that we might merely describe or explain. Furthermore, we can go beyond the surface quality of attributes we consider to be different from one another. The referential quality of metaphor enables us to consider two different qualities at the same time, for the purpose of showing not merely how they differ, but for showing how they relate. Thus, we can show how two ideas relate *through their apparent difference or through what we consider to be their apparent difference.* Metaphor provides a way for a more conscious understanding of complex or conflicting ideas, such as sets of cultural experiences, by refiguring mere descriptions (explanations) into re-descriptions (understandings). Ricoeur explains that attention to metaphor enables us to interpret behind the text, as it were, when we move beyond mere description to interpretation. His support for the poetic nature explains the value of discourse because it enables interpreters to gain access "to language aspects, qualities, and values of reality that do not have access to directly descriptive language and that can be said only thanks to the complex play of the metaphorical utterance and the ordered transgression of the ordinary meaning of our words (Ricoeur, 1997, p. 11). Because metaphor addresses the indirect, it is metaphorical redescription that draws our attention to nuances and attributes we might have missed otherwise in more superficial pursuits.

Ricoeur makes another point about metaphorical re-description that can be applied to cultural relations. When we redescribe two ideas by virtue of their relationship to each other, we create a sense about the two that enables us to become involved mimetically in them in their making, *as linguistic participants.* Likewise, when we engage in redescribing cultural attributes by virtue of metaphorical references, we are explaining how those attributes relate to one another, so we can use those explanations for understanding one another better. We feel welcomed into a social world we understand: *we become involved then linguistically as cultural participants, where we refigure a social world into a communal world.* Ricoeur's point is that through our language participation in remaking the world into a world we can understand, we become even more able to participate in the world. The "field of sensory, affective, aesthetic, and axiological values...makes the world one that can be *inhabited"* (emphasis in original; 1997, p. 11).

Narrative as Understanding

A major concept in Ricoeur's work is that narrative action shapes and organizes human experience as ethical action—action that is consciously attentive to others (1985, 1987, 1992). He frames his theories of action as intersecting with his moral theories (1992). He points out that narrative thus provides the means for framing action as ethical action (1992). His work can explain how narrative is the means for our engaging in public life as *public* intellectuals (Abascal-Hildebrand, 1999a).

By extension, his work on narrative provides us with understandings about what we first imagine are cultural differences. When plotted together through metaphoric reference, supposed differences become more comprehensible as commonality, and enable complex cultural relations to be developed at an intellectual level, "From this intelligible character of the plot, it follows that the ability to follow a story constitutes a very sophisticated form of *understanding* (emphasis in original)" (Ricoeur, 1997, p. 4).

Ricoeur writes, too, that narrative refigures time (Ricouer, 1984, 1985, 1987). While narrative not only provides the means for us to take what we understood from the past into a future where we act with understanding, narrative also provides the means for our challenging our own as well as others' conceptions of the past, itself. We can realize that how and what we thought was merely a first order conception of how and what we might think, and we can realize that new thoughts are actually conceptions of history reformed. Narrative also refigures theories of action and moral action against the backdrop of time (Ricouer, 1992).

Hence, narrative enables us to form events of our lives into referenced sets of events, as a plot, that acts back upon our narrative capacity to plot a unity of understanding and action. Altogether, narrative relates to action through a reconstitution of the background assumptions that shaped earlier action and that might shape future action. Ricoeur explains the connection between narrative and constitutive cultural relations, "narrative structure joins together the two processes of emplotment, that of action and that of character" (1992, p. 146). We know more about action from a critique of, and attribution to why we do what we do through the way we plot events and portray experience.

> We form a dialectic among life events which we call history, a life history. Thus, just as events are not distinct from one another (they fit together in a plot), persons are not distinct from their experiences, or from one another (they owe their being to forms of community). We portray the relationship among our experiences through the qualities we display—thus we portray experience as identity, and identity as character, always within historical and communal frameworks (Abascal-Hildebrand, 1999a, p. 16).

My view is that narrative unites the ethical with the intellectual, in that narrative enables us to replot our practice plans within a view of just social institutions—social texts we form and can re-form.

Metaphor, Narrative, and Imagination for Community as Text

Ricoeur writes of the ethical implications for validating an intellectual conception of action as social text, one that is both anthropological and philosophical, and therefore both critical and interpretive, instead of only validating empirical forms of action. He contends this is vital because too often "we find ourselves forced to reword our conventional concept of truth, that is to say, to cease to limit this concept to logical coherence and empirical verification alone" (1997, p. 12). In other words, understandings gained in metaphorical redescription are valid for reclaiming understanding, through a critical, hermeneutic, ontological and textual conception of just cultural relations to get beyond positivistic tendencies for superficial renditions of difference and commonaltiy. He argues that "to see something as...is to make manifest the *being-as* (emphasis in original) of that thing" (Ricoeur, 1997, p. 20). To *realize* that two cultural systems have a metaphoric relationship that illustrates their commonality is to *see* those systems henceforth as complementary and not as divisive, and to *form* vital intellectual and practical applications.

Ricoeur writes about imagination as that capacity for novel applications (innovation) as that which arises for us in language, from its various aspects, so that we can reference two ideas together in such a way that the ideas fuse into a new idea. Thus we not only speak metaphorically, we make metaphoric utterances (1997)—we draw together words and phrases, but we also draw together ideas about cultural configurations. Likewise, imagination makes it possible to critique forms of community we might have understood separately so that we can remake community forms, since imagination is "where critical distance is fully conscious of itself, imagination is the very instrument of the critique of the real"...as "we try out new ideas, new values, new ways of being in the world" (1997, p. 174). Imagination's "projective function" enables us to continuously remake the communal text of our actions because imagination is "part of the very dynamism of acting" (1997, p. 177).

Altogether, then, I contend that a critical interpretive orientation toward imagination, as the means within language for prompting our vivid utterances and for refiguring our vital reconceptions of difference and commonality, are what make a generative, constitutive multiculturalism. We cannot generate communities from the acritical, dichotomous, "thin skin of superficial mores" (Ricoeur, 1975, p. 280) that is typically claimed in a rush to consensus that isolates difference from commonality.

It is not difference itself we ought to seek; we ought to seek alignments of difference and look for those references that mark the alignments that make new meanings about possible commonality. We will still be able to appreciate and signify what is unique among differences, but not be fixed among differences. Meaning systems that pivot on the *interpenetrative, referential and narrative relationship* between difference and commonality, through the interpretive processes that enable us to imagine such references and sets of references, are more likely to provide us with the "thick description" that anthropologist Clifford Geertz (1983) characterizes in his work on interpretive community anthropology.

The comparison I have made here among metaphor, narrative, and community for the purpose of putting forth a textual theory of community is based on each notion—metaphor, narrative, a textual community—as deriving from *new ways of understanding—especially new ways of imagining*. I contend that the referential mode that metaphor provides for imagining different qualities can be aligned with the referential ways sets of events can also imaginatively act back upon each other to plot a narrative. At the same time, metaphor, narrative, and community as *text* align to signal the referential character of shared experiences, which enable people to form commitments to one another, in mutual recognition of one another's needs.

The redescription that takes place in achieving understanding also enables the participation of persons, since it is they who thereby *make* a metaphor of commonality and difference. Making metaphor together—seeking commonality out of apparent differences—is akin to the way in which narrative refigures action—making possible new constitutive conceptions of community.

References

Abascal-Hildebrand, M. (1999a). The public intellectual as political educator. *Educational Studies*, 30 (3/4), pp. 261–273.

———. (1999b). Narrative and the public intellectual. *Educational Studies,* 30(2: 3), p. 18.

Aristotle. (1954). *Poetics.* (Ingram Bywater, Trans.). New York: The Modern Library. (Original work published 1459)

Bellah, R.N. (1992). *The broken covenant* (2nd ed.). Chicago: University of Chicago Press.

Bernstein, R. (1983). *Beyond objectivism and relativism: Science, hermeneutics and praxis.* Philadelphia: University of Pennsylvania Press.

Gadamer, H. (1975). *Truth and method.* New York: Seabury Press.

Geertz, C. (1983). *Local knowledge.* New York: Basic Books.

Ricoeur, P. (1975). *Political and social essays.* Athens, Ohio: Ohio University Press.

———. (1984, 1985, 1987). *Time and narrative, Volume I, II, III.* Chicago: University of Chicago Press.

———. (1992). *Oneself as another.* (Kathleen Blamey, Trans.). Chicago: University of Chicago Press.

———. (1997). *From text to action: Essays in hermeneutics, II.* (Kathleen Blamey and John B. Thompson, Trans.). Northwestern University Series in Phenomenology & Existential Philosophy. Evanston, Illinois: Northwestern University Press.

Chapter Seven

Foundational Studies in Teacher Education: A New Imperative

Magnus O. Bassey

School Demographics

Public school demographic trends have changed dramatically in the United States. According to national and regional reports, minority student populations have increased over the past few decades (Hodgkinson, 1989). Students in American schools "represent a rainbow of colors, languages, backgrounds, and learning styles" (McIntyre, 1993, p. ix). Statistics show that by the year 2010, about 40 percent of the school age population in the United States will be persons of color (Gay, 1993; McIntyre, 1993; Bassey, 1996). Children of color will constitute the majority of students in the states of California, Texas, Arizona, New Mexico, and Florida (McIntyre, 1993; Bassey, 1993, 1996, 1997). Indeed, it should be pointed out that minority children are already a majority in 23 out of the 25 largest school districts in the United States (Gay, 1993). Children in Los Angeles school districts speak some 184 different languages (Hodgkinson, 1989).

American Schools As Sites of Disenfranchisement of Poor and Minority Children

Despite the above statistics, minority children are the most disenfranchised by American schools' ascriptive mechanisms (Oakes, 1985; Haney, 1993; Bassey, 1993, 1996, 1997; Books, 1994, 1998). What, we may ask, are the ascriptive methods through which schools in the United States disenfranchise and disempower poor and minority children?

Schools in America disempower poor and minority children through practices such as tracking, unequal funding of schools, biased testing, and language codes (Haney, 1993; Bassey, 1993, 1996, 1997). Tracking, for example, functions as a ranking system and legitimizes differences based on race, gender, and social class (Oakes, 1985). It locks students into positions of social hierarchy and limited opportunity (Kreisberg, 1992; Haney, 1993; Kanpol, 1994; McLaren, 1994; Bassey, 1993, 1996, 1997). Tracking perpetuates class inequalities through selection and allocation of status. According to Oakes (1985), tracking alienates poor and minority students, undermines their social aspirations as well as their self-worth. She maintains that students who are poor and most often come from minority backgrounds are the most disempowered and disenfranchised by school tracking procedures and concludes that "the conduct of schooling benefits those at the upper societal levels and burdens those at the bottom" (Oakes, 1985, p. 203; see also Kozol, 1991; Bassey, 1996). Analyzing the 1990 United States census, the Children's Defense Fund (1992) estimated that 39.8% of black children and 32.2% of Hispanic children live under poverty. Oakes (1985) adds that tracking legitimizes inequality by socializing poor and minority students into accepting the inequality of the larger society. She maintains that children in low tracks who most often are minorities and poor (Oakes, 1985; see also McLaren, 1994; Books, 1994, 1998), are often taught behaviors and skills that make them suitable only for menial employments or in the words of hooks (1994), minority children are often given the type of "education which merely strives to reinforce domination" (p. 4). Whereas students in high-track groups, who most often come from privileged families devote more time to learning activities, homework instruction, and less off-task activities (Oakes, 1985; McLaren, 1994).

Disempowerment and disenfranchisement of poor and minority students are further exacerbated by the funding of public schools largely through local property taxes supplemented by state contributions and small federal grants. This arrangement makes the basic goal of quality public education for all students impossible indeed, because as all school districts are not equally wealthy, per-pupil expenditures vary greatly throughout the country (Books, 1994, 1998; Bassey, 1996; Payne & Biddle, 1999). Consequently, local school districts pay more for the education of some students than for others. Hence, disparities exist between urban, rural, and suburban school districts within the states depending on the racial and economic make-up of the people in particular school districts (Kozol, 1991; McLaren, 1994; Kanpol, 1994). Kozol (1991) has carefully documented the savage inequalities existing between one school district and another in the United States and concludes this about the state of Illinois: "Total yearly spending...ranges today in Illinois from $2,100 on a child in the poorest district to above $10,000 on a child in the richest" (p. 57). The system Kozol laments, "bears the appearance of calculated unfairness" (p. 57). Kozol also found that the poor schools were segregated and patronized mainly by the poor and minorities. Indeed, the urban schools Kozol visited were 95 to 99% nonwhite. Consequently, he warns that social policy in the United States as far as it "concerns black and poor children, has been turned back several decades" (p. 4). He goes on to say that "these revelations could not fail to be disheartening" because "these urban schools were, by and large, extraordinarily unhappy places" (p. 5). Indeed, disparity in school funding in America is not only horizontal, it is vertical as well; that is, disparity exists between urban, suburban and rural areas of the same state; within the states themselves and between school districts in the same state. For instance, while the state of New Jersey funded its schools to the tune of $8,118 per student in 1995, Arkansas funded its own schools only to the tune of $3,599 per student during the same period (Payne & Biddle, 1999). Similarly, school funding in Alaska differed by $12,737 between the rich and poor districts in 1995. In Montana, the difference was $9,171; in New York, $7,571 and in Wyoming, $7,400 (Payne & Biddle, 1999). Indeed, Payne and Biddle (1999) maintain that in the United States a few students who happen to live in rich communities are attending public schools which are funded at the rate of $15,000 per student per year while others have to make do with $3,000 or less. Correspondingly, studies have shown that huge disparities in school funding also produce huge disparities in academic achievement of students (Payne & Biddle, 1999). This perhaps caused Murnane and Levy (1996) to ponder aloud by asking: "Would schools be better if they had more money? The question is becoming embarrassing....For most of the nation's superintendents, school principals, teachers, and parents, the answer is obvious—

more money can buy the things that improve education" (Murnane & Levy, 1996, p. 48). It is therefore no wonder why Payne and Biddle (1999) argue that, of all the disadvantages associated with schooling, poverty impacts on students' achievement the greatest. They explain that poor children are uniquely handicapped because their homes provide little access to books, writing materials, computers, and other educational support materials, which are commonplace in most affluent homes. Poor children are also often afflicted by diseases and pain due to lack of health insurance, which most affluent American children take for granted. "What this means," Payne and Biddle (1999, p. 7) conclude, "is that poor children have a *much* harder time in school than either affluent or middle-class children." Books (1998) maintains forcefully that poor children who study in dilapidated buildings and poorly funded schools learn in many different ways that they do not matter. In an earlier article in 1994, she had argued that American society was in an age of "social triage" because the gap existing between rich and poor schools was so great that it was morally indefensible particularly for a nation founded on Judeo-Christian and democratic principles. She concluded that the unequal funding of schools in the United States has led to conditions, which "contribute to dehumanization, marginalization, and other forms of socially induced misery" (Books, 1994, p. 37).

Another source of disempowerment of poor and minority students is the continued reliance on intelligence tests for academic placements, even though these tests devalue and disenfranchise poor minority students because they are often very culturally and linguistically biased in favor of middle-class nonminority students (Oakes, 1985; Haney, 1993).

Besides, research has shown that the school system implicitly reinforces and rewards middle-class values, attitudes, and behaviors. These include the way of talking, acting, socializing, values, and styles of dress (Bourdieu, 1973; Bernstein, 1977; Swartz, 1977; Freire, 1993; McLaren, 1994; Bassey, 1996). For example, in his ground-breaking study, Bernstein (1977) found that because the elaborated and universalistic language patterns of the middle-class predominate in school, middle-class students are better able to participate in school activities, as the home language of the middle class is similar to the language spoken in school. On the other hand, poor and minority children who are not as competent in the language of the school find it difficult to follow classroom instructions and consequently perform poorly in their academic work. This means practices associated with schooling are sometimes responsible for poor children's failure in school. Hence, McLaren (1994) has argued that in America, a child's school chances are dependent on the child's social class. He notes that:

> the structural constraints that characterize schooling and the wider society reinforce inegalitarian stratification—that schools are reduced to credentializing-mechanisms, protected enclaves that favor the more affluent. The "best" schools nurture cocoons of yuppie larvae, facilitating entry of certain students into more privileged locations in the labor market; the worst simply lock the doors to those privileged locations for students already disproportionately disadvantaged. (p. 9)

Consequently, Giroux (1988) has concluded that the fundamental public services generally associated with schooling, such as the empowerment of individuals regardless of race, class, faith, or gender, are undermined by the very contradictions of schooling itself. In another of his works he argues: "The notion of schooling as a vehicle for social justice and public responsibility has been replaced by the imperatives of the marketplace and the logic of the test score." "Making it in the schools," he continues, "is now defined in terms fashioned out of the language of Wall Street, it has become competitive, individualistic and heartless." He concludes that, "[t]he result is often a notion of schooling that has a great deal to do with oppression and too little to do with educating those who are not rich, white, or native speakers of English" (Giroux, 1989, p. 728).

A New Imperative for Foundational Studies in Teacher Education

The disenfranchisement of some students in our schools by schools' ascriptive mechanisms has resulted in some students' veiled existence and invisibility due to what Marcuse (1964, p. 208) calls, "confinement of experience [and] restriction of meaning." In other words, these students' "sense of the rootedness of knowledge in experience diminishes [as well as their] comprehension of the ways in which persons bring meaning into being and constitute their shared realities" (Greene, 1978, p. 22), because as Ricoeur (1991) explains, experience is ontological and therefore cannot be separated from other experiences. He advises that we must consider experience as a whole especially while engaging in critical appraisal and interpretation of our *being* in order to understand the unity between narrative and experience. Indeed, Marcuse (1964) had argued many years earlier that "individuals identify themselves with the existence which is imposed upon them and have in it their own development and satisfaction" (p. 11). This identification, according to Marcuse (1964), is not an illusion but reality which constitutes a progressive stage of alienation in which the subject alienated is swallowed up by its alienated existence. In other words, "the forms of community life created in schools and the power arrangements existing in classrooms strongly shape the identity of students and teachers" (Pietig, McCormack, & Grinberg, 1996, p. 19). This argument is given credence by Taylor (1994), who states that for minorities, self-knowledge is at stake in contemporary American society as a result of discrimination because self-image is determined not only by our own perception of ourselves but also by the image that others recognize in us and communicate to us. He states, "our identity is partly shaped by recognition or its absence, often by the *mis*recognition of others." He goes on to argue that "a person or group of people can suffer real damage, real distortion, if the people or society around them mirror back to them a confining or demeaning or contemptible picture of themselves." He concludes, "Nonrecognition or misrecognition can inflict harm, can be a form of oppression, imprisoning someone in a false, distorted, and reduced mode of being" (Taylor, 1994, p. 25). Arcilla (1995) explains Taylor's position in the following words:

> The thesis of Taylor's essay is that my self-understanding, for example, is determined not only by my own image of myself but also by the image that others recognize in and communicate to me. If there is an incongruity between these images because others fail to recognize or misrecognize the self-image that I recognize, and if these others have the power to influence me, then my self-understanding could become seriously distorted as I accept features of the image that the others project. Such features could reduce the image that I recog-

nized in myself, thus crippling my potential to flourish in or improve my world.
(pp. 160–161)

It is for this reason that some feminist theorists have argued that women in patriarchal societies have been made to deplore their self-image and internalize their own inferiority to the extent that when some of the obstacles in their way are removed, they most often are unable to take advantage of any existing opportunities before them. Consequently, these women perpetually suffer the pain of low self-esteem (Taylor, 1994). It has also been said that white society has for centuries painted a demeaning picture of black people which some black people have adopted as true images of themselves. Black self-degradation then becomes an instrument of black self-oppression (Taylor, 1994). A similar analogy has been made concerning indigenous and colonized peoples. It is argued that since 1492 Europeans have painted a picture of colonized and indigenous peoples as inferior and uncivilized, and, following conquests, Europeans have been able to impose inferior images on conquered and indigenous peoples which most conquered and indigenous peoples have found difficult to overcome (Taylor, 1994). Similarly, in his ground-breaking comparative study of education in various countries of the world, Ogbu (1978) found that the kind of school failure experienced among minorities in the United States, the West Indians in Britain, the scheduled castes in India, and the Maoris in New Zealand is the result of adaptation by these minorities to the limited opportunities offered by their dominant hosts. Frustrations generated within the dominant social structures of these societies for their minority segments have led to negative adaptations of these minorities as a solution to their oppressed status. Indeed, recounting her schooling experience in the United States, hooks (1994) noted:

The classroom was no longer a place of pleasure or ecstasy. School was still a political place, since we were always having to counter white racist assumptions that we were genetically inferior, never as capable as [our] white peers, even unable to learn. (p. 4)

Degradation as we know robs people of their identity; imposes rigid, stultifying identities, and deformed consciousness on its victims (Birt, 1997). Indeed, as Taylor (1994) has aptly pointed out, "misrecognition shows not just a lack of due respect [but] it can inflict a grievous wound, saddling its victims with a crippling self-hatred" (p. 26).

Solution to the Problem of Self in American Schools

Given the above discussion, I propose that foundational studies in teacher education should be reconceptualized to prepare teachers who would keep their students awake to their consciousness. That is, foundational studies should prepare teachers who would be concerned with the *existence* of their students in both their historical and social contexts, for as Dewey (1998/1938) once noted, education should promote the sense of individual self-worth (see also Greene, 1978, 1990, 1991, 1992; Banks, 1991; Sleeter, 1991). Foundational studies should set itself the task of objective reflection or explicit objective inquiry of how some students struggle with school's ascriptive problems. This means, that foundational studies should prepare teachers who would encourage their students to ask existential questions such as Who am I? Why am I here? Where do I belong?, and How can I find my place in history? This recommendation is informed by Fanon (1963), who stated that the struggle for human liberation is invariably a struggle for a liberated identity, and on Butts's (1993) suggestion that "[t]he fundamental character of a profession is the capacity of its members to make informed judgments about the public good and to promote the general welfare as well as the individual welfare of particular persons for whom they have responsibility" (p. 31). Students should be taught to answer existential questions through the study of philosophy, history and literature. Such learning should take cognizance of "the concrete and the temporal, the existential process, the predicament of the existing individual arising from his [sic] being a synthesis of the temporal and the eternal situated in existence" (Kierkegaard, 1944, p. 267). In other words, education should empower individuals and groups by taking seriously their "strengths, experiences, strategies, goals and struggles" (Sleeter, 1991, p. 6). This implies helping students to understand themselves, for as Kierkegaard (1959) once noted: "One must know oneself before knowing anything else. It is only after a person has thus understood himself [sic] that life acquires peace and significance" (p. 46). Greene (1978) expressed a similar concern when she said that freedom depends on the opportunity to make one's own sense of the world. She pointed out that teachers should help their students to be wide awake. Wide-awakeness, according to Schutz (1962), denotes "a plane of consciousness of highest tension originating in an attitude of full attention to life and its requirements" (p. 213). Thoreau (1854, 1946) described wide-awakeness as an effort to throw off sleep:

> Why is it that men give so poor an account of their day if they have not been slumbering? They are not such poor calculators. If they had not been overcome with drowsiness, they would have performed something. The millions are awake enough for physical labor; but only one in a million is awake enough for effective intellectual exertion....To be awake is to be alive. I have never yet met a man who was quite awake. How could I have looked him in the face? We must learn to reawaken and   keep ourselves awake, not by mechanical aids, but by an infinite expectation of the dawn, which does not forsake us in our soundest sleep. I know of no more encouraging fact than the unquestionable ability of man to elevate his life by a conscious endeavor. (p. 90)

Delpit (1995) argues that teachers should be attentive to the voices of their students (particularly minority students) by creating situations that stimulate questioning and the construction of meaning particularly for understanding the culture of power. She informs us that students should be taught the specific language codes which they need in order to participate fully in American political life. She warns, however, that such teaching should neither be hollow nor rest on a shaky foundation. Instead, such learning must be anchored in meaningful communicative endeavors. In other words, while minority students should be given the resources of expert teachers, they must be allowed to articulate their own visions of the world and to understand the arbitrariness of power relations in American society. Indeed, as Dewey (1938/1998) had written many years earlier, "The ideal aim of education is creation of power of self-control" (p. 75). Dewey spoke of the need for students to delve into their past in order to understand the problems of the present. By this

Dewey meant the utilization of subject matter content found in the experience of the learner for the purpose of learning. But Arcilla (1995) argues that there is often tension between self-knowledge, the politics of recognition, and learning. Arcilla (1995), however, resolves this conflict himself by arguing that educators would minimize such tensions in the classroom if they "reduced our investment in recognizable terms of self-understanding, making such terms less worth fighting over." That is,

> by appreciating and cultivating aporias of self-understanding not as preliminary moments on the way to a clearer, more authentic definition of ourselves, but as themselves more authentic, honest ways of acknowledging the mystery that we are—that we exist. (p. 168)

This mystery, according to Arcilla (1995), is inscribed in each of our proper names.

Freire (1994), however, warns us that in order to transform the world, there must be reflection and action because mere perception of reality that is not followed by critical intervention cannot lead to transformation of objective reality. To transform objective reality for poor and minority students in our schools, therefore, teachers should act as public intellectuals (Giroux, 1988; Kanpol, 1994; McLaren, 1994; hooks, 1994). A public intellectual is here defined as one who merges intellectualism with activism. He or she is one who understands the social order enough to want to change it. In which case, teachers should have the knowledge, the vocabulary, and the conceptual framework to educate students in democratic processes. Accordingly, teacher education preparation should probe ideological and political perspectives of education and schooling. Abascal-Hildebrand (1999) argues that teachers should be public intellectuals who act with a social aim in mind because they are members of social networks. She explains that as public intellectuals, teachers should acknowledge and carry out the action dimension of the ideas they teach. She forcefully argues that foundational scholars are the most strategically placed educators to prepare teachers to become public intellectuals. As she explains:

Our interpretive capacities ... serve as the means for acting as public intellectuals. Our interpretive capacities enable our understanding of the action dimensions needed for changing public institutions so it is more possible for all in a
community to participate democratically. (p. 5)

She goes on to add that foundational scholars are always engaged in language because language is our *house of being.* We are engaged in language even in our apparent silence because language is the only means of
understanding our thoughts. It is through language that we become participants in public life and discourse. Language provides us with the opportunity to bring our pasts into the present, thoughts into actions, and to
use the past and the present to project the future (Abascal-Hildebrand,
1999). Indeed, Taylor (1994) argues that human identity is created dia-
logically in response to our relations with others. This being the case, it
is important for foundational studies to prepare teachers who would bring
into dialogue voices of all those who have been silenced, marginalized,
and excluded (Giroux, 1988; Freire, 1994; McLaren, 1994; Kanpol,
1994; hooks, 1994). Indeed, Freire and Giroux (1989) maintain, "Educational programs need to provide students with an understanding of how
knowledge and power come together in various educational spheres to
both enable and silence the voices of different students" (p. ix). Our
teacher education programs, therefore, should prepare teachers who
would see education as an empowering force which must address what
Kanpol (1994) calls "cultural politics." This means, our teacher education programs should prepare teachers who would challenge dominant,
oppressive values in our society: teachers who would be willing to relate
their professional views to the needs and concerns of their students:
teachers who would help students to believe in their own self-worth, and
teachers who would motivate students to overcome injustice, discrimination, and hardship so that students can become what they want to be
(Kanpol, 1994; hooks, 1994).

Furthermore, foundational studies should prepare teachers who
would encourage all students to succeed in school, because "human beings can achieve autonomy and efficacy once they learn how to inquire,
to communicate, and to use their cognitive capacities" (Greene, 1978, p.
8). Foundational studies should equip teachers with the skills to analyze

events and structures and teach them how to deal effectively with a world that is always changing. In other words, foundational studies should concern itself with teaching teachers how to become fully functioning individuals, which means, teaching teachers how to develop critical inquiry skills, because such skills could bring about individual self-awareness and empowerment, and empowered individuals can confront oppressive social structures and instigate wider change in society (LeCompte & de-Marrais, 1992). Indeed, foundational studies can become a crucible within which teachers give voice to their own concerns and lives and connect with others (Hursh, 1992).

The Teaching-Learning Process

It is the position of this writer that teachers should help their students to become the best that they can be through intellectual and emotional growth. This means, that the child's introspective ability and self-knowledge should be seen by teachers as important in the learning process (Maslow, 1971). Indeed, for learning to be meaningful, the "whole" person must be involved. This is to say, both the mind and feelings must be involved in the learning process because, according to Brown (1971), "there is no intellectual learning without some sort of feeling, and there are no feelings without the mind being somehow involved" (p. 4). In this case, both the affective and cognitive domains must flow together because the purpose of education is to convey meaning. Indeed, Johann Heinrich Pestalozzi summed up this point in the early part of the nineteenth century in the following words:

> For it is my opinion that if public education does not take into consideration the circumstances of family life, and everything else that bears on a man's [sic] general education, it can only lead to an artificial and methodical dwarfing of humanity. (cited in Nel & Seckinger, 1993, p. 396)

It is important for learning to be connected with students' personal belief systems and prior experiences because Freire (1993) makes the point that the "school system should know and value the knowledge of class, the experience-based knowledge the child brings to it" (p. 4), because if learning is not made relevant to students' real life experiences, school becomes a place where students learn only compliance to adult authority, and consequently students experience subject matter that is boring. This is why Greene (1978) argues that "the life of reason develops against a background of perceived realities" (p. 2). Hence, concepts should be related to events that are pertinent to the lives of students or to their cultural knowledge, for humanistic psychologists make the point that learning is likely to occur if students realize that the subject is related to the maintenance and enhancement of the self (Morris & Pai, 1976). In his book, *Experience and Education,* Dewey (1938/1998) cogently defined educative experience as one in which students and teachers find meaning in their own lives:

> I have taken for granted the soundness of the principle that education in order to accomplish its ends both for the individual learner and for society must be based upon experience—which is always the actual life-experience of some individual. (p. 113)

Indeed, Greene (1978) concludes that "learning must be a process of discovery and recovery in response to worthwhile questions rising out of conscious life in concrete situations" (p. 19).

Summary

This chapter argues that foundational studies in teacher education should prepare teachers who would awaken students' consciousness, particularly those students who have been disenfranchised by schools' ascriptive mechanisms. For indeed, as students are shaped by their world, they must learn how to control and reshape their own future. I make this recommendation believing, as Ognibene (1998) has noted, "Foundations personnel, and those they teach, should become communities of hope who believe in and work to create a better world" (p. 7).

References

Abascal-Hildebrand, M. (1999). Narrative and the public intellectual. *Educational Studies,* 30(1), pp. 5–18.

Arcilla, R. V. (1995). For the stranger in my home: Self-knowledge, cultural recognition, and philosophy of education. In W. Kohli (Ed.), *Critical conversations in philosophy of education* (pp. 159–172). New York: Routledge.

Banks, J. A. (1991). A curriculum for empowerment, action, and change. In C.E. Sleeter (Ed.), *Empowerment through multicultural education* (pp. 125–141). Albany, NY: State University of New York Press.

Bassey, M.O. (1993). Multicultural education: Its unexplored philosophical themes. *The Western Journal of Black Studies,* 17(4), pp. 202–208.

———. (1996). Teachers as cultural brokers in the midst of diversity, *Educational Foundations,* 10(2), pp. 37–52.

———. (1997). Multicultural education: Philosophy, theory and practice. *The Western Journal of Black Studies,* 21(4), pp. 232–241.

Bernstein, B. (1977). *Class, codes and control. Vol.111: Towards a theory of educational transmission.* London: Routledge & Kegan Paul.

Birt, R. (1997). Existence, identity, and liberation. In L.R. Gordon (Ed.), *Existence in Black: An anthology of Black existential philosophy* (pp. 205–213). New York: Routledge.

Books, S. (1994). Social foundations in an age of triage. *Educational Foundations,* 8(4), pp. 27–41.

———. (1998). School funding: Tinkering with equity in times of ghettoization,*Educational Foundations,* 12(4), pp. 53–68.

Bourdieu, P. (1973). Cultural reproduction and social reproduction. In R.K. Brown (Ed.) *Knowledge, education, and cultural change: Papers in the sociology of education* (pp. 71–112). London: Tavistock.

Brown, G. I. (1971). *Human teaching for human learning.* New York: Viking.

Butts, R. F. (1993). A rejoinder to Tozer's draft position paper. *Educational Foundations.* 7(4), p. 31.

Children's Defense Fund. (1992). *Child poverty data from 1990 census.* Washington, D.C.: Children's Defense Fund.

Delpit, L. (1995). *Other people's children: Cultural conflict in the classroom.* New York: The New Press.

Dewey, J. (1938/1998). *Experience and education.* West Lafayette, IN: Kappa Delta Pi.

Fanon, F. (1963). *The wretched of the earth* (C. Farrington, trans.). New York: Grove Press.

Freire, P. (1993). *Pedagogy of the city.* New York: The Continuum Publishing Company.

———. (1994). *Pedagogy of the oppressed.* New York: The Continuum Publishing Company.

Freire, P., & Giroux, H. (1989). Pedagogy, popular culture, and public life: An introduction. In H. A. Giroux, R.I. Simon, & Contributors (Eds), *Popular culture: Schooling and everyday life* (pp. vii–xii). New York: Bergin & Garvey.

Gay, G. (1993). Building cultural bridges: A bold proposal for teacher education. *Education and Urban Society,* 25(3), pp. 285–299.

Giroux, H. A. (1988). *Teachers as intellectuals: Toward a critical pedagogy of learning.* New York: Bergin & Garvey.

———. (1989). Rethinking education reform in the age of George Bush. *Phi Delta Kappan,* 70(9), pp. 728–730.

Greene, M. (1978). *Landscapes of learning.* New York: Teachers College Press.

———. (1990). Multiple voices and multiple realities: A reviewing of educational foundations. *Educational Foundations,* 4(2), pp. 5–19.

———. (1991). Retrieving the language of compassion: The education professor in search of community. *Teachers College Record,* 92(4), 541–555.

———. (1992). The passions of pluralism: Multiculturalism and the expanding community. *Journal of Negro Education,* 61(3), pp. 250–261.

Haney, W. (1993). Testing and minorities. In L. Weis and M. Fine (Eds), *Beyond silenced voices: Class, race, and gender in United States schools* (pp. 45–73). Albany, NY: State University of New York Press.

Hodgkinson, H. (1989). *The same client: The demographics of education and service delivery systems.* Washington, D.C.: Institute for Educational Leadership.

hooks, b. (1994). *Teaching to transgress: Education as the practice of freedom.* New York: Routledge.

Hursh, D. (1992). Multicultural social studies: Schools as public arenas for understanding diversity. *Social Science Record,* 29(1), pp. 31–42.

Kanpol, B. (1994). *Critical pedagogy: An introduction.* Westport, CT: Bergin & Garvey.

Kierkegaard, S. (1944). *Concluding unscientific postscript.* (D. F. Swenson & W. Lowrie, trans.). Princeton, NJ: Princeton University Press.

———. (1959). *The journals of Kierkegaard.* (A. Dru, trans.) New York: Harper.

Kozol, J. (1991). *Savage inequalities: Children in America's schools.* New York: Crown Publishers.

Kreisberg, S. (1992). *Transforming power: Domination, empowerment, and education.* Albany, NY: State University of New York Press.

LeCompte, M. D. & deMarrais, K.B. (1992). The disempowerment of empowerment: Out of the revolution and into the classroom. *Educational Foundations,* 6(3), pp. 5–31.

Marcuse, H. (1964). *One-dimensional man: Studies in the ideology of advanced industrial society.* Boston, MA: Beacon Press.

Maslow, A. H. (1971). *The farther reaches of human nature.* New York: Viking.

McIntyre, D. J. (1993). The ethical responsibilities of meeting students' diverse needs: A foreword. In M.J. O'Hair and S.J. Odell (Eds.), *Diversity and teaching* (pp. ix–x). Fort Worth, TX: Harcourt Brace Jovanovich, Inc.

McLaren, P. (1994). *Life in schools.* New York: Longman.

Morris, V. C., & Pai, Y. (1976). *Philosophy and the American school.* Boston, MA: Houghton Mifflin Company.

Murnane, R. J., & Levy, F. (1996). Why money matters sometimes: A two-part management lesson from East Austin, Texas. *Education Week,* 16(2), pp. 36–37.

Nel, J., & Seckinger, D.S. (1993). Johann Heinrich Pestalozzi in the 1990s: Implications for today's multicultural classrooms. *The Educational Forum,* 57(4), pp. 394–401.

Oakes, J. (1985). *Keeping track: How schools structure inequality.* New Haven: Yale University Press.

Ogbu, J. U. (1978). *Minority education and caste: The American system in cross-cultural perspective.* New York: Academic Press.

Ognibene, R. (1998). Social foundations and school reform networks: The case against E. D. Hirsch. *Educational Foundations,* 12(4), pp. 5–27.

Payne, K. J., & Biddle, B.J. (1999). Poor school funding, child poverty, and mathematics achievement. *Educational Researcher,* 28(6), pp. 4–13.

Pietig, J., McCormack, M. & Grinberg, J. (1996). Conversations in the field: Social foundations and the student teaching experience. *Educational Foundations,* 10(2), pp. 5–22.

Ricoeur, P. (1991). *From text to action.* K. Blamey and J. B. Thompson (Trans.). Evanston, IL: Northwestern University Press.

Schutz, A. (1962). *The problem of social reality: Collected papers 1.* (M. Natanson, Ed.). The Hague: Martinus Nijhoff.

Sleeter, C. E. (1991). Introduction: Multicultural education and empowerment. In C.E. Sleeter (Ed.), *Empowerment through multicultural education* (pp. 1–23). Albany, NY: State University of New York Press.

Swartz, D. (1977). Pierre Bourdieu: The cultural transmission of social inequality. *Harvard Educational Review,* 47(4), pp. 545–555.

Taylor, C. (1994). *Multiculturalism: Examining the politics of recognition.* (A. Gutmann, Ed.). Princeton, NJ: Princeton University Press.

Thoreau, H. D. (1854,1946). *Walden or life in the woods.* New York: Dodd, Mead & Company.

Chapter Eight

A New Class of Heroes: Fallout from the Clinton-Lewinsky Scandal

Clinton Collins

Just as the resignation of Richard Nixon under threat of impeachment and conviction proves that "the American constitutional system works," the impeachment and acquittal of William Clinton proves, once again, the system works. Nixon threatened American democracy, not because of ineptness. He probably represented America's most astute politician of the post-World War II era. But his political instincts leaned more to the authoritarian than the democratic. And he had the political skill to bend a democratic system to give himself extraordinary powers. The American system worked in his case because the combination of press scrutiny and an enraged legislature and judiciary put a stop to his antidemocratic practices.

Bill Clinton also has proved an astute politician. Judge Richard A. Posner, a Reagan appointee to the United States Court of Appeals for the Seventh Circuit, sees Clinton as having accomplished "a useful if not entirely willing" consolidation of the Reagan revolution. Posner recently authored a much-praised account of the Clinton-Lewinsky scandal, *An Affair of State: The Investigation, Impeachment and Trial of President Clinton*, in the form of a long judicial decision in response to whether the experience has left the nation better or worse. Posner sees Congress's pragmatic decision to impeach Clinton but not convict him, as an inspired solution, for it upheld the rule of law, deservedly darkened Clinton's historical reputation, foiled the right wing's attempt to win a victory in their self-proclaimed cultural war, and proved that America remains a vibrant republic. Posner writes, "If some people have been encouraged by Clinton's survival in office to commit perjury and obstruction of justice, others...have learned that one can get into a lot of trouble by committing them" (Posner, 1999, p. 263).

Posner notes that "if the mystique of the presidency has been diminished, the republic seems perfectly able to function with an unmysterious chief executive." He believes that, as a nation, "we have learned that powerful, intelligent, articulate, well-educated and successful people who would like us to submit to their leadership, whether political or intellectual, are, much of the time, fools, knaves, cowards, and blunderers, just like the rest of us" (Posner, 1999, p. 265).

As a libertarian, Posner seems much more sanguine about the diminishing of government than I, which accounts for his joy in Clinton's consolidation of what he regards as the Reagan revolution. But I share his faith that this scandal has done more to strengthen than weaken America. The one egregious error in our constitutional system, in both Posner's and my own view, came when the U.S. Supreme Court allowed Paula Jones's civil suit against Clinton to go forward while he held the office of president. But even there, I believe that the court has learned from this experience, and will probably reverse itself if given another opportunity. In addition, Americans have shown almost universal approval of the expiration of the poorly constructed Independent Counsel Law.

But while most of the nation seems to have put the scandal behind them, I think one issue raised by Clinton's political opponents casts some light on the significant educational issue, of "how can we explain this to our children?" Adults in this situation had a rare opportunity to expose their children to a serious public discussion of moral values. Their lament indicates that many adults don't want their children—or others' children—privy to adult conversations about moral values, particularly those that concern sexual conduct. Instead, they would prefer to protect children's innocence.

In a recent article, Audrey Thompson (1998) critiques many proposals for what she calls "child-centered" education on the ground that they seek to preserve the young in their innocence, or return them to an earlier state of innocence. Thompson uses as examples recent writings on the boarding schools set up for Native Americans, and a residential high school program set up for dropouts entering the Job Corps. She notes that though teachers in such child-centered education projects seek to protect students from the corrupting aspects of adult society, they do so by means that create goals for learning, which do not aptly represent the students' goals.

In that respect, however, child-centered education, which Thompson traces back as far as Rousseau's *Emile*, does not differ from more traditional forms of schooling that do not assume the innocence of the young, but rather see them as potential threats to the adult social order. For example, a 1994 collection titled *Values and Public Policy*, edited by Henry J. Aaron, Thomas E. Mann, and Timothy Taylor of the Brookings Institute, contains an essay by David Popenoe of Rutgers University in which he writes, "Every society must be wary of the unattached male...for he is universally the cause of numerous social ills. The good society is heavily dependent on men being attached to a strong moral order centered on families, both to discipline their sexual behavior and to reduce their competitive aggression" (1994, p. 98).

At the risk of over-generalization, one could divide the "...ends for schooling other than the students' own" into two broad categories: for advocates of traditional education, to preserve cultural traditions in the face of the threat posed by the unsocialized young; and, for advocates of child-centered education, to reform society by bringing up a new generation free of its evils.

Those two motives become confounded in a fascinating way in a recent book by conservative film critic Michael Medved, and his wife Diane, a child and family psychologist. The Medveds title their book *Saving Childhood: Protecting Our Children from the National Assault on Innocence*. The assault that concern them includes "our news-saturated homes" in which they find it hard for Americans "to escape the sad tales of Jon Benet Ramsey and Jennifer Dubroff—not to mention every shocking detail concerning Lorena Bobbitt, O.J. Simpson, Timothy McVeigh, and even Princess Di and the president of the United States." Yet they urge parents to shelter their children from this dismal reality.

The argument becomes murky, however, when the authors attack the cult of self-esteem which they believe now dominates public schools. They write, "At the moment, our society seems to be obsessed with the importance of 'self-esteem,' but we argue that as significant as it may be for children to believe 'I'm a great kid,' it's even more crucial for them to believe that 'It's a great world.'"

Can the Medveds be telling us of the world's greatness in the face of the bombardment they claim all Americans receive with tales of crime and perverse sexuality? I think the Medveds intend to say that if we can raise the next generation to accentuate the positive aspect of our social life, perhaps the negative aspects will go away. And one of those negative aspects we should avoid in the education of children consists of building up the value of the self in contrast to building up the value of God's creation.

But accentuating the positive comes at the dear cost of manipulating the environment of the young so that they learn as little as possible of the negative. Understandably, from the Medveds' perspective, it doesn't help to have a president of our country who commits adultery with a much younger employee, lies to the press and to a grand jury in order to cover it up, and encourages his lover to cover it up as well. But despite their efforts to write a self-help book, the Medveds offer no serious way for parents to deal with that problem.

George Lakoff, in *Moral Politics: What Conservatives Know That Liberals Don't*, explains the dilemma faced by conservatives like the Medveds in confronting the Clinton scandal. According to Lakoff, to conservatives, accountability and punishment form the very structure of a moral society. What Lakoff calls the conservatives' "stern father" model contrasts with liberals' model of the "nurturing parent." Liberals, according to Lakoff, tend to respond to a leader's transgressions by demanding retribution rather than punishment: having him do more "good deeds" for the people betrayed, such as Clinton's list of desired social programs in his 1999 State of the Union speech. Thus, while the majority of Americans approve Clinton's performance as president, despite reservations about his personal morality, many conservatives believe that preservation of basic values in American society demands his punishment. In this regard, both liberals and conservatives received half a loaf.

Early in 1999, Dean Merrill, vice president and publisher for the International Bible Society, told a reporter:

I think every adult who is right now telling pollsters, "Oh well, if he lied, whatever, I don't really care," still gets pretty ticked off when their 8-year-old lies to them.... If we continue on in this direction, it's going to be a dead-end street for us. We'll just generate more frustration, and we'll come to feel like we can't believe anybody anymore. (quoted in Smith, p. 10)

The quote illustrates many adults' concern about how the Clinton scandal will affect young people. I also think it illustrates perhaps the most hypocritical way in which parents relate to their children, viz., insisting that they always tell them the truth. The same article quotes child psychologist Cathleen Brown pointing out, "As soon as [people] develop a certain amount of power, usually around age 4, we'll start testing out lying." This agrees with David Nyberg, who in his book, *The Varnished Truth: Truth Telling and Deceiving in Ordinary Life*, suggests that deception is a part of ordinary social discourse and always has been. He notes that language is built for something besides truth telling: It's there to establish intimacy with and distance from other people. And, for Nyberg, people need the distance as much as they need the intimacy.

Parents who insist that their children always tell them the truth show a fundamental lack of respect for the young. They try to prevent their children from applying conversational strategies children have learned in communication with others to their communication with parents. While numerous studies suggest that everyone lies, and on a daily basis, that doesn't present the total picture. Virtually every communication combines the attempt to inform others with the desire to put a spin on that information that favors the interests of the speaker. This even occurs in court testimony under oath. The possibility of hearing the unadulterated truth from *any* person comes in at close to zero. Most people wouldn't know what constitutes unadulterated truth even if they wanted to present it.

Parents often provide children with their first lessons in how to lie, putting off the child's concerns when the parent feels distracted by other matters. Cathleen Brown gives good advice to parents when she suggests that they don't set traps for their children, for example, by asking "Did you do this?" when they already have evidence that convinces them that the child did do it.

Dr. Charles V. Ford, who teaches in the medical school at the University of Alabama, Birmingham notes that "one of the things we lose when we become depressed is our capacity to lie to ourselves about how good we are" (Ford, 1996, p. 252). Perhaps that explains attacks on self-esteem as an educational goal: in their depression, the attackers resent those who feel better about themselves.

I don't hesitate to hypothesize that every American president has lied to press and public. That most have not done so under oath reflects that most have not testified under oath during their presidency (and suggests that perhaps our laws should not require them to do so).

Once undermine the absolutist belief that lying is wrong, however, and the whole absolutist view of the foundation of society begins to shake. Fear of the young, or its obverse, the attempt to shelter them, makes at least partial absolutists out of the majority of adults. Otherwise, no one would have suggested that the Clinton scandal posed any enduring threat to the republic. A recent interview in the *New York Times* quoted Richard Posner saying:

> A worthwhile legacy of the impeachment drama...might have been to take not only this President but the Presidency itself down a peg, to take the President off his pedestal so that our politics can become perhaps more pragmatic, less striving for some exalted notion of leadership. (Greenhouse, 1999, p. 14)

I, too, wish that the nation's politics, as well as its child-rearing practices could become more pragmatic.

Can someone who has serious character flaws nevertheless perform well as president? I think that many have. One reason for this, I think: the current American presidency has become almost an impossible job. Only a person somewhat monomaniacal may have a chance of succeeding at it. (Witness, for example, Edmund Morris's recent biography of Ronald Reagan, *Dutch*.) But if our political heroes have feet of clay, perhaps that provides a better kind of hero for a democratic society. Perhaps, then, young people in America may come to recognize that the strength of their society comes from the people themselves more than from their leaders.

References

Ford, C.V. (1996). *Lies! Lies! Lies! The psychology of deceit.* Washington, D.C.: American Psychiatric Press.

Greenhouse, L. (1999). Interview with Richard A. Posner, *New York Times Book Review*, Sept. 25,1999, p. 14.

Lakoff, G. (1996). *Moral politics: What conservatives know that liberals don't.* Chicago: University of Chicago Press.

Medved, M., & Medved, D. (1998). *Saving childhood: Protecting our children from the national assault on innocence.* New York: Harper/Collins.

Nyberg, D. (1993). *The varnished truth: Truth telling and deceiving in ordinary life.* Chicago: University of Chicago Press.

Popenoe, D. (1994). Multiculturalism and public policy. In Henry J. Aaron, Thomas E. Mann, & Timothy Taylor (Eds.), *Values and public policy* (pp. 81–112). Washington, D.C.: The Brookings Institute.

Posner, R. A. (1999) *An affair of state: The investigation, impeachment and trial of President Clinton.* Boston: Harvard University Press.

Ringle, K. (1999, January 21). *Lexington Herald-Leader*, p. A11.

Smith, S. (1999, February 18). Knight-Ridder news service, *Lexington Herald-Leader*, pp. 10–11.

Thompson, A. (1998). The adult and the curriculum. In Steve Tozer (Ed.) *Philosophy of education, 1998* (pp. 183–191). Urbana, IL: The Philosophy of Education Society.

Chapter Nine

Global Education from an Ecological Perspective: To Become a Global Citizen

Hye-Kyeong Pae

Through technological advances, the sharing of information and communication has made many parts of the world more accessible. We are accustomed to hearing people speak of the world getting smaller, of the future of living in the "global village." The economic, political, social, and environmental systems have become interconnected to such a degree that it is of urgent and universal importance to develop world-awareness, because events in one place may have an effect on everybody in the world. This trend requires a better understanding of the world as a series of interconnected and symbiotic systems, because recognition of interdependence is no longer the purview of a limited group. For example, issues such as population, pollution, toxic waste, acid rain, global warming, groundwater contamination, deforestation, fuel shortage, AIDS and other communicable diseases, refugees and illegal immigration, human rights, and drug trafficking have become global problems which threaten life on earth (Jarchow, 1993). In order to function well in the worldwide culture, it is imperative that students develop a global perspective or global awareness as to how other cultures function in the world. A global perspective is defined as the capacity to view events, issues, and problems that take place in any part of the world as an integrated whole with an interdisciplinary approach. Thus, global awareness is a lifelong endeavor in understanding the world community and the interdependence of its people and ecological, social, economic, and technological systems. However, little attention has been given to how a global perspective evolves.

A large body of research has discussed and debated over the significance of global education within the context of social studies program. However, it has never come to substantial fulfillment, because global education has been discussed within the limited scope of international education or multicultural education, seeing its perspective as an essential objective of global education and an outcome of a formal curricular process (Hendrix, 1998; Savitt, 1993; Case, 1993; McCabe, 1997). A significant void in the extant body of knowledge lies in documenting global education from an ecological perspective; such an analysis sheds light on the wide-ranging surrounding conditions and learning experiences by highlighting the family setting, school and peer-group context, and the social and cultural context. To appreciate the complex network that constitutes a student's world, it is necessary to go beyond the unidirectional view of the student's context because his or her environment is constantly changing in relation to its many components.

The purpose of this chapter is to explore global education from an ecological perspective as constant interactions between individuals and their environments, including families, schools, peer groups, the mass media, and neighborhood. The goal of the chapter is threefold: (1) to achieve a better understanding of how a global perspective evolves from the sources of information about the world and other people; (2) to develop insights into the holistic view of global education from an ecological perspective; and (3) to explore the ramifications of relationships between global education and an ecological point of view within the array of an ecosystem. In the remaining parts of this chapter, I briefly review relevant research and theory of global education and ecological systems. Application of global education into ecosystems theory and its implication for practice in ecosystems are also discussed.

The Scope of Global Education

In response to a growing interest in and recognition of the significance of global education, academic efforts have primarily been made under the rubric of both international education and multicultural education in school. Hendrix (1998) claims that international education programs are less likely to be successful in helping students understand global interdependence and in coping with the challenges of an increasingly interconnected world. International education in itself is an insignificant achievement, as Hendrix (1998) points out, because increased knowledge or accumulated information of other nations, geographic areas, cultures, and peoples does not guarantee increased respect for or commitment to others. For example, an international business curriculum might fail to shift a student's own cultural sphere to acquire a global perspective and a corresponding change in consciousness, focusing instead on a material positioning, distribution, logistics, pricing, and segmentation. In addition, traditional pedagogies in international issues may result in the danger of eurocentricism or American supranationalism emerging by placing the United States in the center as the largest economy in the world.

Likewise, the effectiveness of multicultural education may be limited because its cultural emphasis within the United States can bypass issues of political and economic justice (Hendrix, 1998). A multicultural approach, no matter how challenging in itself, does not promise understanding of global interconnectedness or interdependence.

In spite of the merit of each approach, neither sufficiently addresses the requirement of global educational development. Scholars have tried to differentiate global education from international education and multicultural education in order to signify the tenets of global education. During the last three decades, significant resources and efforts for pedagogical reform have been devoted to implementing global perspectives into a social science curriculum in order for students to prepare their future lives in a global age (Case, 1993; Hanvey, 1979; Kniep, 1989; Kniep, 1986; Tye & Kniep, 1991; Ramler, 1991). The avenue to a global perspective has included a distinction between nationalism versus globalism, working definitions and philosophy of global education, curriculum and instruction, and teacher education. Scholars have called attention to the need to see globalization as more than a simple expansion of Western capitalism, philosophical issues of globalization along with the role of education, and the world paradigm shifts to a global society (Featherstone, 1990; Jameson and Miyoshi, 1998; Case, 1993; Hanvey, 1979; King, Branson, & Condon, 1976; Kniep, 1987; Anderson, Nicklas,

& Crawford, 1994; Harris, 1986; Merryfield, 1991; Merryfield, 1998; Tye & Tye, 1992; Bruce, Podemski, & Anderson, 1991).

A great deal of effort has been made to conceptualize global education by scholars. For example, Hanvey (1979) identified cross-cultural awareness as an important dimension of global awareness. According to Hanvey, one of the principal goals of global education is enhancing awareness of diverse ideas and practices to be applied in the world community, and examining how such ideas and practices might be viewed from other vantage points. Hanvey conceptualizes five elements of a global perspective: perspective consciousness, knowledge of world conditions, cross-cultural awareness, knowledge of global dynamics, and awareness of human choices.

In a similar vein, human values, global systems, global issues and problems, and global history have been conceptualized by Kniep (1989) as the focus of global education. Case (1993) classifies two interrelated dimensions of a global perspective into substantive and perceptual elements. The substantive dimension includes knowledge of interconnected global systems, international events, world cultures, and global geography. The perceptual dimension is involved with the cultivation of attitudes reflecting open-mindedness, empathy for others, anticipation for complexity, resistance to stereotyping, and freedom from chauvinistic and ethnocentric bias.

According to Tye and Tye (1992, p. 6), global education is conceptualized as "the study of problems and issues that cut across national boundaries, and the interconnectedness of the systems involved...[and] the cultivation of cross-cultural understanding, which includes development of the skill of perspective-taking; that is, being able to see life from someone else's point of view" (p. 6). With these working definitions of global education, scholars assert that global awareness should become the first new fundamental skill of the twenty-first century.

Other scholars have set forth a thematic framework for curriculum plans and sample lessons, recommended strategies used in various countries for teaching global issues, and a thorough and practical guide for building a global education curriculum (Anderson et al., 1994; Harris, 1986; Kniep, 1987).

Teacher educators have developed programs, courses, and instructional materials to prepare social studies teachers to integrate global perspective into their teaching and learning (Johnston & Ochoa, 1993; Bruce et al., 1991). For example, Merryfield (1991) calls attention to the actual practice of social studies teachers as they teach global perspectives in order to understand the context of their instructional designs, and examines multiple perspectives on the content of classroom practice by conducting qualitative analysis. Viewing teachers as curricular-instructional gatekeepers, Merryfield believes that a better understanding of teachers' theories and practices illuminates the field of global education and improves social studies education. The way teachers make sense of global issues and arguments is more likely to influence how they teach in classrooms. Johnston and Ochoa (1993) indicate a framework of four selected areas of research in teacher education: critical perspectives, teacher reflection, pedagogical content knowledge and beliefs, and cognitive developmental studies of teachers. Freeman (1986) also discusses a number of in-service teacher training programs and focuses on important process issues that are often overlooked.

McCabe (1997) seeks a multi-disciplinary approach, including psychological and anthropological perspectives, to understand how a global perspective is developed and evolves. In order to form a comprehensive understanding of global education, he calls for psychological and anthropological processes which contribute to perspective or attitude formation and growth and provide a sense of social reality of others which can be used as a source of comparison for an individual's own experience and view of the world.

Jarchow (1993) documents ten global thrusts that must characterize American education in the twenty-first century to develop globally aware citizenry: (1) a global curriculum, (2) study abroad, (3) faculty exchange, (4) use of an international student as a resource of culture in American education, (5) extension of Model United Nations concept at all grade levels, (6) foreign language, (7) the Peace Corps, (8) a mission statement of achieving a global perspective, (9) technology integration in education, and (10) emulating leading schools. Jarchow notes that achieving a global perspective with the above thrusts would lead to the notion that we are part of a world community with shared values, hopes, and dreams.

To sum up, the primary goals of global education are to build understanding and respect for peoples and countries outside the United States, to transcend ethnocentric bias and ideological rigidity, to provide an understanding of the dynamics of cultural and economic imperialism and oppression, to create awareness of the earth as an interrelated and holistic system, and to prepare all students to be effective citizens in a global age. As Tye and Tye (1992) observe, a global literate views humankind as a singular entity interconnected across space and time, the earth as humankind's ecological and cosmic home, and global social structure as one level of human social categorization. Having overviewed a selected range of research studies of global education, I now discuss an ecosystem theory in the following section.

Ecological Systems Theory: A Brief Background of the Ecosystem

Student learning is influenced by individual, social, historical, and cultural factors. A relevant body of theory and research starts with Bronfenbrenner's (1977) ecological model of human development. This model is based on a transactional view that emphasizes the interplay between the individual and his or her immediate and outlying environment. This approach serves as a framework for this chapter because its interactional view is in accordance with the understanding of the process of an individual's global perspective development, and with its emphasis on the internal dynamics of components in an ecosystem. To understand a context requires a consideration of both first-hand events that impinge directly on a student and considerations of outlying environments that affect an individual indirectly, because individual development depends on social and environmental contexts, along with biological and psychological influences.

The conceptual groundwork of Bronfenbrenner's ecological system theory stems from both symbolic interactionism and contextualism. To view an individual as a holistic unity, it is fundamental in education to understand the interplay of the individual's historical, sociocultural, psychosocial forces. This transactional view is related to interactionism. Interactionism is a philosophical viewpoint used to understand and to predict human behavior, which reflects both intra-individual qualities (e.g., traits, idiosyncrasies) and relevant characteristics of the individual's environment (Golstein, 1994). Symbolic interactionism, associated with George Herbert Mead and his student Herbert Blumer, focuses primarily on individuals as they interact within the context of daily lives. The central tenet of interactionism is that the sources for the initiation and direction of behavior come primarily from the continuous transaction between the person and the circumstances that he or she encounters.

The other model, a contextual approach, goes back to Lev Vygotsky. For Vygotsky (1978), the clue to understanding children's development is in their social processes; that is, cognitive growth depends on children's interaction with social settings around them. The contextual approach proposes not only the interaction of two separate entities of the student and society, but also a network of *child-in-social context*. Accordingly, contextualism views the *student-in-social context* as the main unit of analysis. The underlying assumption of contextualism is that the social and cognitive realms are inextricably connected. Global social-cultural-historical influences and proximal social influences, particularly parents and other significant adults, are the main source of cognitive development. These interactional and contextual features focused on *person-plus-surroundings* are the roots of ecological system theory (Bronfenbrenner, 1977; Golstein, 1994).

The term ecology derives from the Greek *oikas* (household or living place), and its original use is employed in the area of biology, as a description of organism-environment interaction. Theory and research dealing with both physical and social environment have been explored to conceptualize the ecology of human development (Golstein, 1994).

Bronfenbrenner's Ecosystem

Bronfenbrenner's ecological model shows the richness and depth of the various layers of a human's environment by characterizing it as a series of nested and interconnected structures. Bronfenbrenner views students as active individuals, not passive receptacles, who develop in the constant interaction with their environment. Bronfenbrenner identifies four interconnected systems that frame all human interactions and influence human development: microsystem, mesosystem, exosystem, and macrosystem. In Bronfenbrenner's model, the student is at the kernel of the sphere of influence, which contains various levels that are interconnected in meaningful ways. A microsystem, at the center of the model, refers to the complex of direct interaction between the student and the immediate environment (i.e., student and home; student and family). In most cases, this consists primarily of family members and their home surroundings.

The next level, a mesosystem, comprises the pattern of interrelations or links among major settings beyond family. For instance, interactions between student and school or student and peer groups constitute a mesosystem. A mesosystem assumes a variety of forms and combinations that include "other persons who participate actively in both settings, intermediate links in a social network, formal and informal communications among settings, and, again, clearly in the phenomenological domain, the extent and nature of knowledge and attitudes existing in one setting about the other" (Bronfenbrenner, 1977). Ecological theory holds that the desirable maintenance of mesosystems is essential for proper individual development.

The third level, an exosystem, represents social settings that affect the student, which include both formal and informal social structures such as the neighborhood, the mass media, agencies of government, communication and transportation facilities, and social networks. These settings are not directly connected to the particular student as an active participant, but they affect the student's microsystem in an indirect manner. According to Bronfenbrenner (1977), an exosystem refers to "one or more settings that do not involve the developing person as an active participant, but in which events occur that affect or are affected by what happens in the setting containing the developing person."

The perspective of an exosystem shares the idea with Cortes's (1981) notion of a "societal curriculum." Cortes believes that students learn in schools as well as outside of school through the societal curriculum. He defines societal curriculum as "a massive informal curriculum of families, peer groups, neighborhoods, churches, organizations, institutions, mass media, and other socializing forces that educate all of us throughout our lives" (1981, p. 25). Although Cortes deals with family and peer group's influence on a student's development, his focus is primarily on overarching societal curricula, such as engagement in media use, including the hypermedia, because television, film, and the Internet are the most common environment in a student's life.

Finally, a macrosystem refers to the cultural or subcultural context in which all the other systems are embedded. Most macrosystems are informal and implicit in the society member's ideology. The concrete manifestation of macrosystem is the economy, society, education, laws, politics, and religion.

A macrosystem, the highest level of the ecological model, differs from the previous primary systems in a fundamental way. While the three preliminary systems deal with the immediate contexts containing the specific person and interrelations with them, the macrosystem deals with ideological patterns of the culture or subculture. However, all components of ecosystems are in holistic unity rather than combinations of separate elements. The macrosystem, though it remains away from the students' day-to-day activities, represents a cultural ideology or identity which governs what they should be taught and what goals are important to achieve. These levels of environmental influences and their reciprocal connections are key elements in understanding the nature of ecological view of global education. In terms of a research area, cross-cultural studies are the most common form of investigation from the perspective of the macrosystem (Bronfenbrenner, 1977).

So far, the basic tenets of the ecosystems have been discussed. How does global education fit in the framework of the ecosystem? Discussed below is an application of global education into the system.

Global Education within the Ecological Systems Framework

Global education is multifaceted and embraces manifold layers of process in an ecological perspective. Global education includes the concept that everyone retains myriad citizenships, which include family, community, state, nation, and even world (Risinger, 1998). These inherent multiple citizenships require students to see the world through multifarious perspectives and understand multiple realities with the ability to make choices in light of global issues. Global education embraces the same goals of harmony, equity, and justice for the world's citizenry.

Since the ecological model shows the multifaceted contexts that can influence global perspective development, the model emphasizes the importance of moving gradually beyond the fundamental student-parent relationship to include the effects of other relationships that the student develops in myriad ways. A student's family, school, peer group, and the mass media all influence a global perspective development.

To enhance global understanding, it is fundamental to note that students learn about global issues and other cultures from various communication sources in both a formal and informal context. Table 1 summarizes the major sources of information, by levels of ecosystem. These sources are not equally powerful in all situations. In general, the extent of influence on students in communication may depend on student's age, the level of cognitive development, and immediate environmental factors.

Table 1. Major Channels of Communication in Global Education

Sources of Information	Level of Ecosystem
Oral medium by parents, peers, and teachers	Microsystem, Mesosystem
The formal educational system	Mesosystem
Broadcast and print media	Exosystem
International travel	Exosystem, Macrosystem
Popular culture and art	Macrosystem

Microsystem: Global Education Begins at Home

The first sociocultural level, a microsystem, lies closer to the child per se in its proximal social and physical settings. This level involves the day-to-day interactions with parents, siblings, and other significant figures at home.

In the theory of human ecological development, the environment is described as a set of coherent structures and systems. Any effort to provide children with a global perspective and help them understand global issues must be based on a thorough understanding of the children themselves, including their relationship with family members. Among fundamental underpinnings to global education, family is the most fundamental setting and interconnected system that frame all human interactions and influence global perspective development.

Parents are, without a doubt, in the most powerful position to educate children about global education for two major reasons. First, they can be positive role models and mediators because children's perceptions and attitudes are formed in the beginning years of life at home. Second, parents are usually the persons with whom children form their intimate relationships, and the nature of these earliest relationships will have a major impact throughout one's life. Accordingly, a student's global perspective reflects open-mindedness, empathy for others, perspective-taking, and respect for diversity.

Figure 1 (p. 153) shows a whole picture of an ecosystem that encompasses the holistic global perspective development. Each component is not mutually exclusive, but rather interconnected.

Mesosystem: The Choice Schools Must Make

Although family members, to some extent, infuse a particular perspective on a student at an individual level, teachers also play a dominant role in fostering a global perspective at both an individual and group level. The goals of global education are hardly successful unless students begin in the earlier grades to learn the essential concepts and to cultivate attitudes reflecting awareness of global dynamics, subject content knowledge about global history, geography, religion, and language, and so forth.

Along with such innovations to the elementary curriculum as technology implementation, cooperative learning, and interdisciplinary instruction, global education should be a criterion of a complete social studies program (Taylor, 1997). Although global education has been incorporated in the upper levels of schooling, the need for its inclusion, based on research on cognitive development of the young child, is recognized as vital (Swiniarski, Breitborde, & Murphy, 1999).

Taylor argues that school principals must be active in providing leadership, encouragement, and funding in global education (Taylor, 1997). Using their knowledge about the needs of the community, principals are also encouraged to lead the way in contacting local business, civic organizations, and citizens to assist in the efforts of the schools. It is important to note that teachers and principals are urged to examine their own biases and worldviews, not to emphasize a particular viewpoint on an issue. They should carefully examine the instructional materials and activities adopted for global education. Through understanding the issues and concepts fundamental to global education and being sensitive to the virtues of good citizenship, a global educational program can be successful.

Exosystem: Multiple Perspectives on Multiple Realities

Home and school do not monopolize global education because students continuously receive a barrage of information about transnational and transcultural issues outside these institutions. The community's provision of services also makes a network in many ways. The students may not have immediate contact with these systems and, thus, are indirectly affected by them.

An exosystem is composed of various components such as societal organizations, churches, social clubs, and the media. Each component provides various information, such as values, norms, and attitudes. The influence of informal educational forces, especially the mass media, has become critical for learning and living in complex settings, as students are engaged in the media for a significant amount of time. For example, many studies show that students spend more time watching television than they spend in formal schooling (Keith, Reimers, Fehrmann, Pottebaum, & Aubey, 1986; Stromna, 1991; Quesade & Summers, 1998). The barrage of information delivered by communication channels shapes a viewpoint of global issues.

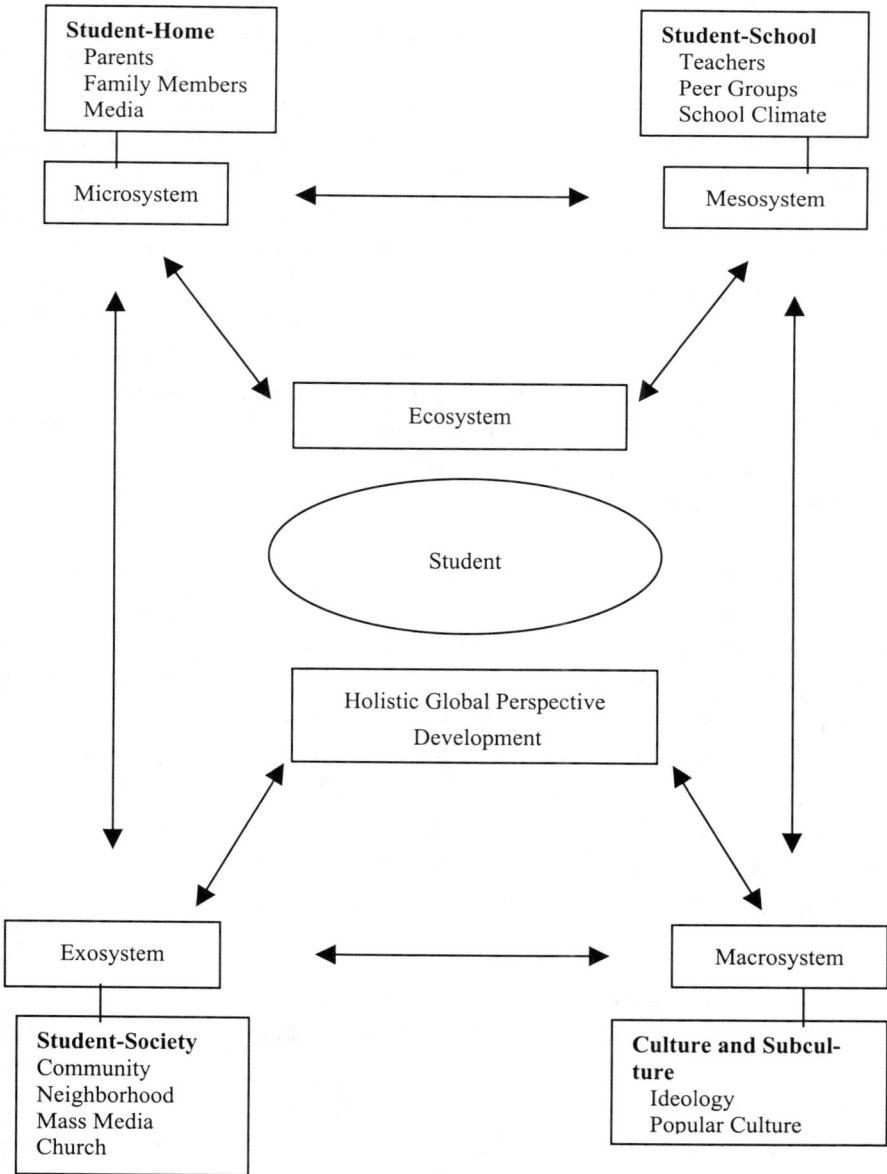

Figure 1. A Framework for Main Factors Associated with the Ecosystem Modified from Bonfenbreenner (1977).

Specifically, the mass media are a primary agent by which students perceive and interpret other cultures and values through a process of categorization. Since many people rely on the media for information gathering about events, issues, and cultures of foreign countries resulting from limited firsthand experiences, the media have become powerful in creating and shaping images about other people and their nations. At times, the media as a cultural mechanism promote stereotypes and biases (Pae, 1999b). For example, in a content analysis of U.S. news magazines, with a special emphasis on the presence of loaded words and slanted expressions in news articles, Pae reports that the overall language used to depict the Arab and Asian political leaders is skewed toward negative portrayals, and that there are split images of the leaders, depending on their political orientations and U.S. foreign policy. Accordingly, the way of portraying other groups in the media may have an impact on how we interpret the issues of international relations, determining our perspectives of the world.

Again, an ecosystem is an interconnected and reciprocal system. Media use falls in both the microsystem and exosystem because individuals are influenced by the powerful role of the media in shaping perceptions and attitudes toward an outer world, through both overt and covert messages, from early childhood to later adolescent to adulthood.

The educational components of an exosystem, therefore, represent the lifelong societal learning process. The much quoted African adage, "It takes a whole village to raise a child" trumpets the theme of an ecological view of human development. A community or village is a microcosm of the world's people as well as part of a global infrastructure.

Macrosystem: To Promote Global Literacy
and to Overcome Cultural Myopia

A global perspective is, in part, developed as a result of cultural transmission and acquisition. Culture creates normative codes or rules which become keys for constructing and interpreting other cultures. Norm or cultural symbols make up the environmental stimuli which create perceptions during a process of cognition and suggest a way of understanding how a person might develop a frame of reference which in turn provides the basis for the development of global perspective. The ideological, economic, historical, and political evaluations and conditions make up different macrosystems. Cultural variations and situational opportunities and circumstances can also influence the course and expression of students' global perspective development. The macrosystem rarely affects students' development directly but, instead, interacts with individual and situational factors.

The global citizenship that requires the development of both a sense of global belonging and a series of global civic values constitutes a fundamental objective of any global perspective development effort. What are, then, civic values? They entail a "sense of shared interest and shared engagement; an acceptance of the individual and national responsibility that comes along with a community of a planet; and a recognition of the ways in which all cultures contribute to the common good" (Savitt, 1993). In short, participation, engagement, and respect are virtues of citizenship that underlie any democratic regime. A failure of global citizenship could undermine a broader community in the increasingly interdependent world of the future.

Table 2 presents the emergent themes or concepts in an ecosystem. The virtues required to be a global citizen under the category of student-centered microsystem include international socialization, open-mindedness, perspective-taking or perspective consciousness. While the themes of the mesosystem primarily regard a knowledge-base on international issues and problems acquired in schools, the themes of the exosystem involve multiple perspectives and reflexive thinking with an emphasis on the role of community or society. The macrosystem deals with the outcome of successful global education as an overarching concept: cross-cultural understanding, intergenerational responsibility, overcoming of cultural myopia, and a gain of global literacy.

The macrosystem also deals with awareness of consequences of British and American imperialism. Spring (1998) argues in his powerful critique of globalization and neoliberal initiatives that European colonialism provided the foundation for the modern global economy and disseminated European ideas about education, science, and technology. The spread of English as the global language becomes, he contends, of particular importance. For example, Prime Minister Tony Blair (quoted in Spring, 1998, p. 7) claims that English is "the language of international politics, of international business, of professional and scientific exchange, of travel and—now—of the internet...Three quarters of the world's mail is written in English. Four fifths of the information stored on the world's computers is in English." Within this context, students need to be informed of the consequences of cultural imperialism and hegemony.

Table 2. Worldwide Paradigm Shift Toward a Global Society in an Ecosystem

Microsystem	Mesosystem	Exosystem	Macrosystem
- International socialization - Open-mindedness - Perspective-taking/ Perspective consciousness - Universal and diverse human values - Holistic perspective through critical thinking - Empathy for others	- Awareness of global dynamics - Subject content knowledge about global history, geography, religion, and language - One's own viewpoint of global interdependence and interconnectedness	- Multiple critical perspectives - Reflexive thinking - Involvement and decisions within the local and global community	- Cross-cultural understanding - Recognition of the complexity of cultural diversity - Intergenerational responsibility - To overcome cultural myopia and to widen the horizon of own cultural perspectives - Acknowledgment of global unity - Understanding of cultural imperialism and hegemony - Gain of global literacy

Note: Most concepts in the table were regrouped from Merryfield's (1998) conceptualization of global education.

Implications for Practice in Ecosystems

Given the interconnections that make up the ecosystem, global education as an ecological unit calls for a number of implementation options as to how it constitutes the successful development of the global education. The following question emerges from the tensions inherent in the ecosystem: How does this ecological framework fit within the context of the current educational realms in America? In short, the problems or tensions generated from the ecosystem lie in the compatibility of this framework with current educational practices.

In American education, such concepts as active, cooperative, and discovery learning, and integrative and critical thinking have received increased attentions as strategies to transform a student from a passive receptacle to an active participant in educational settings. These methods and strategies parallel the objectives and anticipated outcomes for global education.

As shown in Figure 1 (p. 153), a student is the centerpiece of the framework because he/she is the chief client served by education. A student is strongly influenced by his/her own ability and achievement as well as his/her environmental factors, including the home and family, school, community, and cultural components. Within the system, a student's global perspective is the ultimate outcome, due to a number of important interactions that occur among the student, home, school, and community.

The possible implementation options are summarized in Table 3. With regard to a home and family component, an active family involvement becomes an important element in fostering a global perspective. As the primary influence on the life of a student, the family should be the basic agent upon which other socializing agents build. In this model, the home and family includes a number of variables, especially as related to the school. Each family needs to be understood in terms of its cultural ecology. Various structural and dynamic elements of the family should serve to create an atmosphere conducive to learning and to mediate learning. For example, making international issues and various viewpoints an important and frequent topic of conversation at home helps promote a global perspective. Parents should develop patterns of paying attention to a variety of their children's behaviors, achievements, and talents. Placing values on multiple realities associated with global issues is critical to foster a global perspective.

What constitutes a desirable relationship between family and school? The basic prerequisite of the microsystem is a continuity between home and school in discussion of global awareness. The school category includes a number of key elements associated with student learning. These

Table 3. Implementation Options in an Ecosystem

Ecosystem	Primary Setting	Implementation for Practice
Microsystem	Home	Active Family Involvement Active participation in global issue-related conversation Encouragement of open-mindedness
Mesosystem	School	Implementation into curricula Systematic Teacher Education
Exosystem	Mass Media	Societal Curriculum Cultivation of Media Literacy
Macrosystem	Culture	Cultural Pluralism Biculturalism Multiculturalism

elements include the makeup of the faculty, curriculum and instruction, overall school climate, and overall school leadership. Among these elements, as Merryfield (1998) notes, teachers serve as curriculum-instructional gatekeepers. Merryfield (1998) gives some clues in implementation of global education in the curriculum as follows:

- to make connections across cultures, world regions, and civilizations and across global issues instead of teaching them separately;
- to identify historical antecedents to current world issues, events, and problems, and identify the processes of cultural diffusion and borrowing over time;
- to link global content to the local community;
- to teach tolerance and appreciation of cultural differences.

Integrating global education into the curriculum should be coupled with systematic teacher education, including both preservice training and in-service education. Greater attention should be paid to how teachers make instructional decisions as they plan and teach. Teachers may vary in how they perceive their overall roles in planning instruction and curriculum, because teachers usually work alone behind closed doors with their own classes (Tye & Tye, 1992). This problem suggests change of the locus of control from the individual teachers to the school, which calls for the development of new leadership roles within the school, new forms of collaboration among staff members, and more field orientations in preservice education (Tye & Tye, 1992). It also suggests some changes in how teachers spend their time devoted to such things as problem solving, inquiry, and general sharing. Finally, it points to the need for a careful examination of the emerging role of technology, with the rise of Internet use.

Along with the concurrent influences on children by families and schools, the community also plays a key role in global education. A number of variables include both of the immediate neighborhood and of the broader community. The elements encompass the social-political-economic systems of community, the socioeconomic status of the neighborhood, the social services available for students, and the non-school education systems such as public libraries, mass media, and museums, and the peer groups.

The exemplary societal curriculum facilitates open-mindedness, anticipation of complexity, resistance to stereotyping, empathy for others, and nonchauvinism. Among the variables in an exosystem, the mass media have become an important force simply because they take up a good deal of students' time. Therefore, I propose the development of media literacy as a critical choice in implementation options. A media-literate person is skillful in analyzing media codes and conventions, criticizing media stereotypes, values, and ideologies, and thus reading media critically (Pae, 1999a). From the point of view of a constitutive definition, media literacy is the ability to analyze, interpret, and evaluate media messages and to become aware of media as a source of information and stereotypes about other people, countries, and occupations. From an operational point of view, media literacy is defined as students' borrowing and adapting critical thinking methods to understand and evaluate the overt and covert messages of the media (Pae, 1999a). Therefore, well-developed media literacy becomes a base for successful global education.

The concept of "One Planet, One People" signifies the quest to find mechanisms in this world to connect us to one another. As use of the Internet on a daily basis progresses in the world, we are moving towards a multi-national, multi-racial society without national boundaries. With many different nationalities mingling in America, the concept of "One Planet, One People" portrays the Twenty-first century. It emphasizes the will to overcome national differences, and acknowledges individuals' hopes and dreams.

Conclusion

This chapter offers contexts and categories for understanding how a global perspective evolves, with a holistic approach to learning about and acting on the world's issues and problems. All environments of students are composed of complex interconnections among personal, social, cultural factors, which are called ecosystems. The most important part of an ecosystem is the interrelatedness of the elements within the system.

Global education is a collaborative endeavor, as it involves diverse people with different interests. To educate students to live in a democratic society with a sensitivity to and appreciation of local and national needs framed within a world perspective, global education should be part of a worldwide effort to educate for world citizenship. The goal of global education is, hence, to foster the growth of the confident student in accepting challenges and taking the responsibilities required for effective citizenship in the global village. To be meaningful, global education needs the holistic involvement of families, educators, and policy makers in implementing their central ideas in homes, schools, communities, and larger agencies. In order to secure a sound cornerstone for the global educational process, the standards or expectations of parents and teachers should be concerted considerations in promoting a global perspective. With this concern, the upshot of the process will emerge from holistic ecological transaction. Equipped with global awareness, students can go beyond their own ideological preference or rigidity, and overcome their own cultural myopia.

References

Anderson, C.C., Nicklas, S.K. & Crawford, A.R. (1994). *Global understanding: A framework for teaching and learning.* Alexander, VA: Association for Supervision Curriculum Development.

Bronfenbrenner, U. (1977). Toward an experimental ecology of human development. *American Psychologist,* 32, pp. 513–531.

Bruce, M.G., Podemski, R.S. & Anderson, C.S. (1991). Developing a global perspective: Strategies for teacher education programs. *Journal of Teacher Education,* 42 (Jan.), pp. 21–27.

Case, R (1993). Key elements of a global perspective. *Social Education,* 57(Oct.), pp. 318–325

Cortes, C.E. (1981). The societal curriculum: Implications for multiethnic education. In James A. Banks (Ed.), *Education in the 80's: Multiethnic education* (pp. 24–32). Washington, D.C.: National Educational Association.

Featherstone, M. (Ed). (1990). *Global culture, nationalism, globalization, and modernity.* Newbury Park, CA: Sage.

Freeman, R. E. (Ed.). (1986). *Promising practices in global education: A handbook with case studies.* New York: National Council on Foreign Language and International Studies.

Golstein, A.P. (1994). *The ecology of aggression.* New York: Plenum Press.

Hanvey, R. G. (1979). *An attainable global perspective.* New York: Global Perspectives in Education.

Harris, R. (Ed.). (1986). *The teaching of contemporary issues.* Paris: UNESCO.

Hendrix, J. (1998). Globalizing the curriculum. *Clearing House,* 71(May/June), pp. 305–308.

Jameson, F., & Miyoshi, M. (Eds.). (1998). *The cultures of globalization.* Durham, NC: Duke University Press.

Jarchow, E. (1993). A global perspective: A choice American education must make, *National Forum: Phi Kappa Phi Journal,* 73(Fall), pp. 23–24.

Johnston, M., & Ochoa, A. (1993). Teacher education for global perspectives: A research agenda. *Theory into Practice,* 32(Winter), pp. 64–68.

Keith, T.,Reimers, T.,Fehrmann, P.,Pottebaum, S.M., & Aubey, L. (1986). Parental involve-ment, homework, and TV time: Direct and indirect effects on high school achievement. *Journal of Educational Psychology,* 78(October), pp. 373–379.

King, D., Branson, M.S., & Condon, L.E. (1976). Education for a world in change: A working handbook for global perspectives, *84/85 INTERCOM,* New York: Center for Global Perspectives of the New York Friends Group, Inc.

Kniep, W. M. (1986). Social studies within a global education, *Social Education,* 53, pp. 399–404

———. (Ed.). (1987). *Next steps in global education: A handbook of curriculum development.* New York: Global Perspectives in Education.

———. (1989). Global education as school reform *Educational Leadership,* 47, pp. 43–45.

McCabe, L.T. (1997). Global perspective development. *Education,* 118, pp. 41–46.

Merryfield, M.M. (1991). Preparing American secondary social studies teachers to teach with a global perspective: A status report. *Journal of Teacher Education,* 42, pp. 27–32.

———. (1998). Pedagogy for global perspectives in education: Studies of teachers' thinking and practice. *Theory and Research in Social Education,* 26, pp. 342–379.

Pae, H.K. (1999a). *Media literacy: A critical pedagogy to promote global perspective.* Pa-per presented at the 16th Annual Conference of Intercultural Communication., Miami, FL.

———. (1999b). *Split images: Portrayals of political leaders of the Arab and Asian countries in major U.S. news magazines.* Paper presented at the 82th Annual Convention of Association for Education in Journalism and Mass Communication, New Orleans, LA.

Quesade, A., & Summers, S. (1998). Literacy in the cyber age: Teaching kids to be media savvy. *Technology and Learning,* 18, pp. 30–31.

Ramler, S. (1991). Global education for the 21st century, *Educational Leadership,* 48, pp. 4–46.

Risinger, C. (1998). Global and the worldwide web. *Social Education,* 62, pp. 276–277.

Savitt, W. (1993). The interdependent patriot: Education for the global citizen. InWilliam Savitt (Ed.), *Teaching global development: A curriculum guide* (pp. 3–12). Notre Dame, IN: The University of Notre Dame Press.

Spring, J. (1998). *Education and the rise of the global economy.* Mohwah, NJ: Erlbaum.

Stromna, C.A. (1991). Television's role in the socialization of African American children and adolescents. *Journal of Negro Education,* 60, pp. 314–327.

Swiniarski, L., Breitborde, Bary-Lou, & Murphy, J. (1999). *Educating the global village: Including the young child in the world.* Upper Saddle River, NJ: Prentice-Hall.

Taylor, H. (Ed.). (1997). *Getting started in global education: A primer for principals and teachers.* Alexandria, VA: National Association of Elementary School Principals.

Tye, K., & Kniep, W. (1991). Global education around the world, *Educational Leadership,* 48, pp. 47–49

Tye, B.B., & Tye, K.A. (1992). *Global education: A study of school change.* New York: State University of New York Press.

Vygotsky, L. (1978). *Mind in society: The development of higher psychological process.* Cambridge, MA: Harvard University Press.

Chapter Ten

Rethinking Virtual Community as a Pedagogical Enterprise

Huey-li Li

The recent movement toward universal access to the Internet has rapidly facilitated our (in)voluntary and frequent involvement in group mailing lists, bulletin boards, Internet Relay Chat, and Usenet newsgroups. In this libertarian cyberspace, we establish connections with people who share our interests or concerns. Often, we refer to these sites of social congregation as virtual communities. The very term "virtual communities" implies the elusiveness of these Internet groups. On the one hand, mirage-like "virtual communities" are to be distinguished from traditional "real" communities, which are based on commonality, face-to-face interaction, and physical proximity. On the other hand, various virtual communities springing from the existing telecommunication infrastructure have initiated and sustained the ongoing transformation of "real" communities at the global level (Jones, 1993; Harasim, 1993). Jean Baudrillard points out that virtual communities simulate real communities, and such simulation could be "more real than the real." Paul Virilio further states that virtual communities could replace "real" communities (Baudrillard, 1988; Wilson, 1994).

John Dewey claims that community, embodying a matrix of human relationships, is a pedagogical enterprise. In view of the flourishing of virtual communities, it is essential to examine the pedagogical contexts and practices of online virtual communities. In this chapter, I specifically focus on the spatial, temporal, and social dimensions of virtual communities. I argue that virtual communities, to a large extent, reflect and endorse the cultural values of the professional middle classes. As a result, the burgeoning of virtual communities in classrooms and schools is likely to enhance the effects of the current class structure and confute the educational significance of cultural diversity. To ensure the openness of virtual communities, the concerned educator must attend to human agency in the construction of virtual communities.

Community as a Pedagogical Enterprise

John Dewey regards education as "the process of forming fundamental dispositions, intellectual and emotional, toward nature and fellowman" (Dewey, 1916). This process cannot take place in a social vacuum. In view of the interconnections between the words *common, community,* and *communication,* Dewey points out that "men live in a community in virtue of the things which they have in common; and communication is the way in which they come to possess things in common" (Dewey, 1916). To Dewey, a spirit of cooperative community is essential in forming our fundamental disposition because a matrix of interactive human relationships facilitates the individual's continuous growth. He argues that "we are born organic beings associated with others, but we are not born members of a community. The young have to be brought within the traditions, outlook and interests which characterize a community by means of education; by unremitting instruction and by learning in connection with the phenomena of overt associations" (Dewey, 1897, p. 154). In his own words, Dewey stated that "education being a social process, the school is simply that form of community life in which all those agencies are concentrated that will be most effective in bringing the child to share in the inherited resources of the race and to use his own powers for social ends" (Dewey, 1897, p. 78). To Dewey, community is as much processes as it is substance. He argues that "we must take the child as a member of society in the broadest sense, and demand for and from the schools whatever is necessary to enable the child intelligently to recognize all his social relations and take his part in sustaining them" (Dewey, 1897, p. 78).

As discussed above, Dewey believes that community is a pedagogical enterprise, and educational institutions such as schools must function as a "community in microcosm" in order to sustain and improve the larger society. At macro level, there has been an increasing population dedicated to the establishment of virtual communities. Concomitantly, schools have emerged as a proactive agency, conferred with the power to ensure universal access to the Internet, thereby promoting the continuing development of virtual communities. However, most educators have not yet made concerted efforts to explicate the pedagogical nature of virtual classrooms and virtual schools and their relationship to various virtual communities in the larger society. In what follows, I attempt to examine the continuity and discontinuity of our conceptualization of human communities in the cyber age.

Howard Rheingold defines virtual communities as "social aggregations that emerge from the Net when enough people carry on those public discussions long enough, with sufficient human feeling, to form webs of personal relationships in cyberspace" (Rheingold, 1994). Virtual community, to a large extent, is congenial to Dewey's conception of community. After all, commonality and communication can be viewed as the dual foundations of virtual community. However, questions regarding the generic paradigm(s) and normative validation of virtual community as a pedagogical enterprise still remain somewhat unexplored and unanswered. More specifically, it is not clear what type of public discussion we deem conducive to the establishment of virtual communities. Nor can we be certain about the requisite length of public discussion for forming and sustaining the community. Above all, "sufficient feeling" as a constitutive component of virtual communities is so vague that we could question the existence of almost all virtual communities. Clearly, virtual community is such an illusive concept that we can hardly reach a universal agreement on its definition. As a result, it is difficult to determine how virtual community should shape the formation of human disposition and how school should prepare students for their participation in the continuous development of virtual community.

In *Imagined Communities*, Benedict Anderson argues, "All communities larger than primordial villages of face-to-face contact (and perhaps even these) are imagined. Communities are to be distinguished, not by their falsity or genuineness, but by the style in which they are imagined" (Anderson, 1991). In light of Anderson's insight, I will explore how the style of virtual communities is imagined and how the style shapes the pedagogical process within and beyond virtual communities.

The Spatial and Temporal Dimensions of Virtual Communities

The establishment of various virtual communities relies upon the Internet and computer-mediated communication systems (CMCS) that free us from both spatial and temporal constraints to engage in communication and to form communities. To a large extent, the formation of most virtual communities is not independent of off-line communities. In fact, some virtual communities overlap with off-line physical or "real-life" communities. However, as virtual communities have no territorial physical space, the ephemeral existence of virtual communities appears to be based on the members' "consensual hallucination" (Gibson, 1984). Furthermore, scientists such as Hans Moravec have started to envision the transformation of human consciousness into a computerized information pattern (Moravec, 1988). As discussed above, the making of virtual community implicitly suggests the ongoing movement to replace or even displace materiality of human community by virtuality. E. Soja points out:

> The spatio-temporal structuring of social life defines how social action and re-lationship (including class relations) are materially constituted, made concrete. The constitution/concretization process is problematic, filled with contradiction and struggle (amidst much that is recursive and routinized). Contradictions arise primarily from the duality of produced space as both out-come/embodiment/product and medium/presupposition/product of social activity. (Soja, 1989, p. 129)

In the case of virtual communities, the contradictions embedded in the constitutive process often result from the tension between on-line and off-line communities and the entanglement of disembodied and embodied communicative processes.

Undoubtedly, virtual communities could sustain their corresponding and overlapping off-line communities. In fact, the Internet and computer-mediated communication systems (CMCS) have served as an internal communication system in many educational institutions, professional organizations, and even family systems. As mentioned before, advocates for virtual communities such as Howard Rheingold suggest that the longitude of cyberdiscourse is the key factor for forming virtual community. Consequently, members' long-term commitments to virtual communities also compel them to curtail their face-to-face interaction with the other members within corresponding off-line communities and beyond (e.g., family, coworkers, and neighbors). To a certain degree, the primacy of computer-mediated communication indicates a depreciation of face-to-face communication within the local or institutional community. At the same time, it is not surprising that many groups of people have been devoted to the establishment of virtual communities that are independent and separate from "real-life""communities.

Evidently, the establishment of virtual communities demands a time commitment. J. Rifkin states that "the computer is a form of communication like script, print, and the telephone, but it is also a time tool, like the clock on the wall. As a timepiece, the computer...establishes a new set of accelerated temporal demands on human behavior" (quoted in Rifkin, 1987, p. 15). Furthermore, while Internet communication facilitates both synchronous and asynchronous communication, it is obvious that "efficiency" and "immediacy" are the benchmarks of computer-mediated communication. Steve G. Jones points out that the Internet, like other electronic media, has led to the fragmentation of time. Specifically, he states that "[I]nstead of time as a continuity, as a movement with regularity that grows from and in turn builds up our sense of interaction, time is experienced as atomistic and discontinuous; time is not spent *with* others, it is spent *on* or *for* others, or even for ourselves" (quoted in Rifkin, 1987, p. 15).

Above all, cyberdiscourse based on the interconnection between human and machine simultaneously extends and confines our communicative capabilities. More specifically, communication in virtual communities has reduced the totality of our "beings" to immediate and animated images, voices, and text. Texts, signs, and electronic images are the primary communication medium in the virtual communities. The coding and decoding of the texts, signs, images, or combinations of these, inevitably filter out what would be nuances of face-to-face communication in a setting where communicators share the living space. Consequently, it is conducive for on-liners to disembody and objectify the other members of virtual communities and to perceive the communities as "belonging" to them (McLaughlin, Osborne, & Smith, 1995). In Jean Baudrillard's words, "every individual sees himself promoted to the controls of a hypothetical machine, isolated in a position of perfect sovereignty"(Baudrillard, 1988). Such "perfect sovereignty" clearly undermines the reciprocal nature of human communication.

As discussed above, the spatial and temporal dimensions of virtual communities have extensive impacts on teaching and learning. Above all, it should be noted that the development of information processing systems corresponds with the rise of the professional-managerial class; and both information technology and the professional-managerial class appear to contribute to the reproduction of the current class system (Ross, 1994). Basil Bernstein's study of how pedagogical practices sustain a class system is insightful for our exploration of the pedagogical nature and process of virtual community. Bernstein argues that "Class relations constitute inequalities in the distribution of power between social groups, which are realized in the creation, organization, distribution, legitimation, and reproduction of material and symbolic values arising out of the social division of labor" (Bernstein, 1977, p. viii). He further makes a distinction between visible pedagogy and invisible pedagogy. According to Bernstein, visible pedagogies are realized through strong classification and frame, while invisible pedagogies are realized through weak classification and frame. Specifically, classification refers to "the degree of boundary maintenance between contents," and frame refers to "the degree of control teacher and pupil possess over the selection, organization, pacing and timing of the knowledge transmitted and received in the pedagogical relationship" (Bernstein, 1971, p. 205).

On the one hand, visible pedagogy requires strong classification of space. Seating arrangements, school facilities, and instructional apparatus all have their specific, designated functions. On the other hand, in the case of invisible pedagogies, "spaces and their contents are weakly classified. This means that the *potential space available to the child is very much greater*. The privacy embodied in space regulated by visible pedagogies is considerably reduced" (Bernstein, 1997). Ever-extended space and a fragmented temporal dimension, as the distinguishing characteristics of virtual community, embody the invisible pedagogies that foster what Durkheim termed "organic solidarity" in modern society. The promotion of universal access to the Internet indicates the strong possibility of transforming the traditional classroom into a virtual classroom, which could be a microcosm of a virtual community. A virtual classroom supported by a computer-mediated communication system (CMCS) certainly could create ever-expansive space for learning and teaching (Hiltz, 1994). In the meantime, CMCSs enable teachers to document and monitor students' ongoing learning processes. Consequently, students could subject themselves to continual surveillance from teachers.

Moreover, the flexibility of asynchronous communication mirrors "self-pacing" as the trademark of the virtual classroom and renders sequencing and pacing rules more implicit. Nevertheless, asynchronicity of virtual communication still demands immediate responses in modern industrial societies. This is why computer industries constantly push for the acceleration of speed, and students as well as teachers are inclined to expect immediate feedback in virtual classrooms.

As mentioned before, the Internet and CMCSs are simply piggy-back media. Virtual communities and virtual classrooms do not create their own physical space. However, a physical space is indispensable for any of us to launch into a virtual community/classroom. Bernstein points out that new middle class parents expect their children to complete homework, which often is based on textbooks.[1] However, "the textbook requires...an official pedagogic context in the home. That is, a space—a silent space—and this is not usually available in the homes of the poor" (Bernstein, 1990, p. 77). Likewise, while children from low-income families could gain access to the Internet in school, there is no guarantee that they will have "a silent space" (including facilities) to enhance their skills even though the public may be willing to supply them with laptops.

Bernstein's conception of invisible pedagogies sheds light on the reproduction of the new middle class in a modern industrial society.[2] As virtual classrooms embody invisible pedagogies and invisible pedagogies reflect the new middle professional-managerial class value, we certainly need to be cautious about how virtual classrooms could sustain the current class structure and contribute to further class stratification.

The Social Dimension of Virtual Communities

As discussed before, John Dewey argues that community facilitates individual development. G. Simmel also points out that the actualization of individuality is based on the individual's contribution to the collectivity (Simmel, 1950). In other words, social interactions are essential to the formation of both individuality and collectivity. Various net communities certainly reflect diversified social interactions in human communities. However, social interactions in virtual communities depend upon computer-mediated communication. As Steve G. Jones points out:

> CMC... not only structures social relations, it is the space within which the relations occur and the tool that individuals use to enter that space. It is more than the context within which social relations occur (although it is that, too) for it is commented on and imaginatively constructed by symbolic processes initiated and maintained by individuals and groups. (Jones, 1995, p. 16)

Like the establishment of many modern nations, the construction of virtual communities has been imagined through shared cultural practices (Anderson, 1991). Inhabitants in and visitors to various virtual communities, to a large extent, share common concerns and interests even though they disperse in different times and spaces. While their sharing of common interests and concerns could reinforce community solidarity, it is essential not to undermine the significance of "the accidents of proximity" which form traditional communities (Healy, 1997). For example, the accidents of proximity may not allow free association, but involuntary association often reveals heterogeneity in the given community. Bellah and others point out that the association of today's professional middle class often is based on their shared lifestyle. To them, "Whereas a community attempts to be an inclusive whole, celebrating the interdependence of public and private life and of the different callings of all, lifestyle is fundamentally segmental and celebrates the narcissism of similarity" (Bellah, Madsen, Sullivan, Swidler, & Tipton, 1995, p. 66). Following their argument, David Healy refers to virtual communities as lifestyle enclaves (Healy, 1997).

Moreover, while inhabitants and visitors can be connected and form conviviality in virtual communities, it should be noted that they can be easily disconnected as soon as they are not communicating. In other words, the vicissitudes of virtual communities make it difficult to sustain the collectivity that presumably could nurture individual development. In addition, computer-mediated communication has enhanced the fluidity of our identity. It is simple and easy for us to disguise our identity while participating in cyberdiscourse. To a certain degree, Foucault is correct when he asserts that anonymity could free the individual subject from the sociopolitical and sociocultural bonds which attempt to fix his or her identity (Foucault, 1991). While disguised identity may facilitate genuine self-disclosure, deceptive identity could contribute to a misrepresentation of voices, which certainly can misguide the development of collectivity.

On the other hand, while net communities are virtually interconnected, cyberdiscourse is not exempted from parochialism. Dialogue between different net groups is not uncommon; however, cyberdiscourse often is more inviting to likeminded cyborgs who share the same or similar concerns, interests, and values. Consequently, various disconnected net communities have chartered cyberspace. Although destructive collision between divergent net groups has been avoided, fortresslike virtual communities have averted confrontational yet fruitful dialogue between them.

Furthermore, Internet as a medium of public discourse has not mediated existing imbalanced power relationships between various groups. Technically, universal accessibility to the Internet can be an attainable goal, and user-friendly technology can easily transform us into cyborgs trotting on the information superhighway. However, the diffusive power of modern technology does not guarantee equivalence of relationship. An inclusive cyberdiscourse should not disclaim and silence noncyborgs' resistance toward cybernetic interconnections. Nor should cyborgs attempt to speak for noncyborgs. Without noncyborgs' direct participation, cyberdiscourse is somewhat limited and exclusive. Virtual communities can offer public space for political soapbox oratory and street marching; however, it is unlikely that virtual social and political movements can generate and then transpose transformative forces outside cyberspace.

Conclusion

To a large extent, the Internet and computer-mediated communication disable us from setting boundaries "between the real and virtual, between time zones and between spaces,...between our sense of self and our sense of our changing roles" (Shields, 1996). Virtual communities, like traditional communities, could provide us with "context within which personal identity is formed, a place where fluent self-awareness follows the currents of communal conversation and contributes to them" (Bellah et al., 1995, p. 135). Upon examining the temporal, spatial, and social dimensions of virtual communities, I caution that virtual community as a pedagogical enterprise may not contribute to the equal sharing of cultural power. Nor could it foster a long-lasting recognition of culture diversity in the human community. As virtual community certainly will not disappear in the new millennium, it is important for educators and their students to undertake a more critical inquiry into the pedagogical nature and process of virtual communities.[3]

Notes

1. To Bernstein, the new middle class refers to the following agencies/agents of symbolic control: (1) Regulators: Members of the legal system, police, prison service, church; (2) Repairers: Members of the medical/psychiatric services and their derivatives, social services; (3) Diffusers: Teachers at all levels and in all areas including mass and specialized media; (4) Shapers: Creators of what counts as developments within or change of symbolic forms; (5) Executors: Civil service—bureacrats.
2. Due to limitation of space, this chapter does not examine the empirical evidences which support or dispute Bernstein's theory. However, I do not therefore suggest that Bernstein's theory has universal applicability. Here, I only intend to show how Bernstein's theory is helpful for us to inquire into the cultural and pedagogical construct of virtual community.
3. I wish to thank Sue Horn for her valuable editorial assistance with this chapter.

References

Anderson,B. (1983,1991). *Imagined communities: Reflections on the origin and spread of nationalism*, revised ed. London: Verso.

Baudrillard, J. (1988).*The ecstasy of communication.* New York: Autonomedia.

Bellah, R., Madsen, R., Sullivan, W.M., Swidler, W. M., & Tipton, S.M. (1995). *Habits of the heart: Individualism and commitment in American life.* New York: Harper & Row.

Bernstein, B. (1971). On the classification and framing of educational knowledge. In B. Bernstein, *Class, codes, and control: Vol. 2.* London: Routledge & Kegan Paul.

———. (1977). *Class, codes, and control: Volume III.* New York: Routledge.

———. (1990). The structuring of pedagogic discourse. In B.Bernstein, *Class, codes and control: Volume IV.* New York: Routledge.

———. (1997). Class and pedagogies: Visible and invisible. In A. H. Halsey, H. Lauder, P. Brown, and A. Stuart Wells (Eds.), *Education: Culture, economy, and society.* Oxford: Oxford University Press.

Dewey, J. (1897). My pedagogical creed. *School Journal*, Vol. LIV.

————. (1916). *Democracy and education: An introduction to the philosophy of education.* New York: Macmillan.

Foucault, M. (1991). *The Foucault effect: Studies in governmentality with two lectures by and an interview with Michel Foucault.* In G. Burchell, C. Gordon, and P. Miller (Eds.), Chicago: University of Chicago Press.

Gibson, W. (1984). *Neuromancer.* New York: Bantam.

Harasim, L.M. (Ed.). (1993). *Global networks: Computer and international commnication.* Cambridge: MIT Press.

Hayles, N.K. (1996). Boundary disputes: Homeostasis, reflexivity, and the foundations of cybernetics. In R. Markley (Ed.), *Virtual realities and their discontents.* Baltimore: Johns Hopkins University Press.

Healy, D. (1997). Cyberspace and place: The internet as middle landscape on the electronic frontier. In D. Porter (Ed.), *Internet culture.* New York: Routledge.

Hiltz, S.R. (1994). *The virtual classroom: Learning without limits via computer networks.* Norwood, NJ: Ablex.

Jones, S.G. (1993). The internet and its social landscape. In S.G. Jones (Ed.), *Virtual culture: Identity and communication in cybersociety* (pp. 7–35). Thousand Oaks, CA: Sage.

————. (1995). Understanding community in information age. In S.G. Jones (Ed.) *CyberSociety: Computer-mediated communication and community.* Thousand Oaks, CA: Sage.

McLaughlin, M.L., Osborne, K.K., Smith, C.B. (1995). Standard of conduct on usenet. In S.G. Jones (Ed.), *Cybersociety: Computer-mediated communication and community* (pp. 90–111). Thousand Oaks, CA: Sage.

Moravec, H. (1988). *Mind children: The future of robot and human intelligence.* Cambridge, MA: Harvard University Press.

Rheingold, H. (1994). *Virtual community: Homesteading on the electronic frontier.* New York: HarperPerennial.

Rifkin, J. (1987). *Time wars.* (New York: Touchstone Books, 1987) cited in S.G. Jones (Ed.), *Virtual culture: Identity and communication in cybersociety.* Thousand Oaks, CA: Sage.

Ross, A. (1994). The new smartness. In G. Bender and T. Druckrey (Eds.), *Culture on the brink: Ideologies of technology, dia center for the arts discussion in contemporary culture, no. 90.* Seattle, WA: Bay Press.

Shields, R. (1996). Virtual spaces, real histories and living bodies. In R. Shields (Ed.), *Cultures of internet* (pp. 1–10). London: Sage.

Simmel, G. (1950). *The sociology of G. Simmel.* (K. Wolff, Trans.). New York: Free Press.

Soja, E. (1989). *Postmodern geographies: The reassertion of space in critical social theory.* London: Verso.

Wilson, L. (1994). Cyberwar, God, and television: Interview with Paul Virillio. In D. Porter (Ed.), *Internet culture* (pp. 6–22). New York: Routledge.

Part Three

Centering the "Other"

Chapter Eleven

White Identity Development in Preservice Teacher Education

Lanese Kwegyir Aggrey

> The legal system can force open doors, and sometimes, even knock down walls, but it cannot build bridges. That job belongs to you and me. We can run from each other, but we cannot escape each other.
>
> —Thurgood Marshall (1992)

The American Council on Education (ACE) recently released a report entitled "Transforming the Way Teachers Are Taught." This report, developed by a task force of ACE-appointed professionals in the field of education, is a call and a challenge to college and university presidents to put every effort into "major improvements in the quality of education provided to teachers and school leaders" (ACE, 1999). Throughout this report, the Task Force clearly outlines what it sees are the problems with American education at the primary and secondary level. Their conclusion is that any effort to improve and change the nation's schools must begin with the teachers and how these teachers are prepared for their classrooms. Page after page outlined their view of the characteristics that effective teachers possess and what they felt constituted "competent professional knowledge" (ACE, 1999). It is an impressive document, filled with strong words and admonitions. Yet with all the time, money, and research necessary to generate this report, very little is mentioned about the necessity for preparing teachers for the culturally rich classrooms they will face.

This is not surprising. Despite all the rhetoric surrounding teacher education reform in this report and many others like it, our education students are still graduating without receiving training that will provide them with a solid foundation of knowledge needed to effectively teach the nation's diverse student population. Although there are scholars who consistently illustrate the need for teachers to receive training in multicultural education practices, it is uncommon to find "mainstream" educational organizations paying more than lip service to this pressing issue.

Studies show that there will be a need for 2.5 million (!) new teachers over the next 10 years (ACE, 1999). And while an overwhelming majority of students preparing to be teachers are white and female, it is also estimated that in the next 20 years, 25% or more of the students entering their classrooms will "come from ethnically/ racially/ culturally and economically diverse groups" (Fuller, 1994; Bennett, 1999). Without some form of training, most of our nation's teachers are left with popular culture as a primary source of information about the students entering their classrooms. Sandra Lawrence and Beverly Tatum illustrate this point when they state:

> Student teachers have had limited contact with people of color. Their knowledge of communities of color is often misinformed by stereotypes or distortions communicated in the media and by family and friends. Their own educational experiences have been monocultural rather than multicultural, with major omissions concerning the contributions and achievements of people of color. This limited perspective leaves white educators ill-equipped to prepare their own students, both white and of color, to function effectively in a multiracial society. (Lawrence & Tatum, 1997, p. 163)

With this in mind, is it realistic to expect that our preservice teachers will possess the tools necessary to effectively teach *all* students in their classrooms without some formal training to prepare them to do so? My hypothesis is that the study of racial identity development is one critical component in the preparation of teachers for diverse classrooms. Given the reality of the racial makeup of the nation's teachers, devoting time to the study of white identity development is a necessity. According to Lawrence and Tatum:

> When white teachers fail to acknowledge their own racial identity, this lack of acknowledgement becomes a barrier to understanding and connecting with the

development needs of children of color. It is the teacher who does not acknowledge his or her own racial or ethnic identity...who will not recognize the need for children of color to affirm their own. (Lawrence & Tatum, 1997, p. 163)

Is training in racial identity development the only training teachers need to prepare for multicultural classrooms? Absolutely not. I simply argue that in addition to a variety of conceptual, theoretical, and practical knowledge, exploration about one's own identity is equally important. Multicultural education has been conceptualized by researchers in the field as encompassing several different dimensions. Banks and Banks (1997) describe the dimensions as: content integration, the knowledge construction process, prejudice reduction, an equity pedagogy, and an empowering school culture. Reduction of prejudice, particularly in teachers, is a dimension of multicultural education that is crucial, yet often ignored.

In recent times a small but growing number of scholars have begun to address the concept of racial identity development as an important link in the reduction of prejudice among preservice teachers (Banks & Banks, 1997; Ladson-Billings, 1991; Lawrence & Tatum, 1997; Titone, 1998; Wade, 1998; Dilworth, 1992). These studies find that white preservice teachers often "distance themselves from racism" (Sleeter, 1995; Wade, 1998). While they may recognize and outwardly acknowledge themselves as white, "they often fail to acknowledge or understand the privileges their white skin grants them" (Lawrence & Tatum, 1997, p. 164). It is necessary for white preservice teachers to recognize that "Whiteness *does* have content inasmuch as it generates norms, ways of understanding history, ways of thinking about self and other, and even ways of thinking about the notion of culture itself. Thus whiteness needs to be examined, historicized and its consequences need to be examined" (Frankenberg, 1993, cited in Kincheloe, Steinberg, Rodriguez, & Chennault 1998, p. 32). With this "self" reflection, will come a clearer understanding of "what it may be like for those who are outside of white culture" (Rodriguez, 1999, p. 20).

The purpose of this chapter is to continue the work of others in exploring white racial identity and its relevance to teacher education programs. I readily acknowledge the limitations of this work by recognizing that concepts such as race and identity are problematic in that they are socially constructed and highly subjective. While there are a plethora of theories surrounding ways to improve teacher education, I am limiting my focus here to white identity development as an aspect of teacher education reform.

While several models of racial identity development theory exists, Janet Helms described it as:

> ...a sense of group or collective identity based on one's *perception* that he or she shares a common racial heritage with a particular racial group...racial identity development theory concerns the psychological implications of racial-group membership, that is belief systems that evolve in reaction to perceived differential racial-group membership. (Helms, 1990, p. 3)

Underlying these models are some basic assumptions: First, that racism and prejudice are an integral part of life in the United States and permeate all aspects of our culture and institutions. Second, people who are socialized in the United States will inherit the biases, stereotypes, racist attitudes, prejudices, and beliefs knowingly or unknowingly. Third, the stage of racial identity development in a cross-cultural encounter affects the process and outcome of that encounter (Sue & Sue, 1990). Considering the racial makeup of the nation's teaching force and student bodies, these assumptions have serious implications for teachers in classrooms with diverse populations.

Teaching is never a neutral act! Everything from curriculum to the classroom environment speaks volumes about a teacher's perspective. White identity development, just as with any facet related to the classroom dynamic, is relevant and worthy of examination (Titone, 1998). In spite of the good intentions of most teachers, there *is* an "impact of racism on teacher expectations, classroom practice and school climate" (Lawrence & Tatum, 1997, p. 162). Ignoring this fact will not change the reality of American society, nor will it help to improve the nation's schools.

I have witnessed preservice teachers in my classrooms exemplify the attitudes of white teachers in their assertion that "I am free of prejudice and besides I would not *dare* treat any child differently from another."

Rahima Wade calls this attitude a "brick wall," an attitude of resistance to issues of diversity. Examples of other brick walls may include "my attitudes won't affect my students" or "I'm not going to be teaching *those* students anyway." These brick walls impede the process of growth and knowledge for the preservice teacher and shortchange students of *all* races. To hide behind a brick wall is an act of "dysconscious racism," a phrase coined by Joyce King, to describe an act which "tacitly accepts dominant white norms and privileges." She states that dysconscious racism "is...an impaired consciousness" which hinders our ability to examine issues of race as a deliberate act (King, 1990, p. 128).

We must be willing to risk personal discomfort if we are to move forward with teacher education reform. Carlton Brown states, "Teachers must develop the ability to reflect on their own actions, observations and responses to experience and to apply these reflections and their academic knowledge to the design and implementation of new approaches to teaching" (Brown, 1992, p. 11).

I believe that most teachers enter this profession for altruistic reasons and with the best of intentions with the welfare of their students uppermost in their minds. Given this, many will bristle at the use of the term "racism" when discussing teacher education practices. Incorporating white identity development as part of the curriculum in teacher education programs will not be easy. American culture generally treats certain subjects as taboo for public discussion; systemic racism and prejudice is definitely one of those taboo topics. In addition white identity development challenges white students, most of whom are relatively young, to examine the harsh realities of American society in ways many students may not ever have experienced. It was not unusual for my preservice teachers to resist concepts such as these, or to be overwhelmed by them. Tatum writes that in the teaching of her class, *The Psychology of Racism*, "white students often struggle with strong feelings of guilt when they become aware of the pervasiveness of racism in our society. Even when they feel their own behavior has been nondiscriminatory, they often experience 'guilt by association'" (Tatum, 1994, p. 4). In the teaching of this course, we have to make the students feel they are in a safe environment to explore these feelings without judgment or fear of condemnation. In addition, students will need a variety of ways to process their emotions, perhaps journal writing or some other method that allows them to vent their feelings safely. In other words, this is a class that must be taught with great care and patience.

This course would require a commitment of support from the administration of the institution where it will be taught. Administrators must also ensure that faculty teaching this course are themselves well-versed in racial development theory and are actively working on their own level of racial awareness. It is very difficult, if not impossible, to teach what you don't know.

The benefits of incorporating a course such as this as a requirement would be tremendous, although perhaps in intangible ways. After this course, preservice teachers should be able to better understand American society from multiple perspectives, thereby creating "bridges" between their students and themselves. This type of training must be ongoing however. During a teacher's school career, working through their own issues of self-identity and self-examination should continue, whether through personal relationships as well as professional development work through their school district. White teachers will need the support of everyone, including people of color, as they continue the delicate process of moving through the stages of their identity development. This form of teacher education reform is quite outside the "traditional" model in that it is an intensive, holistic, personal yet collective effort to improve our nation's schools.

What are the risks if we do not incorporate models such as these into teacher education curriculum? Old traditions clashing with new imperatives will produce unmotivated students, at risk for dropping out; frustrated teachers; administrators swamped with complaints from parents; and continued calls for the improvement of our schools. Theories of racial identity development are certainly not *the* answer, but one of many solutions to a complex problem.

In summary, I propose that requiring the study of identity development theory in preservice teacher education will accomplish several objectives: First, it will expose preservice teachers to the existence of racism and prejudice in themselves and others. Second, it will increase their awareness of what it means to be white in America and the impact of whiteness on the world outside themselves. Third, it will increase acknowledgment and understanding of racist practices in education and the effect those practices have on students.

I applaud the efforts made thus far by educational institutions to delve into issues of diversity and multiculturalism. But this is not enough!! We cannot afford to begin and end with examining multicultural education from a safe, intellectual perspective. We must venture into more dangerous ground. We *must* find constructive ways of dismantling systemic and *personal* racism so that all children may learn in a caring and inclusive environment. White identity development theory as a required course can help.

References

American Council on Education. (1999). Transforming the way teachers are taught: An action agenda for college and university presidents. Washington, D.C.

Banks & Banks (Eds.). (1997). *Multicultural education: Issues and perspectives.* Boston: Allyn and Bacon.

Bennett, C. (1999). *Comprehensive multicultural education.* Needham Heights, MA: Allyn & Bacon.

Brown, C. (1992). Restructuring for a new America. In Dilworth, M. (Ed.), *Diversity in teacher education: New expectations.* San Francisco: Jossey-Bass.

Delgado, R., & Stefancic, J. (1997). *Critical white studies. Looking behind the mirror.* Philadelphia: Temple University Press.

Dewey, J. (1916/1944). *Democracy and education.* New York: The Free Press.

Dilworth, M. (Ed.). (1992). *Diversity in teacher education: New expectations.* San Francisco: Jossey-Bass.

Frankberg, R. (1993). Emptying the content of whiteness. In J.L. Kincheloe, S.R. Steinberg, N.M. Rodriguez, and R.E. Chennault (Eds.) *White reign: Deploying whiteness in America* (pp. 31–62). New York: St. Martins Press.

Fuller, L. (1994). The monocultural graduate in the multicultural environment: A challenge for teacher educators. *Journal of Teacher Education*, 45, (4), pp. 269–277.

Helms, J. (1984). Toward a theoretical explanation of the effects of race on counseling: A black and white model. *The Counseling Psychologist*, 12, pp. 153–165.

King, J. (1990). *Black mothers to sons: Juxtaposing African American literature with social practice.* New York: Peter Lang.

Ladson-Billings, G. (1991). Beyond multicultural illiteracy. *Journal of Negro Education*, 60, 2, pp. 147–157.

Lawrence, S., and Tatum, B. (1997). Teachers in transition: The impact of antiracist professional development on classroom practice. *Teachers College Record*, 99, 1, pp. 162–178.

Rodriguez, R. (1999). The study of whiteness. *Black Issues in Higher Education.* May 13, 1999.

Sleeter, C. (1995). Reflections on my use of multicultural and critical pedagogy when students are white. In *Multicultural education, critical pedagogy and the politics of difference.* Albany, NY: State University of New York Press.

Sue & Sue. (1990). *Counseling the culturally different: Theory and practice.* Canada: John Wiley & Sons, Inc.

Tatum, B. (1994). Teaching white students about racism: The search for white allies and the restoration of hope. *Teachers College Record, 95,* 4, pp. 462–476.

Titone, C. (1998). Educating the white teacher as ally. In J. L. Kincheloe, S. R. Steinberg, N. M. Rodriguez, R. E. Chennault (Eds.), *White reign: Deploying whiteness in America* (pp. 159–175). New York: St. Martins Press.

Wade, R. (1998). Brick walls and breakthroughs: Talking about diversity with white teacher education students. *Social Education, 62,* 2, pp. 84–87.

Chapter Twelve

"Sick and Tired of Being Sick and Tired": Exploring How the Story of the Mississippi Freedom Democratic Party Can Enrich Multicultural Curricula

Evelyn Sears

Since its inception in the American Civil Rights era, multicultural educa-tion in the United States has gone through several transformations and developed a variety of offshoots. These transformations have provoked a variety of responses, with the result that multicultural education is fre-quently opposed by critics from both the political right and the political left (Sleeter, 1989). On the one hand, advocates of a modest program of multicultural education see it as "anti-racist" education, or instruction in "prejudice reduction." Advocates of a strong program, on the other hand, "see it as directly connected with political struggle" (Sleeter, 1989). In this view, multicultural educators should promote examination of per-sonal biases, and, in addition, strive to transform schools and society, and inspire students to do the same. My view tends toward this stronger side.

A crucial dimension of such a transformational curriculum is a commitment to inclusiveness and comprehensiveness. To take one ex-ample, African American histories are important segments of the vast ar-ray of materials that need to be included in multicultural curricula. As Vanessa J. Lawrence notes, "The African American is interwoven into the fabric of the United States. To tell the American story without incor-porating the role of African Americans at each and every stage is to tell an incomplete story" (Lawrence, 1997, p. 320). Many of the deepest problems of contemporary American society have grown out of the pol-luted soil of oppressive race relations between white and black Americans. Understanding the complexities and confronting the ugliness of these relationships are necessary steps toward creating a more egalitarian society.

To further our own understanding of multicultural education and America, I want to tell a little-known story about some remarkable, yet very ordinary, people who have had a significant impact upon American political and social life. The story is about the political activities of the Mississippi Freedom Democratic Party (MFDP). To appreciate the scope of the party's achievements, however, the story must first be set within its context.

In the 1960s, many Americans viewed Mississippi as "America's dungeon," and "northerners and southerners alike agreed that Mississippi was in a class by itself" (Dittmer, 1995, p. 9). In 1964, for example, "86 percent of all nonwhite families in the state were living below the official federal poverty level" (McAdam, 1988, p. 25). Approximately one-half of Mississippi's black population lived in houses without running water; about two-thirds of this population did not have flush toilets; and infant mortality rates among Mississippi blacks were nearly two-and-a-half times the national average for whites (McAdam, 1988).

In addition to this horrific poverty, African Americans in Mississippi faced brutal persecution. Eric Burner records that "between 1882 and 1962 the state had achieved the national record for lynchings of blacks, with approximately 538" (Burner, 1994, p. 35). John Dittmer's account varies slightly, but its flavor is similar: "[R]acial violence was a daily reality. Between 1800 and 1940 nearly 600 Mississippi blacks were lynched..." (Dittmer, 1995, p. 13). His further attestation that "no jury would convict a white man for killing a Negro" is chilling. Michael Kenney was a northern college student who volunteered to do civil rights work during Mississippi's Freedom Summer campaign in 1964. He described, in a disturbingly graphic manner, the essence of Mississippi life in a letter to his parents:

> Yesterday while the Mississippi River was being dragged looking for the three missing civil rights workers, two bodies of Negroes were found....Mississippi is the only state where you can drag a river anytime and find bodies you were not expecting....Negroes disappear down here every week and are never heard

about. Things are really much better for rabbits here. There is a closed season on rabbits when they may be killed. Negroes are killed all year round. So are rabbits. The difference is that arrests are made for killing rabbits. (quoted in McAdam, 1988, p. 97)

Mississippi blacks believed that their best hopes for improving their social and economic conditions depended upon gaining access to, and participating in, the political system. Fannie Lou Hamer, a poorly educated sharecropper's wife, expressed this belief poignantly:

I am determined to become a first class citizen...[and] if registering to vote means becoming a first-class citizen and changing the structure of our State's Government, I am determined to get every Negro in the state of Mississippi registered. By doing this, we can get the things we've always been denied the rights to. (quoted in Mills, 1993, p. 79)

Among the crucial rights that Hamer and other African Americans sought were opportunities to participate in American political life by voting and holding political office. Poll taxes and literacy tests were effective mechanisms by which white supremacists excluded African Americans from exercising political influence (Dittmer, 1995). Most black applicants, who could not afford to pay the poll tax, had to take the test several times before they were able to pass and register to vote (Burner, 1994). Moreover, many whites viewed any attempt to register as "a momentous and potentially dangerous act, a public challenge to the established order, an invitation to violence or economic reprisals."(McAdam, 1988). Hamer's situation was typical of that of many blacks. On the day she initially attempted (and failed) to register, her landlord/employer advised her that, if she persisted in her registration efforts, she would be evicted from her home and her job would be terminated. She vacated her house that night, eventually satisfied the stringent voter registration requirements, and devoted the remainder of her life to sociopolitical activism (Mills, 1993).

These were the social and political conditions that led to the birth of the MFDP in the summer of 1964. The party's first task was to educate and register black voters. Second, since the Democrats monopolized pre-civil rights Southern politics, members of the MFDP sought to become

Mississippi's congressional representatives within the national Democratic party. To this end, the MFDP held elections that paralleled those of the regular Democratic party's, and nominated 68 delegates to travel to the Democratic National Convention, which was held in Atlantic City in August 1964 (Mills, 1993).

Upon arriving in Atlantic City, the MFDP delegates sought support from delegates from other states, and conducted a vigil on the boardwalk (Mills, 1993). A meeting with the Democratic party's credentials committee was scheduled for August 22, the weekend before the full convention opened. If the MFDP could gain support from 10% of the committee's membership—11 members—then their challenge could proceed to the convention. Once there, the support of eight state delegations could force a roll call vote. At that time, every state delegation would have to go on record definitively, vocally, and publicly either supporting or opposing the challengers (Dittmer, 1995).

Mrs. Hamer's testimony to the committee, which was broadcast on national television, was potent. She described how she had been beaten by the police, evicted from her home, and shot at because of her voter registration activities. Her moving account closed with these words:

> All of this is on account we want to register, to become first-class citizens....Is this America? The land of the free and the home of the brave? Where we have to sleep with our telephone off the hook, because our lives be threatened daily because we want to live as decent human beings in America? (quoted in Hamlet, 1996, p. 571)

This was just one of many similar accounts that the delegates of the MFDP offered to the committee.

Unfortunately, the MFDP delegates were not well equipped to engage in "major league" politics. President Lyndon Johnson, still feeling the effects of his hard-won battle to enact civil rights legislation, and fearing that southern delegates would defect and support the segregationist Republican candidate, Barry Goldwater, "pulled every string, enlisted every ally, and used all the forces at his command, including the FBI, to defeat the MFDP challenge"(Burner, 1994, p. 184). The MFDP's activities threatened the scrupulously planned scenario by which, according to

Dittmer, the convention "was to be a coronation of sorts" for the president, a smoothly orchestrated celebration of his leadership (Dittmer, 1995, p. 285). Consequently, President Johnson applied his considerable political talents toward thwarting their goals.

At the president's request, the FBI provided surveillance of the MFDP delegation and some of its key supporters. Their methods included telephone wiretaps and microphone surveillance at key meeting locations and hotel rooms (Burner, 1994) and the solicitation of information by posing as reporters—with the cooperation of NBC (Dittmer, 1995). Thus, the president was aware of many developments before they actually happened. Additionally, a congressman persuaded a reluctant Bob Moses to divulge the names of credentials committee members who had pledged to support the challenge. All persons on the list received phone calls threatening political or economic reprisals if they continued supporting the challengers (Dittmer, 1995). As Dittmer (1995, p. 290) notes, "Lyndon Johnson had now decided to play hardball."

A Democratic party subcommittee proposed that the MFDP be given two seats as at-large delegates, not as representatives of their home state. Additionally, the subcommittee, without consulting with the MFDP, designated which two members it preferred to serve as the official delegates. The rest of the MFDP delegates were invited to observe the convention as honored guests. In return for this cooperation, the Democratic party promised that, in the future, all state delegations would be elected on the basis of a selection process open to full black participation. This proposal caused tremendous turmoil within the MFDP delegation, and created a split along class lines. Some members (largely middle class) were inclined to accept, while others (mostly working class) were insulted by the "compromise." After bitter altercation, the party declined to accept the deal (Mills, 1993).

An optimistic, idealistic MFDP delegation had traveled to Atlantic City and begun garnering support for its cause. Through its testimonies before the credentials committee the party had successfully and effectively focused national attention on the plight of African Americans throughout the South, as well as in Mississippi. But the duplicity they encountered created significant anguish and disillusionment for many of them. When they returned to Mississippi, the MFDP delegates were weary and dejected, but their work was far from finished. Following a brief respite, they commenced their next task: a congressional challenge of the seating of five newly elected congressmen from Mississippi.

In December 1964, the MFDP formally challenged the seating of the newly elected Mississippi congressmen on the grounds that the elections had been illegally obstructed (Mills,1993). On January 4, 1965, the first day of the new session of Congress, Congressman William Fitts Ryan of New York spoke on behalf of the MFDP. Ryan objected that the oath of office should not be administered to the five representatives from Mississippi. Approximately seventy other members of Congress rose to support this objection. Consequently, the remaining members of Congress took their oaths of office while the representatives from Mississippi watched. Majority Leader Carl Albert, having taken his oath, immediately proposed that the representatives from Mississippi should be sworn in, and a congressional committee should, according to standard procedures, inquire into the alleged election irregularities. After some debate, this motion was passed by a substantial majority, and the five Mississippi representatives were sworn into office (Mills, 1993).

The MFDP's challenge initially was based upon the results of a statewide Freedom Vote that had taken place in November 1964 (Dittmer, 1995). This process, open to all who wished to participate, paralleled the official election. The first Freedom Vote, using homemade ballots and cardboard boxes, had been organized and administered by the Congress of Federated Organizations (COFO) and the Student Nonviolent Coordinating Committee (SNCC), in 1963 (Davis, 1998). The results of this "mock election" were so persuasive that a second, more extensive election, was held in 1964 (Dittmer, 1995).

The Freedom Votes demonstrated two facts. First, they confirmed that, given the opportunity, African Americans would participate in the political process. This directly refuted the white supremacist claim that most southern blacks were content with the status quo and neither desired nor needed political reforms. Second, they verified that African American participation could significantly influence the electoral process. For example, in the small town of Indianola, more votes were cast in the Freedom Vote than in the official election (Dittmer, 1995).

Congress deferred action on the challenge for several months, and in the summer of 1965, the Voting Rights Act was enacted. Opponents of the MFDP challenge suggested that this act rendered the challenge moot. For this and other reasons, when the House of Representatives finally voted on the challenge in September 1965, it was defeated (Dittmer,1995). Clearly, this defeat was a setback for the MFDP. Nevertheless, the challenge gave rise to two notable consequences. First, it kept national attention focused on voting rights issues. Second, it motivated more Mississippi blacks to become involved in the political process (Mills,1993).

Even though the MFDP was largely unsuccessful in meeting its goals in Atlantic City and Washington, D.C., in 1964–65, the party continued to be active on several fronts. In addition to sustaining its voter registration campaign, the MFDP sponsored candidates in local and state elections across Mississippi. The party successfully engineered the election of one of its candidates to the state legislature in 1967 (Davis, 1998). Several party members also filed legal claims against a variety of Mississippi officeholders for continued election irregularities (Mills, 1993). These lawsuits met with varied degrees of success, but they were crucial to sustaining African American political activism, maintaining public attention to the issue of racial inequality, and pressing for enforcement of the recently enacted Civil Rights and Voting Rights laws. As the party's members matured politically, they learned to use the judicial system, as well as the political system, to achieve their goals.

At the 1968 National Democratic Party convention in Chicago, the MFDP allied with several other groups to form the Loyalist Democratic Party. The Loyalists challenged the legitimacy of the regular Mississippi delegates and proved, with careful documentation, that these delegates had been selected by illegal means. The challenge succeeded, and the Loyalists were invited to participate in the convention as Mississippi's officially recognized delegates (Dittmer, 1995).

The MFDP's last foray into national politics took place at the 1972 Democratic National Convention in Miami. Again, the party aligned itself with the Loyalists, but its distinctive voice was largely silenced (Mills,1993). Shortly thereafter, its participation in Mississippi politics also diminished. One reason for its marginalization was its endorsement of socialist policies (Mills, 1993). Another reason is that once the party's initial goals were accomplished it had no real sense of purpose to sustain it. Although some party members still meet occasionally, the MFDP reached its pinnacle in the late 1960s (Davis, 1998). Nevertheless, this extraordinary collection of sharecroppers, small business owners, and other ordinary people dramatically transformed the Democratic Party, America's national political alignment, and Mississippi's political and social life.

There are at least three reasons stories such as this belong in a multicultural curriculum. First, the story of the MFDP represents a sterling example of how common people can generate significant social change. The MFDP was, in the long run, an effective political group. Christine Sleeter, drawing upon a model developed by Dennis Wrong (1979), enumerates the attributes of effective political groups. First, effective political groups have solidarity. They are aware of the common interests that unite them. Second, they "are aware of their collective conflict with another group" (Sleeter, 1989, p. 64). Third, they develop a social organization that is specifically designed to promote their interests. Fourth, they learn to use a variety of power bases (Sleeter, 1989).

The MFDP exemplified all of these traits. Its members were acutely aware of the conditions that oppressed them. They had solidarity. Additionally, the MFDP knew who comprised their opposition, and they were aware that they were engaged in conflict with groups, not merely individuals, who held substantial power over them. Furthermore, the party was created to serve specific purposes and remained vital and active until those purposes had been achieved. Lastly, the party's use of both the judicial and political systems indicates its strategic employment of a variety of power bases.

Multicultural educators who want their students to be politically engaged will need to search long and hard to find a more inspiring contemporary example of successful political activism than that of the MFDP. When teaching about the MFDP we must make it clear that the party suffered many disappointments and defeats. However, the members of the MFDP persevered and ultimately achieved their major goals. African Americans did register to vote. African Americans do hold political offices. In fact, the state of Mississippi now has more African Americans serving in elected positions than any other state (Mills, 1993). Clearly, the MFDP is an excellent example of a group of common people that generated social change.

There is a second reason for including stories like that of the MFDP in a multicultural curriculum. Multicultural educators should be committed to providing their students with as complete and accurate an account of the world as possible. Now, there is no question that curricular decisions always require the excision of some information. It is impossible to include all of the available data about everything in the world in K-12 curricula. Multicultural educators do not deny this constraint. But they do want to ensure that the criteria by which curricula are selected do not continue to be as narrow and biased as they have been traditionally. The story of the MFDP, and others like it, would certainly broaden the curriculum beyond its current boundaries.

A third reason for including stories like that of the MFDP in the curriculum is that it gives students opportunities to reflect on the best, the worst, and the maddeningly ambiguous, dimensions of human character. President Lyndon Johnson's relationship with the MFDP during the 1964 Democratic convention, for example, is a fascinating example of moral complexity.

On the one hand, the president's self-serving machinations against the MFDP delegates, which included outrageous abuse of the FBI, may be perceived by many as disgusting. They are also a brutally realistic lesson in how politics frequently functions. On the other hand, President Johnson's rationale for these actions was that, if he failed to be re-elected because of white flight by southern Democrats, he would not be able to initiate broad reforms, such as the Voting Rights Acts. Hindsight confirms that President Johnson was correct about the likelihood of white flight to the Republican party. Many whites did, in fact, desert the Democratic party, and many continue to support the Republicans today, particularly in the South. Students can gain tremendous ethical insights by pondering the moral ambiguity of President Johnson's behavior in Atlantic City in 1964.

Additionally, the members of the MFDP serve as models of resilience and perseverance we should encourage our students to emulate. The heroes of the MFDP were not accomplished or privileged people.

Most of them had not completed elementary school. The members of the MFDP were people like our students, and like us, people who held little economic, social or political power. And yet, they were people who made a significant mark upon their world. Isn't this what we want our students to do?

The field of multicultural education is, and probably always will be, contested ground. Multicultural education is a dynamic, evolving perspective on humanity and education. The topic discussed in this chapter touches on one small slice of American and African American history. Nevertheless, that thin slice is rich in its educational potential. The challenge that we have as multicultural educators is to learn and share more stories like that of the MFDP. If we tell these stories effectively, we may be able to inspire our students to become noble people committed to building a world in which people of all cultures, classes, and persuasions can regard each other with mutual respect and appreciation.

Note

The saying, "sick and tired of being sick and tired" in the title of this chapter is the epitaph on Fannie Lou Hamer's tomb.

References

Burner, E. (1994). *And gently he shall lead them: Robert Parris Moses and civil rights in Mississippi.* New York: New York University Press.

Davis, T. (1998). *Weary feet, rested souls.* New York: Norton.

Dittmer, J. (1995). *Local people: The struggle for civil rights in Mississippi.* Urbana: University of Illinois Press.

Hamlet, J. (1996). Fannie Lou Hamer: The unquenchable spirit of the civil rights movement. *Journal of Black Studies*, 26, 5 (May), p. 571.

Lawrence, V. (1997). Multiculturalism, diversity, cultural pluralism...'Tell the truth, the whole truth, and nothing but the truth.' *Journal of Black Studies*, 27, 3.

McAdam, D. (1988). *Freedom summer.* New York: Oxford University Press.

Mills, K. (1993) *This little light of mine: The life of Fannie Lou Hamer.* New York: Dutton.

Sleeter, C. (1989). Multicultural education as a form of resistance to oppression. *Journal of Education*, 171, 3.

Wrong, D. (1979). *Power: Its forms, bases, and uses.* South Hampton, UK: Basil Blackwell.

Chapter Thirteen

Good/Bad Girls and the Women Who Teach Them: A Renewed Call for Media Literacy

Lesley Shore

In the spring of 1999, the work of my doctorate complete, I returned to teach at the elementary school where I had taught before, the same school where my daughters had been students.[1] Six years had passed, bringing many changes with them. My first morning supervising recess duty, Lia, a little girl in grade one, caught my eye. There was something about the way she was dressed that struck me as inappropriately provocative: the tank top, the jeans slung low on the hip to expose the navel, the wire choker round the neck, the bare arms striped with wire bracelets, the washable tattoo placed on the apple of the upper arm— these seemed too sexualized for a six-year-old. Remembering my own daughters and their female classmates clad in baggy sweatsuits caked with sand, I mentioned my reaction to the other teacher on recess duty. "Oh no," she gasped in mock alarm, "Lia's mother would be just *horrified* to think that she was dressing her daughter that way."

In the ten years since multinational clothing outfitters have begun retailing clothes for children, clothes for children have all but disappeared. A spring 1999 issue of the *New York Times Magazine* featured a fashion story with infants and toddlers dressed in *haute couture* by Donna Karan and Ralph Lauren—hardly the thing for the sandbox (Marx & Trachtenberg, 1999, pp. 51–60). North American children are being dressed like miniature adults, sexualized before they're out of diapers. My question is: what does it mean for girls?

Contradiction lies at the heart of what it means to be educated as a girl today, culturally and academically. Look like this but act like that. Yet where in the curriculum do teachers problematize and probe that contradiction? How does it feel to be bombarded by media prescriptions about how to look your sexiest and at the same time be expected to attain high career aspirations? A Canadian study maintains that girls in grade six are already worried about how they will manage their future lives (King, Boyce, & King, 1999). Recent American Association of University Women studies (1999a) confirm that girls are still struggling with a traditional view of femininity and the contemporary realities of being a woman. How can we truly educate girls without helping them to understand the double shift that will face them as they enter the work/life force, the doubled nature of their existence, the learned doubleness that becoming an adult woman has come to mean? To read the messages the culture is sending them is to understand that girls are clearly expected to be both Madonna and whore in doing it all.

In the process of developing my own good/bad girl checklist I remember the good girl in me who was a model student, a medal winner, a teacher, a wife, a mother. The bad girl in me got a divorce, thus admitting that I might sleep with more than one man in my lifetime, subjected my children to the stringent economic consequences of divorce, learned painfully to stand up for herself and finally admitted, as the first line of her doctoral dissertation in education, that she never wanted to be a teacher. It is not easy to grant our daughters, personal or otherwise, the pleasures and freedoms we have not experienced ourselves.

Twenty years have passed since Carol Gilligan (1982) published her ground-breaking discovery about adolescent female development: the confidence a young girl may feel at eleven is subtly eroded as she approaches sixteen or eighteen along the continuum of understanding that who she really is and what she really knows from her lived experience no longer count. Irrespective of class or ethnicity (though Gilligan's later studies consistently demonstrated the ways in which Hispanic and African American girls are more able to resist cultural pressure), in order to become a woman, Gilligan's teams found that a girl must trim herself literally and figuratively to fit a media-driven norm and banish her authentic self into hiding, losing her voice.

Researchers who followed Gilligan's lead (Bartky, 1996; Orenstein, 1994; Sadker & Sadker, 1994) documented the many ways that contemporary education is unfair to girls, how it fails to give girls what they need to survive the passage to adulthood with their self-esteem intact. Girls in classrooms experience less eye contact with their teachers, fewer opportunities to respond to questions, more muted praise, less encouragement to go on to higher education, and once at university, cooler relationships with supervising professors who are less likely to encourage and support their work and choices. At the same time that so much is expected of them, so little educational attention is paid to the real pressing social issues in their lives. Girls must do it all, get married, reproduce, and save the world at that. Where are they learning how to do that?

As the messages of the culture sweep over young women in a tidal wave that threatens to engulf them, we are obliged to remember that these same girls spend at least as much time in school as they do being manipulated by the culture. Teachers must open up the possibilities of refusal and rupture in messages the culture brings. Listening to the girls themselves provides a good starting point.

> When it comes to school and education, it is critical that we listen to what our teens have to say about the issues they face....These girls are coming up with important recommendations as they call on schools to improve sex education and challenge the media to present realistic and powerful images of women and girls. (Sandy Bernard, AAUW 1999a, p. 2)

More than two thousand American girls were brought together for the study described in *Voices of a Generation* (1999a). "Girls need a clear definition of girls or women. We are encouraged to be assertive through TV, magazines, and some adults, but we're punished indirectly by the world when we do," wrote one of these girls (AAUW 1999a, p. 19). Another put it this way:

> Media images tell us to be a certain shape and size, our friends and peers want us to like certain things, our parents wish we'd act a specific way. With all the different messages from all different angles, it is sometimes hard for a girl just to find the person she really is. (p. 18)

Gilligan, Lyons, and Hammer (1990) and Gilligan, Taylor, and Sullivan (1995), notwithstanding, almost the same girls remain troubled by almost the same problems. In the last ten years significant energy has been directed toward giving American girls the tools to enter traditionally male-dominated fields of employment. The reality in 1998 was that only "6 percent of women were in nontraditional careers, that women cluster in only 20 of the more than 400 job categories, and two out of three minimum-wage earners are women" (AAUW, 1998, p. 13).

Girls are front and center in mainstream media today. A *Time* magazine cover screams: "Teens before their time: With budding breasts and pubic hair, girls are developing earlier than ever. What's causing it?" (Lemonick, 2000, p. 42). The *New York Times Sunday Magazine* worries about "Making of an 8-year-old woman: How do we understand early puberty? Through the prism of our times" (Belkin, 2000, p. 38). Both articles focus on research published three years ago by Marcia Hermans-Giddens, adjunct professor at the University of North Carolina School of Public Health, which indicated that "today's girls are growing up faster and entering puberty earlier than their mothers did" (quoted in Belkin, 2000, p. 38). While the outward signs of sexual maturity were beginning to appear in significant numbers of girls as early 7 years of age, the average age of menstruation had remained steady at 12.8 years. In the interim Hermans-Giddens has watched as primatologists, endocrinologists, psychologists and anthropologists have scattered to find the answer. Obesity, the hormones in cow's milk, estrogen simulators in environmental chemicals and plastics, pollution, food additives, soft porn, divorce and consequent households where biological fathers are absent, and, last but not least, the media, specifically MTV and advertising, have all been targeted.

"The female reproductive system is exquisitely sensitive to external influence," Hermans-Giddens explains, "as college women who room together know well, because their cycles often mysteriously fall into sync" (quoted in Belkin, 2000, p. 40). Emphasizing that visual images can provoke physiological responses, she explains, "If you watch somebody cut a grapefruit from across the room, you're going to salivate...just one example of how what you see can have a biological effect on your body" (p. 43). Far-fetched perhaps for many to believe, but no more so than maintaining that a father's physical absence can influence his daughter's hormones.

The latency period, normally a time when girls bond with other girls and build up that sense of confidence Gilligan found in girls of eleven, is compromised by this jump-start on adolescence and its concomitant turn toward the opposite sex. Girls of this age do not have the emotional maturity to deal with the complications of heterosexual relationships. Meanwhile "[b]oys," complains a nine-year-old in one of the research projects, "are gaga over girls with breasts" (Lemonick, 2000, p. 32). Presenting as sexually mature increases the possibility of sexual harassment, pregnancy, sexually transmitted diseases, and school dropout. Though we understand that the sexually explicit universe in which we raise North American children today is not healthy, it comes as a shock to understand that visual images can affect biology so profoundly. Many of the children in our classrooms are children whose experience of childhood has been radically compressed.

Time magazine reports that girls as young as five are celebrating their birthdays with make-up parties where they learn to emulate pop idol Britney Spears, herself a recent transformation from "perky ingénue" to "pop tart" (Labi, 2001, p. 56). Older girls celebrate with Britney impersonators who come to teach the guests her dance moves (p. 54). Britney's impact is everywhere as girls insist on coming to school showing some skin (because boys like it), and administrators retaliate by bringing back school uniforms. Joan Jacobs Brumberg comments that "[a]ge-appropriate behavior is something we've lost sense of" (p. 56) and laments that the line between childhood and adulthood is also in danger of being lost.

Little wonder then that a recent Saturday feature page in the Toronto *Globe and Mail* is devoted to "Girls Under the Knife" (MacDonald, 2000, p. R1). "Cosmetic surgery is on its way to becoming a routine self-esteem booster for adolescents eager to emulate their pop-culture idols, and a common birthday or graduation gift from parents who've had a little work done themselves." The girl in the color photograph accompanying this copy looks about 15 years old—she is wearing a blazer and skirt that suggest the uniform of girls' private schools. Along the side of the page, running the length of her body, is "The Makeover

Menu," accompanied by a price list. An 18-year-old who recently had breast implant surgery comments: "It's boosted my confidence a lot. I feel more attractive because I'm more proportioned" (p. R1). One of the sought-after plastic surgeons explains: "These kids are bombarded with images of their idols, like Jennifer Lopez, Britney Spears, and Christina Aguilera. They may not yet be mature girls, but they're mature consumers, with huge buying power. They wonder if their idols may have had cosmetic surgery" (p. R25). The article further reports that sociologists are concerned because teenagers are fixated not on their futures but on the perfection of their body parts.

Support for the problematic effects of advertising is not likely to be found in the glossy ad-filled pages of the mainstream press. Hermans-Giddens regrets that it would be difficult to find a control group of children to study who had not grown up surrounded by billboards advertising underwear. "As a society, we worry about children watching violence but what about all the sex they see?" she asks (quoted in Belkin, 2000, p.43).

A recent Toronto *Globe and Mail* series on pornography explains how, because the Internet has exponentially multiplied access to porn in ways that cannot be monitored or policed, "[t]he average teenager sees something like 14,000 sexual images in a single year" (Cheney, 2000, p. A8). Dr. Al Cooper, a California therapist and academic known as the "Masters and Johnson of cyberspace," continues: "There is an inundation of sex, followed by a long series of buts—'but don't do this' and 'don't do this.' The buts go on and on and on. There is a tremendous, built-in conflict. We sell sex, yet we don't accept it" (quoted in Cheney, 2000, p. A8), particularly not from girls.

"Advertising," explains Jean Kilbourne, "is our *environment*. We swim in it as fish swim in water. We cannot escape it" (Kilbourne, 1999, p. 56). Kilbourne, a professor at the Stone Centre at Wellesley College, is the producer of award-winning documentaries like *Killing Us Softly*, a chilling deconstruction of how ads portray women. Though she has been lecturing to college women for twenty years, heavily ad-dependent publications (like *Time* and the *New York Times Sunday Magazine*) are no more likely to publish her research than they are to inform us of the links between smoking and lung cancer. Kilbourne points out that estimates show that entertainment and publishing conglomerates Time Warner, Sony, Viacom, Disney, Bertelsmann, and News Corporation will shortly control "90 per cent of the world's information, from newspapers to computer software to film to television to popular music. We may be able to change the channel, but we won't be able to change the message" (p. 54).

Kilbourne (1999) has pointed out that advertising is our culture's version of propoganda. It is so subtly and skillfully done that we don't realize that the average North American is exposed to more than 3,000 ads a day, that she/he spends more than three years of her/his life watching TV commercials, that the American tobacco industry successfully recruits 3,000 new smokers every day (the younger the better) to replace smokers who die, that children of three can recognize a cigarette ad for what it is. Kilbourne's interpretation of sex in advertising hearkens back to Gilligan's loss of self and self-esteem: "Just as women and girls are offered a kind of ersatz defiance through drinking and smoking that interferes with true rebellion, so we are offered a pseudo-sexuality that makes it far more difficult to discover our own unique and authentic sexuality. How sexy can a woman [or girl] be if she hates her body?" (Kilbourne quoted in Simon, 2001, p. 57). "The saddest girls," Kilbourne maintains, "are those who choose self-destruction in the name of liberation and rebellion, who see no other way out of the terrible dilemma of having to choose between the stifling false self of the 'good girl' and the more authentic self that society so often labels as the 'bad girl'" (Kilbourne, 1999, p. 31).

It is no accident that the faces in the ads seem younger all the time as advertisers seek to expand their flourishing markets. Kilbourne believes that what they sell more effectively than any product is cynicism, and that preadolescent children are suffering because of it. The hotly disputed Channel One program, which operates in under-funded American schools, costs taxpayers $1.8 billion in lost classroom time but delivers 8 million public school students each day into the hands of the advertisers. This "dance with the devil" (Kilbourne, 1999, p. 45) is the inevitable outcome of cuts to education funding and corporations who are salivating to pick up the shortfall.

Kilbourne advises that the most important thing we can teach in our schools is media literacy, because "a truly critical audience would be less easily manipulated" and things will change only when "a critical mass of people" begin to see things differently (Simon, 2001, p. 59). Our most important philosophical ideas have been co-opted by the advertising industry to sell products. I maintain that teachers can be in the forefront of the movement. Kilbourne seeks to "take back our culture and rebuild a society in which good choices are encouraged" (Pipher quoted in Kilbourne, 1999, p. 13).

In a doctor's waiting room recently, my twenty-one-year-old daughter and I leafed through a two-inch thick copy of the most recent issue of a glossy in-your-face fashion magazine we never buy. I had picked up the magazine with a sense of excitement, a kind of "Ah—a chance to have a peek at what's in style." When, after only a few minutes' wait, the receptionist came to call us into the office, I was surprised at the intense feeling of relief I had—having been given permission to put the magazine down. When I blurted out this confession to my daughter, she understood. We talked about how looking at the ads made us feel inadequate: I felt too old, she felt too fat. For some women and girls the act of reading fashion magazines, whatever else it is, is masochistic. A conversation in a classroom might begin here.

Literary theorists (Willinsky & Hunniford, 1993; Cherland & Edelsky, 1993; Christian-Smith, 1990, 1993) have explained how vulnerable girls reading are to the messages of the texts they read, particularly to the stories of heterosexual romance that are ubiquitous in the culture at large. Girls read not simply for entertainment; they read for their lives. Canadian researchers Willinsky and Hunniford (1993) explained how, with each new reading act, girls try on a new life script. In the first year of the new millennium, I remain haunted by the words Virginia Woolf wrote in 1928, that "literature [was] impoverished beyond our counting by the doors that ha[d] been shut upon women," that "[l]ove was [their] only possible interpreter" (1929, 1977, p. 80). The love story remains the only important story that a female will write with her life in the series romances that are the reading staple of millions of North American girls today, many of whom receive these texts from teachers who help sell them, teachers who are, in Linda Christian-Smith's terms "retailing gender" (1993, p. 2).

Cherland and Edelsky (1993) in Canada and McRobbie (1991) in Britain have found, however, that girls today are more questioning readers than the adult women in Radway's landmark 1984 study of women reading romance. Girls will read against the grain looking for alternative and transgressive messages. British psychoanalytical theorist Valerie Walkerdine explained in 1985 that identity was not achieved in one fell swoop; it was formed as the result of a continuous process of resistance, negotiation, and accommodation deep in the psyche; accommodation which might be destabilized again with each new reading act. Australian researchers Carrington and Bennett, studying girls' reading of magazines in 1996, confirmed that girls were not "the passive victims of a hegemonic culture of femininity" (1996, p. 148).

The complex concept of role model as it applies to adolescent girls demands teachers' continual and serious reconsideration. Naomi Wolf wrote recently that our daughters must grow up with "someone to turn to more powerful in their imaginations than Kate Moss and Calista Flockheart. Maybe we will learn to understand that our salvation, as women, lies in ourselves" (Wolf, 1999, p. 154). What will we tell the girls we teach about the role that relationships with women have played in our lives, how they have sustained and supported our own endangered selves and voices, provided us with role models, echoed and confirmed our dreams?

Speaking at a Toronto girls' school, Wolf asked the teenage girls present: What was your dream when you were nine? They told her of dreaming to drive garbage trucks and win Nobel prizes, of becoming pilots or prime ministers, and indeed, of being able to save the world. Alice Kaplan writes in *French Lessons*:

> When I was in first grade, my sister's friends could hardly stand to ride to school with me in the car. I was loud and unrelenting. I liked to run my own bath water while I sang the song of the rest of my life, endless verses with my own lyrics; I would rule the world, I would sing on a stage, I would travel the seas. (Kaplan, 1993, p. 5)

I suggest there is value in making classrooms safe for the remembrance of such empowering dreams, for life scripts that move beyond the narrow parameters of romance, for recognizing the statistics that indicate that even women who choose to marry will spend long periods of life on their own, for learning to value and honor a diversity of relationship choices.

To be a girl today is to be impaled on the nascent contradictions of mature womanhood, to feel that contradiction acutely, to have few safe spaces to discuss what the contradictions entail. As teachers we must understand and make transparent the much-researched, overdocumented "dangerous" passage to female adulthood (Nathanson, 1991). It is critical for women teaching to honor their potential as role models for the girls they teach. Gilligan's research signaled teenage girls' need to remain in connection with supportive older women as they negotiate their ways through adolescence. Some girls will need to augment the possibilities for relationship that exist in their families. Learning to share trusting relationships with women who are prepared to give of their authentic selves is an important part of girls' education.[2]

In 1985 Valerie Walkerdine asked us to consider how it felt when women teaching in child-centered classrooms had to suppress in themselves the very initiative and independence they were expected to nurture in their students. Kristen Golden, writing nearly ten years later in *Ms.* magazine, reminded women that girls were watching them and forming conclusions on the basis of the way we lived our lives and not how we talked about them (1994, p. 61). "Resistant" girls in Gilligan's studies were vigilantly observant of the women around them and sensitive to their compliance to male authority. The teachers in Gilligan's 1992 study understood that in order to open up possibilities for the kind of resistance and rupture that would help the girls in their classes survive adolescence intact they had to retrace the loss of their own voices. They found that "[u]nless we, as grown women, were willing to give up all the 'good little girl' things we continued to do and give up our expectations that the girls in our charge would be as good as we were, we could not successfully empower young women to act on their own knowledge and feelings" (Brown & Gilligan, 1992, p. 221).

For some women Rosalind Coward's words are resonant:

Living an illusion is uncomfortable, and often women hover on the point of exposing the illusions of their lives. But most back off, preferring the illusions to the difficulty of personal change. And this is ultimately what I mean by complicity. Complicity is about not telling the truth—to other women or to ourselves—and not confronting men about the areas of our lives that don't fit the illusions. This complicity means that women don't pass on information and knowledge about their condition, and disparage those who try to do so (1992, p. 194).

African American and Hispanic women have often provided stronger role models for their daughters. Real life has taught these girls to be skeptical about the promise of romance. Because they have had to cope with more responsibility and less privilege, they are more sanguine about life's possibilities. More grounded in the real world, they are not as likely to be swept away by notions of love and marriage and are less susceptible to the tyranny of body image. The ties of female relationship run strong here, and conversations between mothers, aunts and daughters are more unguarded than they were with the (predominantly white) girls in Gilligan's earlier studies.

"Intellectual freedom depends on material things," Virginia Woolf told the young women of the first women's colleges in 1929, many of whom would graduate and become teachers (1929, 1977, p. 103). How extraordinary that in seventy years of scholarship developed around her thought, so few scholars have picked up on that critical practical message that has become my personal mantra. "Why [was] one sex so prosperous and the other so poor?" Woolf asked (p. 26); "a dinner of beef and prunes will not light the lamp in the spine" (p. 19). The famed five hundred pounds that Woolf insisted a woman needed along with a room of her own was a great deal of money in 1928; were women not entitled to the same material luxuries that men were? Gloria Steinem explained in 1994: "Women have had centuries of training to consider money impure, undeserved, mysterious, not our worry, or, as this mind-set is sometimes reflected even inside current feminism, a male-imitative and politically incorrect concern" (Steinem, 1994, p. 171). Let us not delude ourselves about the progress of twentieth-century feminism until we clearly understand the links between access to money and the long history of misogyny that keeps women in their place.

> Women are one-half of the world's people; they do two-thirds of the world's work; they earn one-tenth of the world's income; they own one one-hundredth of the world's property. (Classroom poster quoted by Orenstein, 1994, p. 247)

Seventy years after Woolf wrote that money meant power, that it was even more important for women than the vote, millions of women and their children in the so-called "developed" world live in poverty. What kind of an education have they had? Training in being good girls from the school and from the culture? Young women today need literacy in financial, relationship, and bodily matters.

I recently had the opportunity to speak to a group of one hundred girls from four different high schools who were delegates to the WOW (Women Offering Wisdom) conference at a suburban Toronto secondary school. The conference was organized by four students in a World Issues geography course as their combined Independent Study Project. These girls listened attentively to Woolf's message and to the personal interpretation of that message that I had made of my own life, the connections I had drawn between marriage, divorce and money, economics, women, and the law. The question period was animated. They all had money stories to share from the women in their own families. "They especially liked how you told them about your own life," the supervising teacher reported afterward. It is more than prurient curiosity that impels this desire to know how other women live their lives.

It is risky business teaching young women today. How far are we prepared to go in sharing the pitfalls of our personal lives? What will happen if we do not share with them what life has taught us? "Can one admit the rhapsodies?" Woolf asked in 1925. What do we teach them to do with their bodies when desire pulses hot within them? Do we teach them to claim their sexuality when it is more and more difficult to get a legal abortion and we know how much children will change the direction of their young lives? "Girls want to learn how to say 'yes' to relationships without automatically saying 'yes' to sex," says AAUW President Sharon Shuster (AAUW, 1999a,b, p. 1). She continues: "They don't want sex to be an all or nothing issue. They're missing the middle ground of affection, intimacy and relationships." What does Michelle Fine's 1988 "discourse of desire" look like in 2001 where we read of college girls embracing lesbianism as a way to accommodate their sexual needs until they graduate and many girls turning to celibacy as a way to stave off the heartbreak of failed romances, in a deliberate attempt to avoid repeating their mothers' mistakes (Nolen, 1999)? Perhaps all we can hope to do is open up safe spaces for discussion of these issues.

It is a question of how we read what we read, of feeling, power and location, as Deanne Bogdan (1992) has explained. In Bogdan's terms there is at least some choice implied in remaining a victim; there is the possibility of situating oneself differently. Do we teach girls how much money they will need in order not to take abuse in exchange for money? Do we teach them how to get the jobs that pay that kind of money? Do we remind them that 80% of the lowest paying jobs (teaching, social work, and nursing) still belong to women and that supporting a family on those salaries will be a challenge?

Thus *seducere*, what Jane Miller (1990) has explained as being seduced by the texts, epistemology, and mythology of Western culture, becomes transformed into *se educare* (Bogdan, 1992, p. 241–244) in Bogdan's terms, to the injunction to get a different kind of education, to be led out of ignorance, to become aware, to wake up, to know thyself, to listen to the still small voice within. This is what we would teach our daughters: how to manage desire differently, how to take apart the culture, how to laugh right in its face, how to balance our checkbooks and our hearts. But first we need to acknowledge, understand and perhaps, for a time, to mourn that we have been swept away for so long.

Notes

1. I am a white, middle-class, fifty-something, Jewish, able-bodied, divorced, the mother of three grown children, western Canadian by birth but now living in Urban Ontario. All of what I know is filtered through the standpoint engendered by that accident of birth and that historical/geographical/social location.

2. It is not within the scope of this chapter to review the current literature on the importance of relationships, and the emotional climate of the classroom to learning. Especially noteworthy is *The Courage to Teach* by Parker J. Palmer for his emphasis on the "who" of teaching as opposed to the "what" and "how." Good teaching does not require leaving one's self at the classroom door and donning a persona. Many teachers teaching today (and I am among them) aim to teach from the most authentic core of who they are.

References

American Association of University Women. (1998). *Gender gaps: Where schools still fail our children*. Washington, DC: AAUW Educational Foundation.

————. (1999a). *Voices of a generation: Teenage girls on sex, school, and self*. Washington, DC: AAUW Educational Foundation.

————. (1999b). Press release. *Voices of a generation: Teenage girls on sex, school, and self*. AAUW website. http://www.aauw.org

Bartky, S.L. (1996). The pedagogy of shame. In C. Luke (Ed.), *Feminisms and pedagogies of everyday life* (pp. 225–241). Albany: State University of New York Press.

Belkin, L. (2000, December 24). The making of an 8-year-old woman. *New York Times-Sunday Magazine*, pp. 38–43.

Bogdan, D. (1992). *Re-educating the imagination: Towards a poetics, politics, and pedagogy of literary engagement*. Portsmouth, NH: Boynton-Cook.

Brown, L.M., & Gilligan, C. (1992). *Meeting at the crossroads: Women's psychology and girls' development*. Cambridge: Harvard University Press.

Brumberg, J.J. (1988). *Fasting girls*. Cambridge: Harvard University Press.

————. (1997). *The body project: An intimate history of American girls*. New York:

Random House.

Carrington, K., & Bennett, A. (1996). 'Girls' mags' and the pedagogical formation of the girl. In C. Luke (Ed.), *Feminisms and pedagogies of everyday life* (pp. 147–166). Albany: State University of New York Press.

Cheney, P. (2000, December). A solitary obsession that can ruin a life. *Toronto Globe and Mail*, pp. A8–A9.

Cherland, M., & Edelsky, C. (1993). Girls and reading: The desire for agency and the horror of helplessness in fictional encounters. In L. Christian-Smith (Ed.), *Texts of desire: Essays on fiction, femininity and schooling* (pp. 28–44). London: Falmer.

Christian-Smith, L.K. (1990). *Becoming a woman through romance.* New York: Routledge and Kegan Paul.

———. (Ed.). (1993). *Texts of desire: Essays on fiction, femininity and schooling.* London: Falmer.

Coward, R. (1992). *Our treacherous hearts: Why women let men get their way.* London: Faber and Faber.

Fine, M. (1988). Sexuality, schooling and adolescent females: The missing discourse of desire. *Harvard Educational Review, 58,* 1, pp. 29–53.

Gilligan, C. (1982). *In a different voice: Psychological theory and women's moral development.* Cambridge: Harvard University Press.

———. (1998a, February 1). *In a different voice: 16 years later.* Paper presented at Branksome Hall School, Toronto, Ontario.

———. (1998b, February 1). *Teaching girls.* Teachers workshop at Branksome Hall School, Toronto, Ontario.

Gilligan, C., Lyons, N., & Hanmer, T. (Eds.). (1990). *Making connections: The relational worlds of adolescent girls at Emma Willard School.* Cambridge, MA: Harvard University Press.

Gilligan, C., Taylor, J., & Sullivan, A.M. (Eds.). (1995). *Between voice and silence: Women and girls, race and relationship.* Cambridge: Harvard University Press.

Golden, K. (1994, May/June). What do girls see? *Ms., 4* (6), pp. 52–61.

Kaplan, A. (1993). *French lessons: A memoir*. Chicago: University of Chicago Press.

Kilbourne, J. (1999). *Can't buy my love: How advertising changes the way we think and feel*. New York: Simon and Schuster.

King, A., Boyce, W., & King, M. (1999). *Trends in the health of Canadian youth*. Canada: Queen's Printer.

Labi, N. (2001). The Britney brigade. *Time (Canada) 157* (5), pp. 54–56.

Laird, S. (1995). Who cares about girls?: Rethinking the meaning of teaching. *Peabody Journal of Education, 70* (2), pp. 82–103.

Lemonick, M.D. (2000). Teens before their time. *Time (Canada) 156* (18), pp. 42–48.

MacDonald, G. (2001, January 13). Girls under the knife. *Toronto Globe and Mail*, pp. R1–25.

Marx & Trachtenberg. (1999, August 1). The brat pack. *New York Times Magazine*, pp. 51–60.

McRobbie, A. (1991). *Feminism and youth culture: From Jackie to just seventeen*. Boston: Unwin Hyman.

Miller, J. (1990). *Seductions: Studies in reading and culture*. London: Virago Press.

———. (1996). *School for women*. London: Virago Press.

Nathanson, C.A. (1991). *Dangerous passage: The social control of sexuality in women's adolescence*. Philadelphia: Temple University Press.

Nolen, S. (1999, February 13). Girls just wanna have fun. *Toronto Globe and Mail*, pp. D1–D3.

Orenstein, P. (1994). *School girls: Young women, self-esteem, and the confidence gap*. In Association with the American Association of University Women. New York: An-chor/Doubleday.

Palmer, P.J. (1998). *The courage to teach: Exploring the inner landscape of a teacher's life*. San Francisco: Jossey-Bass.

Pipher, M. (1999). Foreword. In J. Kilbourne, *Can't buy my love: How advertising changes the way we think and feel*. New York: Simon and Schuster.

Radway, J. (1984). *Reading the romance: Women, patriarchy, and popular literature*. Chapel Hill: University of North Carolina Press.

Sadker, M. & Sadker, D. (1994). *Failing at fairness: How America's schools cheat girls*. Toronto: Maxwell Macmillan.

Simon, C. (2000/2001, January/December). Hooked on advertising. *Ms. 9* (1), pp. 54–59.

Steinem, G. (1994). *Moving beyond words*. New York: Simon & Schuster.

Walkerdine, V. (1985). On the regulation of speaking and silence: Subjectivity, class and gender in contemporary schooling. In C. Steedman, C. Unwin, and V. Walkerdine (Eds.), *Language, gender and childhood* (pp. 203–241). London: Routledge and Kegan Paul.

———. (1990). *Schoolgirl fictions*. London: Verso.

Willinsky, J., & Hunniford, M. (1993). Reading the romance younger: The mirrors and fears of a preparatory literature. In L. Christian-Smith (Ed.), *Texts of desire: Essays on fiction, femininity and schooling* (pp. 87–105). London: Falmer.

Wolf, N. (1999, May 16). The future is ours to lose. *New York Times Magazine*, pp. 134–154.

Woolf, V. (1929, 1977). *A room of one's own*. London: Triad Grafton.

Chapter Fourteen

An Alternative to Criminal Behavior: Educating Inmates as Captive Students or Just Captives?

Angelique Williams
John A. Xanthopoulos

This chapter will offer an overview of various studies showing (1) a correlation between educating inmates and the decrease of recidivism; (2) the significance of educational programs within correctional facilities, past and current issues of implementation, and availability of financial support for inmates' education; (3) a comparison between the average annual cost of housing an inmate and the annual cost of providing higher education in a correctional facility and future savings as a result; and (4) a correlation of recidivism and the negative impact and effects on their families. Statistical data is used to show the importance of education and its impact on our contemporary society from various aspects. Discussions will also include the benefits of higher education for the inmate, the correctional environment, the taxpayer, and using education as a means of crime prevention to eliminate costs to the inmate's family. The main emphasis is based on the theoretical foundation that education not only reduces recidivism, but also prevents future crime, thus reestablishing safe home and school environments.

The implications and goals of this article are to create awareness that education is a highly successful tool in reducing recidivism. It can also serve as inspiration to others in dealing with the diverse and changing inmate population and create more productive citizens, thus a safer society. Moreover, educating prisoners positively impacts the lives of their children, who otherwise often exhibit aggressive behavior, withdrawal, or depression at home and schools. The increase of violence within contemporary society, especially among children, is alarming and suggests a chain reaction in which individual behavior spreads to other groups such as family, friends, and classmates and ultimately to society and the nation as a whole.

The following statistics present alarming facts, which should be taken into consideration by educational organizations and communities that deal with the public at every level:

- Russia and the United States are the world leaders in incarceration rates (Mauer, 1994).
- In 1995, Russia's rate of incarceration was 690 per 100,000, followed by the United States with 600 per 100,000. (Bureau of Justice Statistics, 1997)
- An analysis of the 1997 prison population figures indicates that the U.S. nation's prison and jail population will reach a total of two million by the year 2000 (Bureau of Justice Statistics, 1997).

In comparison:

- Germany's 1995 rate of incarceration was 85 per 100,000, and Japan's rate was 37 per 100,000.

Germany and Japan are paying more attention to the development of preventive measures to deal with the increase of crime and delinquency. Both countries place considerable emphasis on school activities in middle and high schools that fight crime by fostering the development of group consciousness and mutual cooperation. Their belief is that the fight against crime is the responsibility of society as a whole, regardless of the various crime rates, criminal justice policies, or social policies that may have led to this situation (Mauer, 1994).

The growth of incarceration has had its greatest impact on minorities, particularly African Americans. In the ten-year period from 1985–1995, the number of African Americans in state prisons increased by 132% (Bureau of Justice Statistics, 1997). Moreover, teenagers 14 to 17 have become more violent than at any other time in tabulated history, currently committing 165% more murders than they did 10 years ago (Sherman, Gottfredson, MacKenzie, Eck, Reuters, & Bushway, 1997).

These figures have triggered various responses from a variety of experts and the government, and they continue to argue over the cause of incarcerations and the crime rate, especially among juveniles. The National Institute of Justice claimed that illiteracy was the primary cause of crime, noting that juvenile offenders, on average, have a third grade functional reading level, and adult offenders, on average, a sixth grade functioning level (Sherman et al., 1997). The rate of recidivism is 60% or more for released prisoners. Sadly, the response of legislators and policymakers to these facts is to promote the building of more prisons, pass harsher sentencing legislation, and elimination of various programs inside prison and jails, none of which seem to decrease an inmate's level of illiteracy (Elikann, 1996).

Building more prisons in addition to handing down harsher sentences does not alleviate these social problems; instead they compound the problem, making it harder to intervene as time passes. If we, as a society, are serious and want to avoid living next to a prison and protect our children from the accumulations of anger and frustration, intervention and prevention strategies and programs with a heavy emphasis on education must be implemented.

Illiteracy is an increasing problem in America and remains to be addressed. The general belief that implementation of harsher and more punitive measures will combat crime and recidivism is clearly an approach that is failing and will remain unsuccessful, as evidenced by today's increase of crime and recidivism. In 1965 the Congress passed Title IV of the Higher Education Act, which permits inmates to apply for financial aid in the form of Pell Grants to attend college. During the 1970s, research suggested that higher education was responsible for a decrease in rearrests and an increased ability of offenders to obtain and maintain employment upon release (Brunner, 1993).

The United States houses 1.6 million adults in correctional facilities, and approximately 99,682 juveniles are in custody (the total does not include the number of juveniles in lock-ups, and reflects only the result of a 1-day census count at private and public juvenile facilities, adult jails, and state and federal correctional facilities). The majority of these adults and juveniles will be released into society unskilled and undereducated, and they are more likely to reengage in criminal activities (DeComo et al., 1995).

Various researchers have shown that one of the most effective forms of crime prevention and reduction of recidivism is education; however, despite this evidence, many of these educational programs in prison have been partially if not completely eliminated over the past five years. It can be argued that we need to promote policies and procedures that are geared toward success. Education is one of the most essential and promising tools to give inmates the opportunity to become productive members within our society. For a formerly educated individual, the chances of returning to criminal practices decrease, which in turn reduces incarceration and victimization, and it provides the economy with skilled workers (Taylor, 1993).

In the early 1990s elected officials proposed legislation to prohibit federal tuition assistance to inmates. Despite the overwhelming evidence supporting the correlation of higher education and its decrease of recidivism, the U.S. Congress decided upon a provision in the Violent Crime Control and Law Enforcement Act of 1994 that denied all prisoner access to federal Pell Grants. Congress was primarily concerned with the notion of prison becoming a place of leisure that afforded inmates access to higher education at the expense of law-abiding taxpayers (Taylor, 1993). According to the Department of Education (1992), less than 1% of inmates received federal Pell Grants in their final year of availability.

According to the Federal Bureau of Prisons, there is an inverse relationship between recidivism rates and education. The more education received, the less likely an individual is to be re-arrested or reimprisoned. A report issued by the Congressional Subcommittee to Investigate Juvenile Delinquency estimates that the national recidivism rate for juvenile offenders is between 60% and 84%. For juveniles involved in quality reading-instruction programs, the recidivism rate can be reduced by 20% or more (Harer, 1994).

A five-year follow-up study conducted by the Arizona Department of Adult Probation concluded that probationers who received literacy training had a significantly lower re-arrest rate (35%) than the control group (46%), and those who received GED education had a re-arrest rate of

24%, compared to the control group's rate of 46%. Inmates with at least two years of college education have a 10% re-arrest rate, compared to a national re-arrest rate of approximately 60% (Siegel, 1997).

Research studies conducted in Indiana, Maryland, Massachusetts, New York, and other states have reported significantly low recidivism rates for inmate participants in correctional higher-education programs, ranging from 1% to 15.5%. The overall recidivism rate for degree holders leaving the Texas Department of Criminal Justice between September 1990 and August 1991 was 15%, four times lower than the general recidivism rate of 60%. A two-year follow-up report found that the higher degree was inversely related to the level of recidivism. Individuals with associate degrees had a recidivism rate of 13.7%, those with bachelor's degrees had a rate of 5.6%, and those with master's degrees had a rate of zero (Tracy & Johnson, 1994).

The expense of providing higher education to inmates is minimal; New York State estimates that it costs $2,500 per year, per individual to provide higher education in a correctional facility. In contrast, the average cost of incarcerating an adult inmate per year is $25,000. In correctional facilities, higher education is provided primarily by universities and community colleges that provide inexpensive tuition (Consortium of the Niagara Frontier, 1996). It would appear that overall cost to our taxpayers is of primary concern. However, studies show that more money is spent on building prisons rather than to provide inexpensive correctional educational programs that could lower the need for prison space.

In a hypothetical situation ($2,500 per year per inmate in New York State) with one of the highest recorded rates of recidivism upon completion of such a program (15%), the savings from providing higher education are still substantial: The cost of incarcerating 100 individuals over 4 years is approximately $10 million. For an additional 1/10 of the cost (or $1 million), these same individuals could be given a full, four-year college education while incarcerated. Assuming a recidivism rate of 15% (as opposed to the general rate of 40–60%), 85 of the initial 100 individuals will not return to prison, saving U.S. taxpayers millions of dollars each year (Elikann, 1996).

In addition to the millions saved by preventing an individual's return to incarceration and dependence on the criminal justice system, providing higher education to prisoners can save money in other ways. The prevention of crime helps to eliminate costs paid to crime victims and the courts, lost wages by the inmate while incarcerated, and cost incurred by the inmate's family (Tracy & Johnson, 1994).

The RAND Corporation, a public policy think tank based in California, recently released a study showing that of all crime prevention methods, education is the most cost-effective. Higher education has a stabilizing influence on the correctional environment and can help a facility run more smoothly and less violently than other institutions without educational programs (Sherman et al., 1997).

The majority of inmates who are from ethnic and cultural minorities are from low socioeconomic levels and have a history of drug and alcohol abuse. Without education, these individuals will be released without finances and with limited employment opportunities or pressure to support their families or both. Their children, through visiting their parent in prison and observational learning, are more likely to fall into the same pattern as their parent role model. Moreover and of particular interest is the serious problem of increased school violence.

According to the Bureau of Justice Statistics, approximately 10% of reported incidents of nonfatal violence against persons 12 and over occurred in school buildings or properties (Bureau of Justice Statistics, 1992). Recent media coverage portrays the increase of gun use within the school system, and additional research states that many children fear becoming victims of violence at school. Almost a quarter of third to twelfth grade students nationally are worried about being hurt at or near school (Louis Harris and Associates, 1993).

Incidents of actual violent behavior and fear of violence interfere with the learning process of students; additional reasons for concern are the patterns of aggression and violence that often persist into adulthood (Dishion, Patterson, Stoolmiller, & Skinner, 1991). In a report published by the Family and Corrections Network, information regarding demographic data of prisoners shows that incarceration weakens the inmate's family unit, which could lead to an increase of criminality in the following generation. Current educational and social programs are not meeting the needs of children of inmates, despite the higher risk of behavioral misconduct and delinquency (Family and Corrections Network, 1994).

The educational level of a parent is a clear indicator of both the educational achievements of a child and the level of parental involvement in a child's education. As the majority of prisoners are parents, the education of adults in prison can have a positive and long-lasting impact upon the lives of their children. The positive impact of education in prisons should inspire better public education for all citizens, both in and out of our prisons and jails.

With all the evidence available supporting the positive impact of correctional higher education, it is critical that programs be implemented that allow for the maximum number of qualified participants. The reinstatement of federal financial assistance in the form of Pell Grants to inmates is crucial. Alternative and varied sources of funding must also be considered. For example, in New York State a variety of sources, including university assistance, private funding, and the individual financial contributions of inmates and their families has combined to provide the financial support for correctional higher-education programs (Taylor, 1993).

The U.S. Department of Justice reported that almost 1.5 million children had a parent in prison—an increase of more than 500,000 since 1991, and of these children 58% were under the age of 10. Three quarters of state prisoners who were parents had a prior conviction and a majority (56%) had previously been incarcerated. State prisoners who were parents were less likely to be violent offenders than inmates without children. On average, the imprisoned parent is expected to serve more than six-and-a-half years in a state prison or eight-and-a-half years in federal prison. Additionally, the same report states that as of December 31, 1999, an estimated 336,300 U.S. households with minor children had a resident parent in prison. It was found that almost 60% of the parents in state prisons reported having used drugs in the month before their offense, and 25% reported a history of alcohol dependence. Moreover, about 14% reported mental illness and 70% did not have a high school diploma. One month prior to their arrest, 46% had a monthly income of $1,000, and 27% derived their income through illegal activities—i.e. drug trafficking (U.S. Department of Justice, 2000).

The social stigma associated with the incarceration of a family member is another issue that may lead to a variety of psychological problems, such as aggression or depression for all members involved. In schools, children may use degrading statements, exclude the children of prisoners from the group, and make fun of the child whose parent is incarcerated; even adults engage in statements such as "like father, like son" and often set the stage for suspicion when an illegal act (i.e., petty theft) occurs (Schneller, 1976).

A child raised in an environment where drug trafficking and welfare dependence is strong, where physical and verbal violence is frequent, where imprisonment is rampant, and where discrimination by race, ethnicity, and other factors is the norm is likely to act in similar ways. The environment, in combination with other characteristics such as support systems, levels of self-esteem, and expectations, often determines a child's future. The child will imitate behavior through observations within his/her immediate and extended social groups. Thus it is important to connect positive prevention strategies in the form of education.

Albert Bandura's social learning theory emphasizes learning within a social context, by acknowledging the social environment as a stimulus for learning. The concept evolved from the awareness that much learning occurs through the observations and imitations of other people's behavior (Bandura, 1986). It introduces imitation and direct instruction as additional means of acquiring new behavior or changing a current behavior, and its cognitive processes. This acquisition or change of behavior can occur without a specific pattern of positive or negative reinforcement. The knowledge a learner already has, the influence of one's expectations about how one's behavior is evaluated, and the anticipation of probable outcomes is all of importance (Bandura, 1989).

Behavioral acquisition or change applies to both adults and children and is largely the response to their diverse environment and its systematic change. For example, upon the incarceration of the father of a family, the mother has to take over the responsibilities of the absent husband. Children, while mourning the loss of their father, are worried about their father and often blame the other parent or themselves. Sometimes either parent or both are incarcerated, thus leaving the child behind to either live with a grandparent, in foster care, or become homeless. The adjustments for a child with a parent in prison can be devastating and the psychological impact (i.e., feelings of abandonment) is critical.

Although not directly related to prison issues, the U.S. Department of Commerce published in its Census Brief similar findings identifying risk factors many children must overcome, ranging from dropping out of school to becoming involved in crime. Among these specific risk factors are: poverty, welfare dependence, absentee parents, single-parent families, and parents without a high school diploma. The report states that 50% of 16- and 17- year-olds are at risk and suggests, "Those exposed to risk factors are more likely to experience adverse outcomes" (U.S. Department of Commerce, 1997, p. 1).

Various researches have shown the effects of imprisonment upon families, effects that also have an impact on the learning process for both the inmate within the correctional facility and children in school. Although the feelings differ between the inmate and his family members, many are the same. Families may experience feelings of social isolation, fear, powerlessness, unworthiness, abandonment, hopelessness, frustration, anger, and depression. Moreover, being subjected to low self-esteem and low expectations for the future poses another threat to children and their healthy psychological development. In addition to these factors, inmates are also faced with the general hostility found within facilities (Brooks, 1993).

Educating inmates does not guarantee that they will not commit another crime. Just as the problem of crime is complex, the solution to crime must be complex. Each individual prisoner has a unique background, and mixed emotions underline its complexity. Education in and of itself is not enough. One must address basic human needs such as socioeconomic status, mental health, and so on, before education can be successfully applied. Education is just one of various factors which must be addressed. It is very difficult for a person to obtain and maintain a job in our global, technological society without being educated. When one has a criminal record with limited working skills and experiences the negative social aspect of prison, an enormous amount of barriers emerge that an ex-offender must overcome.

A good educational program will teach people many things not reflected on a GED test or high school diploma, such as cognitive skills, social skills, and communication skills. Important factors such as emotional disturbances, inadequate support systems, socioeconomic status, and mental health problems have a profound impact on inmates and their families and their learning process. Education entails much more than just the "basics," and in order to successfully educate we must educate ourselves about the relevant issues at hand. It seems clear that collaboration with families, schools, and the community is crucial in developing effective prevention strategies to decrease recidivism, thus increasing public safety. Psychology courses, multicultural courses, global skills, and communication courses are essential prerequisites to successful teaching within the prison system and within public schools to aid the families and prevent a rise in crime among the younger generation.

Each time we can remove one barrier, we make it easier for that person to become a productive citizen. Correctional educators are most effective when they understand the population they are teaching. Once the students' viewpoint is understood, the teacher can then use history and literature to help students discover for themselves the alternatives that exist for them (Sherman et al., 1997). To successfully limit these barriers, multicultural education is essential in that it addresses culturally diverse communities, social, political and economic education, ESOL, and critical thinking skills. Furthermore, teaching strategies should include emotional, disciplinary, motivational, and academic categories. Current social policies and practices regarding prisoners and their families interfere with an individual's ability to achieve recognition and respect for their work or the ability to perform meaningful work. These interferences endanger the individual psychosocial development and the future of the social group. Social policies and practices should be used to inspire society to care about its members and to foster optimistic ambitions and goals in younger generations.

References

Bandura, A. (1986). *Social foundations of thought and action: A social cognitive theory.* Englewoods Cliffs, NJ: Prentice Hall.

———. (1989). Social cognitive theory. *Annuals of Child Development,* 6, pp. 1–60.

Bandura, A., Carlson, B.E., & Cervera, N. (1991). Incarceration, coping, and support. *Social Work,* 36, pp. 279–285.

Brooks, Margaret K. (1993). *How can I help? Working with children of incarcerated parents. Serving special children, Volume 1.* New York: Osborne Association.

Brunner, M.S. (1993). *National survey of reading programs for incarcerated juvenile offenders.* (NCJ Publication No. 144017). Washington, DC: Office of Juvenile Justice and Delinquency Prevention.

Bureau of Justice Statistics. (1992). *Criminal victimization in the U.S., 1990: Incarcerated parents and their children.* Washington, DC: Author.

———. (1997). *Criminal offender statistics.* [On-line]. Available: http://www.ojp.- usdoj.gov/bjs/crimoff.htm.

Consortium of the Niagara Frontier. (1996). *The benefits to New York State of higher education programs for inmates.* [pamphlet]. Amherst, NY: Consortium of the Niagara Frontier.

DeComo, R., Tunis, S., Krisberg, B., Herrera, N.C., Rudenstine, S., & Del Rosario, D. (1995). *Juveniles taken into custody: Fiscal year 1992 report.* (NCJ Publication No. 153851). Washington, DC: Office of Juvenile Justice and Delinquency Prevention.

Department of Education, National Center for Education Statistics. (1992). *1992 National adult literacy survey.* Washington, DC: National Center for Education Statistics. [On-line]. Available: http://www.ed.gov/NCES/nadlits/overview.html.

Dishion, T.J., Patterson, G.R., Stoolmiller, M., & Skinner, M.L. (1991). Family, school, and behavioral antecedents to early adolescent involvement with antisocial peers. *Developmental Psychology,* 27, pp. 172–180.

Elikann, P.T. (1996). *The tough-on-crime myth: Real solutions to cut crime.* New York, NY: Insight Books.

Families of offenders: A key crime to prevention. Report 1. (1994, July). Family and Corrections Network.

Harer, M.D. (1994). *Recidivism among federal prison releases in 1987: A preliminary report.* Washington, DC: Federal Bureau of Prisons, Office of Research and Evaluation.

Louis Harris and Associates, Inc. (1993). *The Metropolitan Life survey of the American teacher.* New York: Louis Harris and Associates, Inc.

Mauer, M. (1994). *Americans behind bars: The international use of incarceration, 1992–1993.* Washington DC: The Sentencing Project.

Schneller, D.P. (1976). *A prisoner's family: A study of the effects of imprisonment on the families of prisoners.* San Francisco: R&E Research Associates.

Sherman, L. W., Gottfredson, D., MacKenzie, D.L., Eck, J., Reuters, P. & Bushway, S. (1997). *Preventing crime: What works, what doesn't, what's promising.* (NCJ Publication No. 165366). Washington, DC: National Institute of Justice.

Siegel, G.R. (1997). *A research study to determine the effects of literacy and general educational development programs on adult offenders on probation.* Tucson, AZ: Adult Probation Department of the Superior Court in Pima County.

Taylor, J.M. (1993, January 25). Pell grants for prisoners. *Nation.*

Tracy, C., & Johnson, C. (1994). *Review of various outcome studies relating prison education to reduced recidivism.* Windham School System: Huntsville, TX.

U.S. Department of Commerce. *Census brief September 1997.* Bureau of the Census. Washington, DC: Economics and Statistics Administration.

U.S. Department of Justice. (2000*). Sourcebook of criminal justice statistics.* Washington, DC: U.S. Government Printing Office.

Chapter Fifteen

Prison Perspectives on Pedagogy

Beth Hatt-Echeverria

Dear Teachers:

When I was going through elementary and middle school, the size of my classes were very small and I received a lot of one on one instruction from my teachers. My problems and concerns were recognized and dealt with. I was a fast learner and in the 4th grade I was placed in A.G. classes, where 9 other classmates and I left our regular classes 3 times a week to attend more challenging math and science classes. My educational experience was good up until I reached the 8th grade.

Entering 8th grade, I brought with me a whole new range of problems that few of my other classmates were dealing with. I was using drugs on a regular basis even on school nights, dating an older guy who was abusive, which caused me to show up at school on several occasions with bruises on my face from his violence. These problems were causing even more problems at home with my parents.

My teachers no longer seemed concerned for me. Not one ever asked how or where I had received the blackened-eyes and swollen lips. They never questioned me when my grades went from A's to C's and D's. They just kept teaching their curriculum. My mind was so jumbled with other things that their curriculum could no longer hold my interest.

The advice I give to you is to recognize and identify with the lives of your students. Get to know them. Create an "easy" environment where students feel comfortable speaking out; where they are free to express themselves. Most of my years in school, I could always turn to my teachers. Several teachers became my friends, whom I still keep in contact with today.

Things got so bad in my life that I was struggling everyday just to make it. I felt like I could no longer identify with my fellow classmates because I felt so out of place. I quit school two weeks before becoming a sophomore. Empathize, put yourself in their place and genuinely care. You truly can make a difference in someone's life.

—Crystal, 19 year old incarcerated female

The above letter was written as part of an assignment in a class I taught for female youth offenders. Sadly, Crystal's letter does not sound all that different from the others. Each of the women told a story of not feeling cared about or even abused by teachers in school. Furthermore, all of the women in my class dropped out before graduating from high school. My motivation for writing this chapter comes from the stories I have heard through my work with incarcerated youth, especially from the women whom I have taught or, rather, who have taught me. In this chapter, I want to discuss the struggles of caring faced by teachers and students through the educational experiences of incarcerated youth.

The educational history of inmates typically includes one of poor grades in school, behavior problems, and having dropped out (Farrington & West, 1990; Robins & Hill as cited in Farrington, 1996). In fact, 39% percent of the prison population do not have their high school diplomas (U.S. Federal Bureau of Justice Statistics, 1995). They often fulfill the stereotype of the student who does *not* care about school. From listening to them, I hope we can learn more about what it means to care.

Caring in the classroom can take many different forms. It can mean wanting students to achieve and value school to talking with a child during lunch about gardening (Courtney & Noblit, 1994; Rogers, 1994). Within the literature, caring revolves around interacting with others and is typically split into two halves: aesthetic caring and authentic caring (Gilligan, Ward, & Taylor, 1982; 1988; Noddings, 1984). In schools, aesthetic caring often relates to teachers wanting their students to achieve academically and abide by school rules, while authentic caring refers to "relations of reciprocity between teachers and students" (Valenzuela, 1999).

Caring appears simple to accomplish but with large class sizes, low teacher support, and high stakes accountability systems, teachers often struggle to provide for the diverse needs of their students. Consequently, aesthetic care is the deepest level of care many teachers are able to provide. This creates a conflict between teachers and students because students often demand that they be cared for *authentically* before they will care about school (Valenzuela, 1999).

Teachers often assume that students should place the same value on education as they do themselves. This becomes problematic when teachers devalue students who do not achieve academically rather than attempting to understand their students' personal interactions with education and lives outside of school. One example of a typical misunderstanding between teachers and students is when students drop out of school. Often, teachers believe the students are dropping out because they do not care about school. Furthermore, larger society often perceive dropouts as "hopeless and helpless losers" (Fine, 1991, p. 4). This stereotype is frequently tied to Latino and African American youth because their dropout rates range from 40 to 60% (Fine, 1991).

Alternatively, the reality suggests:

> Dropouts could be reconceptualized as critics of educational and labor market arrangements. The act of dropping out could be recast as a strategy for taking control of lives fundamentally out of control. (Fine, 1991, p. 4)

Consequently, how we think about dropouts needs to be shifted from an assumption that these students do not care about school to an attitude that asks why students are dropping out and how education is not meeting their current needs. Rather than placing the blame on students by saying "They do not care," the focus should be on how the educational system is failing *them* by upholding the ideals of education over the pressing needs and concerns of students.

Within this paper, four key themes connected to caring will be discussed: struggles beyond education, alienation, image, and teaching with personal meaning. Figuratively, this paper will be a journey through hallways, rather than classrooms, because it is there where teachers are more likely to encounter the lives of their students. In the hallways, love is found and lost, friendships formed and broken, identities shaped, and personal meanings developed for education (Eckert, 1989). It is in the hallways that teachers find the emotional and relational lives of their students. To depict this point, I use fictional vignettes that are close to the events in their lives.

What I have learned about the educational experiences of incarcerated youth comes from interviews that I conducted over the past three years and from having taught two college-level courses within men's and women's prisons. What is most important is that I learned their stories through relationships that I developed with them. As relating to this chapter, fieldwork is about relationships and caring for the person, rather than just the "data." Consequently, out of respect for these men and women, I do not reveal the crimes that landed them in prison because their crimes *do not* and *should not* define who they are. We must not forget that they are also mothers, fathers, sons, sisters, friends, poets, artists—they are people. By focusing on their crime, we have a tendency to forget that.

Struggles Beyond Education

> The bell rings and students flood into the hall. We see a Black female student, Sherry, arguing with a teacher. Sherry needs to leave her teacher's class early today to get to work on time but her teacher will not let her. He does not understand why Sherry cannot change her work schedule and believes that her attendance in class is more important than her job. He refuses to let her leave before class is finished. He has thirty students waiting on him to begin class so he tells her the discussion is over. He shakes his head and walks back into his classroom while leaving Sherry in the hallway. Sherry glares at him and leaves the building.

I interviewed Sherry in February of 2000. Although the previous vignette is fictional, it is close to the actual events of her life. Sherry grew up being physically and emotionally abused by her stepfather and at the age of 15 escaped by running away. From that point on, she lived on her own. She struggled to have her own apartment and pay her own bills, which made work a higher priority than school. Eventually she needed to quit school because she was not making enough money. At that point, Sherry was raped and her life began to crumble. For reasons unknown to her, Sherry began to act in self-destructive ways. She did not care what happened to her. She became pregnant and involved in an abusive relationship before being sentenced to six years in prison at the age of eighteen.

Sherry's focus during high school was on survival. She had to meet her basic needs of shelter and food before she could focus upon the ideals of education. I asked Sherry if she could remember any teachers taking an interest in her life outside of school. She thought for a second while looking away and quietly replying, "no."

The attitude within most schools is that the school's responsibility is to foster academic achievement. This encourages teachers and administration to connect with the cognitive aspects of students' lives but no further. Unfortunately, a student's struggles beyond school are often pushed out into the hallways and not welcomed into the classroom. What is missing from this perspective is the reality that many other factors contribute to a student's academic performance. For example, a child's overall health, ability to make friends, and self-esteem all influence how a student learns (Comer, Haynes, & Joyner, 1996). Authentic caring focuses upon the whole child and not just their ability to learn.

Alienation

> As we are heading out of the building, we see a female student, Shayla, leaving the principal's office while crying. She walks over to a friend who has been waiting and hugs her. The principal states that she needs to go back to class. He appears frustrated and upset with her. As a student, Shayla often causes problems by lying and, the principal was not about to believe her this time. Shayla walks down the hallway sobbing as the principal goes back into his office. A teacher of Shayla's passes by but does not ask what is wrong because she is late to a parent-teacher conference.

As before, this vignette is a fictional reconstruction of Shayla's experience in dealing with her principal after being raped. She was interviewed during the fall of 1999 within a focus group. I was shocked at how openly Shayla discussed being raped and how much pain was still in her voice. Shayla has been in prison for two years and has three small children. She described how at her high school it was common for students to do drugs during breaks between classes. She also told me about being raped in a men's bathroom at school. The principal would not believe her and, consequently, life at school became miserable for her. Eventually she dropped out due to the emotional ramifications of being raped. She is taking classes in prison to create a better life for her children and to ensure that their educational experiences are better than her own.

Shayla needed someone, whether the principal or a teacher, to believe in her and to listen to her closely. Rather than being perceived as a "problem," she needed someone to care about her regardless of her past and to care about her beyond the classroom. With the amount of security and comfort she lost from being raped at the school, she needed someone to help her gain some of that back. Instead, she found herself even more alone and isolated.

Schools are not inherently places where students feel comfortable and safe. Instead, they can be places of shame, fear, and alienation. Students of color and from working-class backgrounds often find themselves alienated from school. For example, African Americans account for 30% of all school suspensions although they only represent 16% of the student population (Nieto, 1996). Additionally, African Americans are placed in special education classes at double their enrollment rate, but only contribute to 8% of gifted and talented programs. Other groups of color also fare badly; Latino students drop out of high school more often than any other group (Nieto, 1996). Students of color often feel alienated within schools but doors of opportunity can be opened through authentic caring (Valenzuela, 1999).

Image

I was nervous as I drove to the mall to meet Devon. I had interviewed him while he was in prison and was now meeting him a month after his release. I wasn't sure as to what I should expect. I walked around the cafe court a couple of times before I finally saw him. He looked much healthier—the dark circles under his eyes were gone, he stood straighter, and his hair was neatly trimmed. He was wearing Tommy Hilfiger from head to toe. We sat and talked for about an hour. He seemed caught up in making money, buying the new "in" shoes, and getting a beeper. He also mentioned that his speech was "proper" and that people knew he didn't fit in with the other inmates when he was locked up. Image seemed to be everything to him. Education was only about image too. He slept during his college classes in prison but went because he said it "looked good"

—Fieldnotes, spring 2000

A key component often ignored when discussing students is the importance of image. David Harvey (1989) refers to the importance of image as a part of the postmodern condition. He claims that image is highly stressed through consumerist culture and has become closely tied to identity. He states:

> Corporations, governments, political and intellectual leaders all value a stable image as part of their aura of authority and power....Moreover, image becomes all important in competition, not only through name-brand recognition but also because of various associations of 'respectability,' 'quality,' 'prestige,' 'reliability,' and 'innovation.' (p. 288)

The image of the white, upper middle class is often portrayed as correlating to success and respectability. Consequently, styles that oppose this image are often discouraged in schools. Students working against the dominant image are typically stereotyped as the "uncaring student."

> While walking down the hall, we pass two students, Jeremy and Sara. Jeremy is wearing baggy pants, a Tommy Hilfiger shirt, 2 gold chains, and a gold hoop through his ear. One of his front teeth is also gold and has a smiley face indented into it. Sara has short, bright pink hair, a nose ring, and is wearing fish net stockings. The assistant principal walks by and informs us that Jeremy is valedictorian for the senior class and Sara is one of the top students in the advanced physics class. As we walk further, the assistant principal mumbles, "If only we could get them to dress more appropriately."

Image for high school students is often closely tied to their struggle for independence and in forming their own identities while also wanting to feel respected. Image is so powerful for youth that it can persuade them to adopt looks of all kinds. It can encourage students to want to appear "smart," "rebellious," "upper-class," or even as if they do not care about school. An image is all about what you "have," including clothes, cars, stereos, and jewelry.

I have spoken with many male inmates that started dealing drugs at 12 to 13 years of age because it was a way for them to have things such as brand name clothes or create an image they otherwise could not afford. One young man told me that when he was 14 years old he had

$16,000 under his bed. He used the money to not only buy nice clothes and a stereo but he also helped to support his mother and younger sister. Additionally, many inmates have mentioned that drug dealers are looked up to in their communities because they have wealth and help to provide for others in the community. Students sometimes seek to acquire a "positive" image or respect through having expensive things and being able to provide for others rather than achieving in school.

A perfect example of this occurs in the movie *My Family* (Nava & Thomas, 1995). It is a movie about a Mexican American family's struggles in East Los Angeles. One night the father discovers his son has been making money through dealing. The father is extremely upset and begins to remind his son of the struggles he has went through to earn a living and to survive in the United States. He wants his son to achieve dignity through struggling like him. The son replies:

> Fuck dignity. Fuck your struggle. Do you think anybody cares about that here? This [money] is the only thing they care about in this country, not dignity. It doesn't matter how you get it, as long as you get it.

This statement reflects the attitude of many of the incarcerated youth I have spoken to in their quest for respect. Acquiring an education may not mean "success" or respect for many students, which pushes us to explore alternative definitions of success and to consider them as valid— not problematic.

Instructors and Caring

Many of the incarcerated women discussed taking college classes as a way to provide a better life for their children or to keep others from ending up in prison. Their goals revolved around escaping oppression and ensuring that those they care about escape and avoid oppression. To these women, education was not simply about acquiring knowledge but about escaping an oppressed state and ensuring those around them escape it too. Their relationships with others were key in providing meaning to education. Additionally, their relationship with instructors was a key factor in determining whether they continued with a class and how much effort they put into it.

The instructors had personal agendas that included wanting to be a role model, having political ideals concerning prisons, and simply desiring to teach the subject matter. The following are comments from instructors as to why they chose to teach in prison and how they hoped the inmates would benefit by taking their class:

Teacher 1

"I'm there to teach psychology. I want them to learn psychology. However, by going over a lot of the material, if it gives people insights that are meaningful to them—to me that would be wonderful. But I am really uncomfortable with saying that it was my goal to really create that kind of situation." — *Bill*

Teacher 2

"I could have very easily ended up where these kids are. Fortunately, I chose a different path. I could be a role model for these kids....They have this huge stereotype of society in that everybody is against them and everybody wishes them ill or whatever. I try to let them know that there are people out there, like yourself and me, that are looking out for their best interests." —*Theresa*

Teacher 3

"I wanted to diversify my experience and I'd always thought it would be one of my political goals to teach in prison. It's very gratifying. It would be nice to work in advocacy for greater educational opportunity in the prison system." —*Carol*

The first instructor, Bill, believes teaching is about acquiring knowledge (i.e., psychology). He perceives his role as limited to cognition rather than emotions. The women performed the worst in his course and only one student completed the class. Many of the women blamed their poor performance on Bill, stating that he was very boring and did not encourage them to relate the material back to their lives. By ignoring the context of the inmates' lives, he overlooked or ignored the fact that his role needed to be more than simply teaching psychology. He failed students in more than grades by continuing to deny relationships in the classroom.

However, the women spoke highly of the other teachers and performed much better in their classes. They stated that the other instructors were open with them about their own lives and seemed interested in the inmates' lives too. Their teaching styles revolved around developing a relationship with their students.

During group interviews, both male and female inmates stated that they preferred instructors who were interested in their lives and related the subject matter back to their lives. Consequently, the inmates had positive educational experiences in their classes. Through embracing the personal experiences of students, issues of image, alienation, and struggles outside of school become opportunities for growth and caring rather than problems in the classroom.

Conclusion

Shay is exhausted after a day of student teaching. She has class tonight and a ton of papers to grade. She wonders if she even really wants to be a teacher. Her mentor comes into the room and chastises her for not having her lesson plans typed out. Shay feels her lesson plans are the least of her worries at the moment. She grabs her bookbag and walks out of the classroom. On the way, she passes a male, black student who looks like a gang member to her so she clutches her bag tighter and walks faster. Further down the hall, she sees a girl crying in the hall but does not feel like she has time to intervene because she has to get to class on campus.

While walking through the parking lot, she passes one of her students who, unknown to her, has just dropped out. He creates a lot of problems for her in class and she is not in the mood to deal with him. She says, "hi" while hurrying past him to her car. She gets in her car, drives out of the "bad" neighborhood her school resides, and heads home to the suburbs. She feels like crying on the way home for her feelings of being overwhelmed and not understanding why her students do not care about school.

Shay cares about her students in that she wants them to achieve academically. However, she has missed a step. She does not realize that students first want to feel *cared for* before they will *care about* school (Valenzuela, 1999). By caring for her students outside of the classroom, she could provide opportunities for students to feel like they "belong," to be more encouraged about their academic ability among other abilities, to feel "special," to have an adult to talk with, to have a comfort zone at school, to feel safe in asking for help, and to have a reason to come to school. These are just a few of the potential opportunities that can be created through authentic forms of caring.

All kids need these relationships, whether or not they are "good" students. Relationships based upon authentic caring can enhance any student's educational experience; they are important regardless of the child's home life, academic performance, or neighborhood. However, the stories of incarcerated youth in this chapter teach us that relationships based upon authentic caring are especially important for students who lack these kinds of relationships in their lives and face extraordinary struggles beyond schooling.

The perspectives we have heard from incarcerated youth on schooling stress that when relationships are cut from learning, then student ties to schooling are also cut. In having their relational ties to schooling cut, students are free then to deviate. They are free to fail, free to quit, free to get kicked out, and free to not care because no one will notice or else it is the only way to get noticed. As a prison official once stated to me:

> These kids [youth offenders] quit going to school at twelve, thirteen years of age and no one goes after them or even knows what happens to them

Figuratively, we have walked through school hallways and seen students struggling with drug addictions, abuse at home, and attempting to survive independently. Students with baggy pants and gold chains have passed by us while looking at us from head to toe attempting to have a "gangsta" image. Finally, we have passed a young woman crying in the hall because the principal will not believe she has been raped and she feels like there is no one she can talk to. We have only seen a few teachers during our walk that have been talking and laughing with students.

Through this walk, we have heard story after story of youth describing educational experiences void of authentic caring. We have also heard pain, alienation, and bitterness in their stories. Furthermore, we have heard stories that are often silenced either behind prison walls or because they are hard for us, as educators, to hear. I believe most educators truly care about their students but struggle to care because of the structure of the system, too many demands placed upon them, or for various other reasons. Consequently, caring relationships are often an afterthought to academics. Based upon the stories in this chapter, this clearly is not only wrong but can be harmful to students' potential academic performance. However painful or difficult it may be, we must create better relationships between students and teachers if we want all students to achieve academically.

References

Comer, J., Haynes, N., & Joyner, E. (1996). The school development program. In J. Comer, N. Haynes, E. Joyner, & M. Ben-Avie (Eds.), *Rallying the whole village: The Comer process for reforming education.* New York: Teachers College Press.

Courtney, M., & Noblit, G.W. (1994). The principal as caregiver. In A.R. Prillamen, D. Eaker, & D. Kenderick (Eds.), *The tapestry of caring* (pp. 67–85). Norwood, NJ: Ablex Publishing Corporation.

Eckert, P. (1989). *Jocks and burnouts.* New York: Teachers College Press.

Farrington, D.P. (1993). Childhood origins of teenage antisocial behavior and adult social dysfunction. *Journal of the Royal Society of Medicine,* 86, pp. 13–17.

———. (1996). The explanation and prevention of youthful offending. In A. Blumstein and D. Farrington (Eds.), *Delinquency and crime* (pp. 68–148). Cambridge: Cambridge University Press.

Farrington, D.P., & West, D.J. (1990). The Cambridge study in delinquent development: A long-term follow-up of 411 London males. In H.J. Kerner and G. Kaiser (Eds.), *Criminality: Personality, behavior, life history* (pp. 115–138). Berlin: Springer-Verlag.

Fine, M. (1991). *Framing dropouts: Notes on the politics of an urban public high school.* Albany: State University of New York Press.

Gilligan, C. (1982). *In a different voice.* Cambridge, MA: Harvard University Press.

Gilligan, C., Ward, J., & Taylor, J. (Eds.). (1988). *Mapping the moral domain.* Cambridge, MA: Harvard University Press.

Harvey, D. (1989). *The condition of postmodernity: An enquiry into the origins of cultural change.* New York: Blackwell.

Nava, G. (Director) & Thomas, A. (Producer). (1995). *My family* [Film]. New Line Home Video.

Nieto, S. (Ed.). (1996). *Affirming diversity: The sociopolitical context of multicultural education.* White Plains, NY: Longman.

Noddings, N. (1984). *Caring.* Berkeley, CA: University of California Press.

————. (1992). *The challenge to care in schools.* New York: Teachers College Press.

Rogers, D. (1994). Conceptions of caring in a fourth-grade classroom. In A.R. Prillamen, D. Eaker, & D.Kenderick (Eds.), *The tapestry of caring* (pp. 33–47). Norwood, NJ: Ablex.

Rutter, M, Maughan, B., Mortimore, P., & Ouston, J. (1979). *Fifteen thousand hours.* London: Open Books.

Smith, D. (1990). *The conceptual practices of power: A feminist sociology of knowledge.* Boston: Northeastern University Press.

U.S. Federal Bureau of Justice Statistics, Washington, DC, 1995.

Valenzuela, A. (1999). *Subtractive schooling: U.S.-Mexican youth and the politics of caring.* Albany: State University of New York Press.

Part Four

Troubling Differences

Chapter Sixteen

Foundations of Education and Acting Theory? You've Got to Be Kidding!

David M. Dees

As undergraduate education majors across the nation open their foundations of education textbooks at the beginning of each semester, they inevitably are greeted by an obligatory introductory chapter that discusses such issues as the difference between education and schooling, the "profession" of teaching, "Who are America's teachers?" and "What is teaching?". It is this last issue, "What is teaching?" that has challenged educational researchers for decades.

Many educational scholars that have explored issues associated with this question, including Cuban (1982, 1984, 1990), Jackson (1968), Gibboney (1994) and others, contend that there has been insignificant change in the educational discourse regarding the act of teaching. However, some educational scholars such as Eisner (1979), Lee (1993), May (1993), and Pineau (1994) have challenged us to think metaphorically and artistically in attempting to answer this question. These scholars have proposed that teaching is an art form that can be improved upon, studied, and researched from an artistic perspective. However, to date there has been limited educational research that draws specifically from the arts in an attempt to address the question "What is teaching?" This gap serves as the impetus of this chapter.

Konstantin Stanislavski, a cofounder of the Moscow Art Theatre, is considered one of the most important acting teachers and theorists of the past two centuries. Stanislavski, who was "a pragmatic questioner whose books, teaching and productions together reveal the full range of his lifelong search for truth in art" (Cole & Chinoy, 1970, p. 485), created an acting method that was designed to allow actors to address the question,

"What is acting?" The Stanislavski system, later adapted by Lee Stras-berg and called "The Method," has made a major impact on actor train-ing and thinking in this country (Brestoff, 1995, p. 94).

Stanislavski's "method" consists of various techniques that are de-signed to help actors focus on their communication processes. These techniques serve to isolate "different elements of human behavior, such as 'concentration of attention,' 'relaxation,' and 'sense memory'" (Moore, 1991, p. 2) in an effort to help actors develop their artistry. For Stanislavski, an actor who is relaxed and concentrated "in the moment" is in a better physical and mental state to "reach the living spirit" (Stanislavski, 1936, p. 189) of human communication. For Stanislavski, this type of actor is better prepared to "commune" internally, with other actors and with audience members, in an attempt to create meaning on stage.

This chapter, drawing from the writings and techniques of Stanislavski, explores how his philosophical perspectives could inform the question, "What is teaching?".[1] The Stanislavskian concepts, such as the "magic if," the "circle of attention," and the "spirit of the object," are explored in the context of the teacher–student transaction. Additionally, this chapter explores specific exercises that could be utilized in teacher training to help future teachers understand the performative aspects in-volved in the art of teaching. The goal of this chapter is to provide foun-dational scholars with a possible artistic approach to answer the question, "What is teaching?"

External vs. Internal

Stanislavski's systematic approach to this art form was his response and reaction to the "external" approach to acting that became so pre-dominant on the stage during his lifetime. Simply stated, the external ap-proach to acting relied upon standardized and symbolic physical gestures and pronunciations as the means to communicate the character's emo-tional reality on stage. In one great example, Stanislavski describes how he experienced this approach to acting:

Let us say that the pupil could not pronounce the sounds S, KH, and SHTCH. Then the teacher would sit down in front of him, open the mouth as wide as possible, and say to the pupil: 'Look in my mouth. You see what my tongue is doing; it lies on the roots of my upper teeth. Do the same. Say it. Repeat it ten times. Open your mouth wider, and let me look into it to see if you are doing it correctly.'...It cannot be denied that this method develops the voice. But it also does tremendous harm. The habit of saying words without any meaning for the sake of the exercise of sound, and not in order to express inner feelings and thoughts, breaks the direct connection between soul and word, voice and emotion. (Stanislavski, 1948, p. 84)

For Stanislavski, the correct physical and vocal pronunciation is an important part of the acting process. However, similar to the criticisms of the drill-and-skill approach to teaching, Stanislavski questioned the relevance of this approach. The artist should not limit his or her focus to the "external" reality of the character. The inner reality of the role is just as important. Stanislavski believed in the importance of both the inner and outer realities of a character. According to Benedetti (1998):

There are two aspects to the technique of the 'system'; one inner, where the mind and imagination create the thoughts and feelings of the character; the other outer, where the body expresses and communicates what is going on inside. It is no good carrying imaginative and subtle thoughts and feelings inside me if they are not reflected in the minutest detail in my body. (p. 13)

For Stanislavski, one of the main elements for outer expression of the character is physical relaxation. The main elements of the inner reality of the character are represented in the ideas of the "magic if," concentration/observation, and communion with the spirit of the object. Each element is addressed in the following sections of this chapter.

Relaxation

Stanislavski's text, *An Actor Prepares*, written as an actor's account of a year studying at the Moscow Art Theatre, outlines in a practical manner many of the ideas that he believed were important to his system. In one section of this text the director/teacher Tortsov, who is supposed to represent Stanislavski, has a student lift a corner of a piano. While the student is lifting the piano Tortsov requests that he attempt a wide variety of tasks such as multiplying, visualizing the street outside of their building, and singing a song. To achieve any of these assigned tasks the acting student had to lower the piano (Stanislavski, 1936, p. 91). In this section of his text Stanislavski outlines the importance he placed on physical relaxation. For Stanislavski physical relaxation and control of one's muscles allows the actor to better communicate the inner reality of the character. Tortsov continues, "As long as you have this physical tenseness you cannot even think about delicate shadings of feeling or the spiritual life of your part" (p. 92). Physical tension limits the artist's ability to stay in touch with the inner realities that he or she is creating. Therefore, Stanislavski set out to devise techniques that could help actors learn to control some of their physical responses. He believed that through practice and discipline an individual could take control over her or his muscular responses. He notes, "this relaxing of the muscles should become a normal phenomenon. This habit should be developed daily, constantly, systematically, both during our exercises at school and at home" (p. 94). Thus, much of the "outer" focus of the Stanislavski system relies upon teaching actors how to control their physical responses to tension. As an actor takes the stage nerves, concerns about technical elements of the production, and focusing on his or her cues, for example, may create a sense of tension in the actor's body. For Stanislavski, if the actor does not know how to take control of that physical response, the inner reality that has been created through the techniques of the system will get lost in the actor's mechanical physical presence. Physical relaxation is a primary component of the Stanislavski system.

Contemporary actors that have adopted the Stanislavski system utilize several yoga relaxation techniques that teach them how to take control of their physical responses to tension. One of the most popular techniques involves teaching students the power of tension and release. Acting teachers ask their students to find a comfortable position in the room. Then, the teacher asks the students to focus all of their attention and concentration on a specific area of the body. For example, a student may be asked to focus all his or her attention and focus on the right thigh muscle. Then, on a command, the students tighten this muscle for a count of ten. At ten, the students are asked to allow for a complete release of the tension. Upon release, the muscle is more relaxed than before the tension was applied. This tension–release technique continues through with each major muscle grouping. At the end of this exercise, the students typically feel relaxed and are then better able to concentrate on the task at hand. From this exercise, the students learn how to focus and to control their concentration, while also developing control over specific muscle groupings. Over time, with daily exercises that practice this technique, the students can learn how to relax and to control specific parts of their own bodies that hold such muscular tension. This physical control allows for a more clarified representation of the inner realities the artist has been creating. The following sections of this chapter examine portions of the Stanislavski system dedicated to creating the artist's inner realities.

The Magic If

In another section of his text that relives a year in the Moscow Art Theatre, Stanislavski describes a day in which the acting students were asked to visit with the director at his house. As the students were relaxing in his study the director began:

> Our work on a play begins with the use of *if* as a lever to lift us out of everyday life onto the plane of imagination....The aim of the actor should be to use his technique to turn the play into a theatrical reality. In this process the imagination plays by far the greatest part. (Stanislavski, 1936, p. 51)

Stanislavski believed that actors had to develop a keen sense of imagination. This sense could be accomplished through understanding the power of the "magic if." As Brestoff describes, "'If' allows you to modulate from the key of reality into the new key of imagination without violating your sense of truth. 'If' can put us anywhere; past, present, future, Earth, Mars, or in a bottle" (Brestoff, 1995, p. 37). Stanislavski outlined this sense of imagination in the following passage:

I came to understand that creativeness begins from that moment when in the soul and imagination of the actor there appears the magical, creative *if*. While only actual reality exists, only practical truth which a man naturally cannot but believe, creativeness has not yet begun. Then the creative *if* appears, that is, the imagined truth which the actor can believe as sincerely and with greater enthusiasms than he believes practical truth, just as the child believes in the existence of its doll and of all life in it and around it. From the moment of the appearance of *if* the actor passes from the plane of actual reality into the plane of another life, created and imagined by himself. Believing in this life, the actor can begin to create. (Stanislavski, 1948, p. 466)

For Stanislavski, actors need to rekindle the childlike honesty and sense of make believe that each of us once realized and appreciated. Actors need to rely on the "magic if" to pay attention to the external conditions created within the world of the play in order to create an honest emotional character representation. Like his belief in the importance of daily physical discipline, Stanislavski also believed that the actor needed to be consistently developing his or her imaginative powers.

Due to this belief, acting teachers who follow the Stanislavski system have developed series of exercises that help their students to rekindle and refine their sense of imagination. For example, acting students may be asked to imagine that they are on a picnic, resting on a bench, witnessing a catastrophe, walking through gelatin or standing in a balloon. Actors may be asked to verbally describe or physically create these images before their peers. These classroom exercises, continued on a daily basis, help actors to develop their sense of imagination through the creation of emotional and physical responses that match his or her given situation. Stanislavski believed that this sense of imagination could be developed through constant discipline and practice. He also believed that this process helps actors to develop and refine their sense of concentration and observation.

Circle of Attention

The ability to concentrate and focus on stage is a key element for this type of internalized acting. Stanislavski noted, "In order to get away from the auditorium you must be interested in something on the stage...an actor must have a point of attention." (Stanislavski, 1936, pp. 70–71). He believed that actors must learn how to focus on the other actors on stage rather than upon what was occurring in the audience. Stanislavski (1936) described a rehearsal in which the director used a series of lamps to highlight this point. At first, a small lamp was turned on. The actors were asked to describe and to focus on only what was lit in the tiny circle of light. Then, a larger light was illuminated, thus creating a larger circle of light. The actors were then asked to describe and to focus on what was lit in this larger circle. This process was repeated until the actors understood the concept of the circle of attention. Then, without the lights, this process was continued until the actors could learn how to control their own circle of attention. Stanislavski realized that maintaining a specified circle of attention was a difficult and, at times, impossible task. Thus, the actor must learn the skill of refocusing his or her circle of attention when it deviates from the reality on stage. He writes, "Your attention will slip and become dissipated in space. You must collect it again and redirect it as soon as possible to one single point or object" (Stanislavski, 1936, p. 80).

Closely related to this notion of concentration is the power of observation. For Stanislavski, actors should be astute observers of the human condition. He notes:

> After you have learned how to observe life around you and draw on it for your work you will turn to the study of the most necessary....I mean those impressions which you get from direct, personal intercourse with other human beings. This material is difficult to obtain because in large part it is intangible....To be sure, many invisible, spiritual experiences are reflected in our facial expression...but even so it is no easy thing to sense another's inmost being, because people do not often open the doors of their souls...(Stanislavski, 1936, p. 88)

He believed that the actor needed to learn how to focus her or his attention, not only on the life events portrayed on the stage, but also on the diverse individuals each of us encounters on a daily basis. For him, plays are written about people under given circumstances and the role of the actor was to represent that created reality upon the stage. In order to achieve this end actors need to learn how to focus their attention and to observe the "acts, thoughts, and impulses" of real human beings (Stanislavski, 1936, p. 88). This keen sense of observation, matched with broad life experiences, leads to the creation of an "imagic" store of emotional memories that an actor can draw from as he or she creates the inner life of the character that is being portrayed on stage. For Stanislavski, broad life experiences help the actor to grow in this area of personal and artistic development.

> He should know not only what is going on in the big cities, but in the provincial towns, far-away villages, factories, and the big cultural centres of the world as well. He should study the life and psychology of the people who surround him....We need a broad point of view to act the play of our times and of many peoples. (Stanislavski, 1936, p. 181)

Thus, his system requires the consistent observation of others who are different from ourselves. His system also requires a broad internal "imagic" store of emotional memories that the artist can recall and draw from as he or she creates the inner life of a character. Additionally, his system requires a heightened level of concentration as the actor tries to recreate this inner reality on stage. Simply learning how to observe the psychological and physical properties of another human being can be a difficult skill to develop. However, the Stanislavski system also requires the actor to develop his or her sense of concentration in order to bring the inner realities of other people to life on stage.

Acting teachers have created various exercises to help students develop their senses of concentration and observation. For example, students are asked to arrange all of the seats in the classroom into two rows without making a noise. This exercise requires a heightened level of concentration and physical discipline that is quite challenging. Also, by repeating this exercise in the dark, the students' sense of concentration can be taken to another level. Other concentration exercises include having the students name each sound that they hear in the building; or with their eyes closed, touch an object and describe it. In terms of developing the actor's sense of observation, students may be asked to name all of the objects in the room that are the same color. Another exercise is to have a student leave the room while five changes are made within the space.

Upon their return, the student is to identify what changes were made in his or her absence. Each of these exercises helps the students to develop their sense of concentration and observation, which are important elements within the Stanislavski system.

In terms of broadening their "imagic" store of human personalities and emotions, acting teachers ask their students to observe and to imitate human behavior. Some teachers ask their students to go to malls, parks, or other areas in which a wide variety of diverse individuals gather. In this assignment the students are asked to see the world from these individuals' point of view. How do particular people walk? How do they talk? What are their hobbies? Acting teachers may have their students study history books, biographies, and personal stories in an effort to develop this sense of otherness. Developing a keen sense of concentration and observation, matched with broad life experiences, are critical elements for acting artistry within this system.

Spirit of the Object

Another aspect of the Stanislavski system is to understand the sense of communion that should occur between the actors on the stage.

> [I]t is both possible to look at and to see, and to look at and not to see. On the stage, you can look at, see and feel everything that is going on there. But it is also possible to look at what surrounds you on this side of the footlights, while your feelings and interest are centered in the auditorium....It is important that an actor's eyes...reflect the deep inner content of his soul. (Stanislavski, 1936, pp. 184–185)

Successful acting requires an awareness of the entire ensemble. An actor draws off of the energy and of the realities being created by the other actors on the stage. As noted in this section, personal commitment is important for all involved. If one actor is not focussed on communicating the "human soul" of his or her part to the other actors on stage, he or she will affect the interpretation of the others' characters. As Stanislavski describes actors need to develop a "spiritual intercourse" with each other on stage as they try to represent the characters involved in each event. He continues:

> All that is necessary is for two people to come into close contact and a natural, mutual exchange takes place. I try to give out my thoughts to you, and you make an effort to absorb something of my knowledge and experience. (Stanislavski, 1936, p. 189)

This understanding of the spirituality and commitment involved in meaningful acting encounters is hard to teach students. Most acting teachers rely on scene work in class as a means to engage this level of awareness. Additionally, some acting teachers use the mirror exercise to teach students how to engage another person within this heightened level of awareness.

In the mirror exercise, two students stand face-to-face with their hands an inch or so apart and stare into the other's eyes. One student is designated the leader and the other is the follower. Upon the command, the leader makes subtle circular movements with his or her hands and the follower mirrors these movements. After a while, the follower is then asked to become the leader. Over time, with deep concentration, the movements can become more complex and who is leading comes into question. If done well and with a heightened sense of commitment, the students find a connection with each other. When these moments occur the students have connected on a spiritual level that can be quite meaningful. This heightened level of human connection and communication is a difficult concept to teach students. It is also difficult to teach someone how to "commit" entirely to an interpretation of a character, let alone a mirror exercise. However, when this reality is seen and felt, students remember the feelings associated with this type of exchange. They also realize how this level of commitment could be helpful on the stage.

Acting Theory and Foundations

The previous sections of this chapter briefly explored specific elements of the Stanislavski system. As noted, this acting system focuses on the synthesis of the external and internal reality involved with creating a character on stage. The importance of relaxing, concentrating, observing, and being committed to the act of communication are some of the elements of the system that were explored. However, the issue still remains as to the usefulness of this system in the study of educational foundations.

In my undergraduate foundations classes, we have been exploring the question, "What is teaching?" In educational foundations, teaching is explored through a combination of learning theories, personal philosophies, and legal, social and historical perspectives. In reality, foundation scholars rarely discuss the "foundations of the act of teaching." This perspective is, in most cases, left up to our curriculum and instruction counterparts that do not typically address the question "What is teaching?" Rather they tend to explore the "how to" of teaching. This "how to" approach addresses issues such as creating a lesson plan, learning how to ask different types of questions, and understanding how to create learning groups. Thus, exposing future educators to the Stanislavski system may provide some insight into the foundations of the art form of teaching.

For example, as noted earlier, Stanislavski addressed the importance of being relaxed. All of us would agree that we are able to recognize the student teacher or the beginning professional who looks and acts tense in front of the classroom. Additionally, all of us, I am sure, have told that student the importance of being relaxed. But have we given our students the foundational knowledge of how to relax? For Stanislavski, actors, through disciplined techniques and practice, can learn how to control their muscular reactions to tension. This physical discipline allows them to represent the inner reality of a character in a more clarified manner. As foundation scholars, we could also teach our students how to control their muscular responses, so that their inner reality of what they are teaching will be expressed in a more clarified manner. At least, if not specifically utilizing some of the physical relaxation techniques associated with the Stanislavski system in our classes, we can have students engage this material so that they know there are methods of relaxation available to them. In my foundations classes we practice some of the relaxation techniques utilized in the field of acting to help students begin to understand the importance of controlling their physical responses. We do not do the daily practice prescribed by Stanislavski, but we do engage in and address the importance of this topic in relationship to their professional practice.

A second element evoked by the Stanislavski system is the importance of concentration and observation. Most undergraduate programs across the nation require the students to obtain numerous hours of classroom observations. At Kent State University, our students, on average, spend at least 180 hours observing teachers and students in the classroom environment before their student teaching experience. In most cases, we send our students to classrooms with questions to answer for a journal or paper assignment. However, do we spend enough time with our students teaching them how to observe human interactions? Do we help them to develop specific observational skills that will help them when they enter the classroom? Some of the Stanislavski exercises that are designed to develop observational skills could help our students become better at comprehending and appreciating classroom transactions.

The third element highlighted in the Stanislavski system that is beneficial to our future teachers is the issue of concentration. The Stanislavski system relies on actors developing a sense of discipline regarding their circle of attention. For Stanislavski, actors must be able to concentrate enough to adapt to the changing circumstances that occur on the stage. He believes that actors should learn how to "be-in-the-moment." This heightened level of mental and physical awareness is also a powerful skill that may benefit educators. As Eisner (1979) and Van Manen (1991) have described, artistry in teaching requires a "being-in-the-moment" awareness. As foundational scholars, how are we leading the discussion towards the development of this understanding of the educational process? What types of improvisational exercises can we use in our own classes to help students to work on their own "being-in-the-moment" awareness? Again, it appears that some of the Stanislavski exercises can be adapted and developed to help our students explore this heightened sense of awareness.

A fourth piece of the Stanislavski system that serves to inform foundational knowledge towards the act of teaching is the idea of memory recall. As noted above, good actors have a large "imagic" store of emotional responses from which they draw to create a variety of characters. Connected with concentration and observation, Stanislavski wanted his actors to become excellent observers and interpreters of human interactions. These concentration and observation abilities are the same skills we desire for our own students. As we explore issues in multicultural education in our classrooms, do we help our students to "see" and to "feel" the inner realities of oppression? Are we working with our students to develop the skills to "live" from the others' points of view? Are we encouraging them to strive to think what it would be like to see the world as a dyslexic? What would it feel like to hate math? The Stanislavski exercises that explore this domain would serve to help our students develop a wider foundational perspective towards human learning and human experience.

A final element of the Stanislavski system that can inform the foundational question of "What is teaching?" is helping our students to understand the spiritual elements associated with human interactions. Described specifically in his system as the notion of communion, Stanislavski believed that actors need to understand the spiritual nature of meaningful human communication. This heightened state of connection with other human beings is vital to the acting process. Could our own students benefit from seeing the teacher–student relationship in the context of the actor-to-actor connection described in this system? I believe our students will benefit from developing this perspective toward their own classrooms. If we are able to help our students to strive for a "spiritual intercourse" with their students, they will become better equipped to create an environment that is sensitive to powerful learning experiences. In many cases, powerful learning experiences, the "aha" moments that occur in our classrooms, are associated with heightened levels of communication that are occurring between the teacher and the students. Developing an awareness of the communicative power associated with these meaningful and heightened levels of human communication can only serve to enlighten the teacher/student interactions that occur in our own classrooms and in the future classrooms of our education students.

A Creative Mood

Clearly, the foundations of education has never been limited to the specific study of the act of teaching. As the liberal arts in the field of education, foundational studies have served to develop the foundational knowledge of our students through such subjects as history, philosophy, sociology, anthropology, psychology, and gender studies in an effort to create better informed and well-rounded educators. It is my belief that through this liberal arts perspective, foundational studies help future educators to understand the broad, diverse, and salient issues that affect the overall educational process. Simply stated, foundational studies help our students to view the educational process from a more holistic perspective. This holistic perspective, although limited towards acting, was Stanislavski's motivation for creating his system of acting.

With this holistic perspective in mind Stanislavski wrote:

> What I wanted to learn was how to create a favorable condition for the appearance of inspiration by means of the will, that condition in the presence of which inspiration was most likely to descend into the actor's soul. As I learned afterward, this creative mood is the spiritual and physical mood during which it is easiest for inspiration to be born. (Stanislavski, 1948, p. 462)

For Stanislavski, the inspired actor is the best. He believed that he could invent a system that allowed actors to consistently create an environment that encouraged personal inspiration. That should be a similar goal for educational foundations. We should strive to create informed and well-rounded educators who understand how to create classrooms sensitive to inspirational moments of learning. Stanislavski continues:

> One cannot always create subconsciously and with inspiration. No such genius exists in the world...our art teaches us...to create consciously and rightly, because that will best prepare the way for the blossoming of the subconscious, which is inspiration. The more you have conscious creative moments in your role the more chance you will have of a flow of inspiration. (Stanislavski, 1936, p. 14)

Translated to the field of education, by helping our students realize the foundational elements associated with the act of teaching, we are providing them with the tools to find their own flow of inspiration towards the profession. This, in turn, will lead to more powerful educative moments within all of our classroom spaces. To me, that should be one of the primary goals of the foundations of education.

Note

1. The classroom acting exercises highlighted throughout this chapter are taken and adapted from Sonia Moore, *Stanislavski Revealed* (New York: Applause Books, 1991).

References

Benedetti, J. (1998). *Stanislavski and the actor*. London: Methuen.

Brestoff, R. (1995). *Great acting teachers and their methods*. Lyme, NH: Smith and Kraus.

Cole, T., & Chinoy, H. K. (1970). *Actors on acting*. New York: Crown Publishers.

Cuban, L. (1982, October). Persistent instruction: The high school classroom, 1900–1980. *Phi Delta Kappan*, pp. 113–118.

———. (1984). *How teachers taught: Constancy and change in American classrooms*. New York: Longman.

———. (1990). Reforming again, again, and again. *Educational Researcher*, 19, 1, pp. 3–13.

Eisner, E. (1979). *The educational imagination: On the design and evaluation of school programs*. New York: Macmillan.

Gibboney, R. A. (1994). *The stone trumpet: A story of practical school reform 1960–1990*. Albany: State University of New York Press.

Jackson, P. W. (1968). *Life in classrooms*. New York: Holt, Rinehart and Winston.

Lee, K. (1993). Transcendence as an aesthetic concept: Implications for curriculum. *Journal of Aesthetic Education*, 27, 1, pp. 75–82.

May, W. (1993). Teaching as a work of art in the medium of curriculum. *Theory into Practice*, 32, 4, pp. 210–18.

Moore, S. (1960). *The Stanislavski system*. New York: Viking Press.

————. (1991). *Stanislavski revealed.* New York: Applause.

Pineau, E. L. (1994). Teaching is performance: Reconceptualizing a problematic metaphor. *American Educational Research Journal*, 31, 1, pp. 3–25.

Stanislavski, K. (1936). *An actor prepares.* (E. R. Hapgood, Trans.) New York: Theatre Arts.

————. (1948). *My life in art.* (J.J. Robbins, Trans.). New York: Theatre Arts.

————. (1949). *Building a character.* (E. R. Hapgood, Trans.). New York: Theatre Arts.

————. (1961). *Creating a role.* (E. R. Hapgood, Trans.). New York: Theatre Arts.

Van Manen, M. (1991). *The tact of teaching.* Albany, NY: State University Press.

Chapter Seventeen

Educational Reform or Corporate Agenda? State Takeover of Detroit's Public Schools

Monte Piliawsky

> With few exceptions, discussions of school reform have ignored the consequences of poverty and racial isolation on attempts to improve America's inner city schools.
>
> —*Jean Anyon (1997)*

On March 26, 1999, with all 13 House members from Detroit voting against the bill, the Republican-dominated Michigan state legislature took control of Detroit's public school system from the city's African American voters (McConnell & Christoff, 1999). Ostensibly the state legislature transferred governance of the school board from the 11-member, locally elected Detroit Board of Education, to Detroit Mayor Dennis Archer, who appoints six of the seven members of the new "re-form" board (Heinlein, Harmon, & French, 1999). However, the state, not the city, actually controls Detroit public schools (Gregg, 2000).

The Detroit school board's seventh member, appointed by the gover-nor, holds a veto over the board's overriding task of appointing an all-powerful chief executive officer. As the *Detroit News* put it, the "law-makers handed [Republican Governor John Engler] a trump card over Mayor Dennis Archer in the selection of Detroit's school reform czar" (Hornbeck, 1999).

Several subsequent actions demonstrate that the state legislature and governor thoroughly control the Detroit school board. In May 1999, the Michigan state legislature waived its own unanimity stipulation in select-ing the CEO, allowing the Detroit school board to appoint David Adamany, the white president of Wayne State University between 1982 and 1999, to be the interim CEO for Detroit schools (Harmon, 1999). In December 1999, the legislature passed a bill applying only to the city of Detroit, which prohibits school administrators with the rank of department head through principal from belonging to unions (Grigg, 1999).

Significantly, on January 18, 2000, the governor's representative, state Treasurer Mark Murray, the only white member of the Detroit school board, exercised his absolute veto power (Harmon, 2000). Murray overturned a vote of five to zero (and one abstention) by the other six school board members in support of John Thompson, superintendent of the Tulsa, Oklahoma, schools, to succeed Adamany as the permanent CEO of the Detroit schools (Harmon & Cohen, 2000). The headline in the *Detroit Free Press* read, "Engler's Man Bars New Schools' CEO" (Walsh-Sarnecki, 2000). Thus, Michigan followed the design of a growing number of state legislatures, mostly Republican-dominated, which have taken control of large, troubled urban school districts. These cities include Chicago (1995); Boston (1996); Newark (1996); Washington, D.C. (1996); Baltimore (1996); Hartford (1997); and Cleveland (1998) (Arasim, 1999). This essay examines whether the state takeover of Detroit public schools represents an attempt to provide genuine equal educational opportunity for inner-city students, or instead, a public relations strategy to advance the interests of the corporate community.

State Takeover in Detroit

"Few places in the country offer a better perspective [than Detroit] on the interaction between industrial capitalism and the politics of class and race" (Mirel, 1999). Detroit is the poorest major United States city, as well as the largest predominantly African American city in the United States, with a Black-American population of 83% (Hornbeck & Harmon, 1999). The ninth-largest school district in the nation, Detroit public schools enrolled 182,332 pupils in 263 schools in the fall of 1998— 91.3% of whom were African American, compared to 4.3 percent white (Detroit System, 1999).

Detroit has the lowest median household income of any large city in the United States, with 44% of public school pupils living in poverty and 70% receiving school lunches free or at reduced prices (Detroit System,1999). Finally, Detroit is the nation's third most racially segregated large city, behind Atlanta and Cleveland (Brand-Williams, Cohen, & Puls, 1999). In sum, the problems now facing Detroit typify those besetting other large, urban school districts in the United States: "declining enrollments, aging and deteriorating physical plant, high unemployment, relatively small tax base and children who are regularly confronted by violence, drugs and poverty" (Addonizio, 1999, p. 7).

For a third of a century, scholars have debated the reasons for the presumed decline in urban public education in the United States. This controversy is framed by the landmark study, Equality of Educational Opportunity (Coleman, 1966), which concluded that characteristics of students' own home backgrounds and those of other students in their school more adequately explain differences in achievement levels than do educational resources or school environments. Coleman asserted:

> Schools bring little influence to bear on a child's achievement that is independent of his background and general social context;...inequalities imposed on children by their home, neighborhood, and peer environment are carried along to become the inequalities with which they confront adult life at the end of school. (Coleman, 1966, p. 325)

Conservatives have used the Coleman report to question the utility of additional spending to improve public education, pointing instead to family values, cultural norms, and so-called "higher standards" to achieve positive educational outcomes (Gross & Gross, 1985; Chubb & Moe, 1990; Oldenquist, 1983). To illustrate, in his recent essay, "What No School Can Do," James Traub (2000) observed, "Labor economists have had a field day proving that school spending is not correlated with school achievement" (p. 56).

On the other hand, left-leaning "revisionist" scholars have relied on Coleman's findings "to bolster their arguments that public schools are a tool of American capitalism, and that "most reform efforts... [are] superficial" (Mirel, 1973; Katz, 1972). If, as revisionists Samuel Bowles and

Herbert Gintis (1976) claim, schools do not mitigate the power of family influences in determining academic performance, then the result of public education is "to justify and reproduce inequality rather than correct it." Accordingly, revisionists like Christopher Jencks (1972) have adopted the radical stance that since schools only pass on and legitimize inequality, the only solution is a socialist-style redistribution of income. In the debate with conservatives about the underlying function of public schools, the author subscribes to the revisionist position.

The rationale behind the current movement for state takeovers of urban school boards is consistent with the educational philosophy of conservatives. Historian Diane Ravitch (1974) contends that, through the 1930s, American public schools, with their rigorous core curriculum, offered "unprecedented social and economic mobility" to "the descendants of the miserably poor European immigrants." However, according to conservatives, since the 1930s, urban schools have softened their curricula and lowered standards and expectations for the sake of access and social adjustment, thus denying students of color in the last two generations the quality of education accorded their immigrant predecessors (Ravitch, 1983; Labaree, 1988).

The reason for state takeovers of inner-city schools is the emerging conviction by conservatives that school districts controlled by "old-timer insiders" are unlikely to contain the characteristics of "good" schools, particularly a "rigorous regimen of academic courses" (Angus & Mirel, 1999). According to this logic, a "reform" school board composed of strong leaders from outside, and presumably not beholden to the teacher's union, would be free to make the necessary, but unpopular, decisions to remedy the school district's educational problems (Moorlehem, 1999). As Michigan governor, Republican John Engler, put it in February 1999:

> The problem is not the kids. The problem is the system. It is broken. It is corrupt. It's not a matter of resources. It's a matter of management. (Engler, 1999, p. A1)

During the 1999 Michigan legislative debates, lawmakers favoring the state takeover of Detroit public schools, such as Senate Majority Leader Dan DeGrow, argued that the low performances of Detroit students on state tests and students' alarmingly high dropout rates warranted drastic action (Gray, 1999). In addition, supporters such as Senator Virgil Smith, minority party leader from Detroit, stressed the need to attract new companies to the Detroit area, observing that "without quality public schools, investments in the city will not pay off" (Ortiz, 1999, p. A7).

Moreover, Detroit business leaders hoped that better schools would reduce their heavy expense for retraining employees. According to Dave Bing, chair of one of the largest African American owned businesses in the United States, a 1,000-employee manufacturer of auto parts, corporations effectively are being double taxed:

> It's unfortunate that those of us who are in business to make money...have to go through the cost of extensive training that's necessary to get a good employee....It's unfortunate that we have to once again expend the kind of resources that we thought our taxes were doing. ("Businesses," 1999, p. A14)

In rebuttal, opponents of the proposed state takeover contended that it was an undemocratic denial of voting rights to alter the procedure for selecting school board members from elective to appointive without the approval of Detroit residents (Bell, 1999). Expressing the sentiment of several other lawmakers, Representative Gary Peters exclaimed, "I don't believe that you can argue for local control in every city in the state of Michigan, yet carve out an exception for the city of Detroit" (Christoff, 1999, p. A6). As a reporter from the *New York Times* put it, "it smacks of racism for a white Governor and all-white Republican majorities in the state House and Senate to be making decisions for a city" (Bradsher, 1999) where three-fourths of the residents and nine-tenths of the public school students are African American. On July 15, 1999, interim CEO Adamany presented a preliminary School Improvement Plan for Detroit Public Schools. The program included the following eight major elements (Adamany, 1999):

- reduced class sizes in grades K-3 to a range of 13 to 17 students;
- prescribed standards-based core curriculum and instructional program;

- national standardized grade-level tests in core curricular subjects administered at least eight times each school year;
- social promotions ended, with grade-level performance on tests required for promotion to the next grade;
- required summer school for students who do not show grade-level mastery at the end of the academic year;
- school uniform policy for all schools;
- substantial merit bonuses for all personnel (teachers, staff, and principals) in schools that meet district student attendance and test score targets;
- closing of schools that chronically fail to meet student attendance and test scores targets;
- replacing those schools with charter schools.

In terms of pedagogy, the Detroit School Improvement Plan relies on the standards-based approach to school reform, which encompasses "comprehensive benchmarks in core disciplines, curriculum frameworks based on those benchmarks to guide teaching, and assessment systems to help schools continuously reorganize and critique their instruction" (Asher, Fruchter, & Berne, 1996, p. 87). The heart of the proposed Detroit reform program is regular monitoring of student mastery of a system-wide, highly specific, standardized core curriculum through frequent formalized testing. A key element in the program is the linking of merit pay—perhaps more accurately termed production bonuses or profit-sharing—to the improvement of student MEAP scores on a schoolwide basis. The overall goal of the Detroit plan is to produce graduates with skills that make them job-ready.

A Historical Precedent

Assuring a work-ready labor supply has been a constant priority on corporate America's educational agenda. Accordingly, the current state takeover movement can best be understood in light of the major drive of state intervention, during the Progressive era, designed to ensure elite control of America's urban school boards (Cremin, 1961). Indeed, revisionist scholars "trace the problems of urban school systems to the actions of upper-class, business-oriented reformers who, in the late nineteenth and early twentieth centuries, transformed urban school systems in order to satisfy the needs of American capitalism" (Mirel, 1973, p. xiv).

Specifically, between 1890 and 1915, financiers and corporate executives called for state legislative involvement in urban public schools, which were controlled by working-class, immigrant politicians (Cohen, 1964). In language that still resonates with these issues today, revisionist historian David Nasaw explained the logic of other reformers, who alleged:

> It was the fault of neighborhood board members...that adolescent boys were not staying in school long enough to learn 'how to work'....The immigrants and their school boards were held directly accountable for juvenile delinquency, illiteracy, and aimlessness. The schools were failing, and the problem was one of poor management. The solution was to fire the old managers and replace them with new ones. (Nasaw, 1979, p. 109)

At the turn of the century, in virtually every large city, the reform coalition persuaded gerrymandered state legislatures to replace the ward-based election system with small school boards, chosen through nonpartisan, at-large (city-wide) voting districts (Spring, 1997). As a result, the percentage of businessmen and professionals on most of the restructured urban school boards in American cities increased dramatically, from roughly 10% to 75% (Counts, 1927). Moreover, the basic authority in educational policy in most key areas, from teacher certification to curriculum, shifted away from local school boards to state legislatures (Tyack, 1974; Cronin, 1973).

Revisionist scholars further argue that besides placing power in the hands of elites, "turn-of-the-century school reform...reproduced social inequality through biased testing and tracking procedures, and socialized children into the norms and values of a bureaucratized, corporate society" (Mirel, 1973, p. xiv). Surmising that "most of the new [immigrant] students entering high school were...incapable of thriving in the traditional curriculum," states established a new three-tier curriculum based on the tracking principle (Tyack & Cuban, 1995, p. 52).

In this arrangement, immigrant and working-class students received industrial schooling, the 50% of the nation's children whom the Committee on Industrial Education of the National Association of Manufacturers in 1912 referred to as "concrete, or hand-minded children...who can only with extreme difficulty and then imperfectly, learn from abstractions on the printed page" (quoted in Nasaw, 1979, p. 109). The business community hoped that industrial education for future factory workers would allow the United States to compete successfully with Germany in an ever-expanding export market (Graham, 1974).

Move the historical clock up three-quarters of a century. In the 1980s, business elites, reiterating this same concern about the loss of U.S. competitiveness in international trade with Germany (and Japan), argued that the remedy for economic decline was higher academic standards (Murphy, 1990; Berube, 1994). Although the warning in the National Comission on Excellence in Education's highly influential report, A Nation at Risk, of a "rising tide of mediocrity" (p. 5) was not explicit, criticisms about declining academic performance were primarily directed at low-income students of color and at their urban schools.

In the spirit of A Nation at Risk, the current movement for state takeovers of urban schools expresses the worries of business interests that poor schooling in large inner cities leads to costly unemployment, higher crime rates, and an underproductive work force, resulting in reduced corporate profits. The rationale is that economic competitiveness requires workers with greater competence in the basic skills, as well as the personal discipline and work ethic to perform the necessary work. As Louis Gerstner, CEO of IBM, puts it:

> Just as the original industrial revolution 'dumbed-down' work, making it simple and less complex, the modern technology-based manufacturing process 'smartens up' work, requiring more skilled workers....The remedy is straightforward: more and better education. (Gerstner, Semerad, Doyle, & Johnston, 1994, pp. 10–11)

It may be that the educational agenda of business, to maintain a work-ready labor supply, is a symbiotic one, good for both employers and employees. Perhaps, an education in basic skills leading "only" to work readiness represents an improvement in the lives of inner-city students, coming from deeply distressed situations. It may be that the advance up the occupational hierarchy for some among the most disadvantaged will require generational steps, just as one century ago the advance for many immigrants in the United States took place in steps over several generations.

Still, as progressive educators suggest, merely upgrading the basic skills in literacy and numeracy of inner-city students, the stated goal of corporate leaders, may relegate these youngsters to the low-paying employment classifications. In economist Robert Reich's terms, these jobs are "routine production service," such as assembly-line or repetitive data entry work, and "in-person service" jobs, such as janitors, hotel, restaurant, and hospital workers (Reich, 1991).

In balance, the author suggests that the fundamental goal which corporate America envisions for today's urban students, many of whom are persons of color, resembles its educational agenda of one hundred years ago for immigrants: to create a docile, compliant, punctual work force possessing the rudimentary skills to perform low paying jobs near the bottom rung of the employment ladder. According to Anyon, "the poor, immigrant, and native, do not seem to be valued as part of the economy—despite corporate protestations to the contrary" (Anyon, 1997, p. xiv).

Assessing the Detroit School Takeover

The justification offered for the 1999 state takeover of Detroit's public schools was that the poor academic performance of local students warranted such draconian action. The issue of whether the MEAP standardized tests is a valid measure of student academic performance is a complicated one, largely outside the purpose of this essay (Ohanian, 1999; Kohn, 1999; Brooks & Brooks, 1999). However, two responses to the state's claim deserve mention. First, an examination of the MEAP scores shows that Detroit is by no means the worst school district in Michigan.

As indicated in Table 1 (p. 278), the scores of Detroit's poor, overwhelmingly African American, fourth-grade students on the 1998 MEAP reading tests, the year before the state takeover of Detroit public schools, were *only slightly below the statewide average,* with 52.6 percent of Detroit students scoring satisfactory/proficient, compared to 58.6 percent of students statewide. (In 1997, the corresponding gap on students statewide. (In 1997, the corresponding gap on fourth-grade MEAP reading tests was only 2.3 percentage points: 46.7% for Detroit students, compared to 49.0% statewide.)

Table 1: Comparison of 1998 MEAP Scores in Reading for 4th Grade, 7th Grade, and 11th Grade Students in Detroit Public School District and Michigan Statewide (Percent Passing)

	4th Grade	7th Grade	11th Grade
Michigan Statewide	58.6	48.8	58.9
Detroit School District	52.6	32.2	31.8
Difference	-6.0	-16.6	-27.1

Source: David Adamany, "Detroit Public Schools School Improvement Plan," 19 January 2000, Appendix.

Indeed, on the 1998 reading test, Detroit's fourth-grade students actually outscored the students in 240 out of 554 school districts in Michigan, placing seventeenth among the 34 school districts in Wayne County, which, other than the Detroit school district, are overwhelmingly white. In a similar fashion, in the 1998 MEAP science tests for fifth graders, Detroit's students outscored their counterparts in 231 of the state's 554 school districts (*Detroit Public Schools*, 1999).

In actuality, Detroit fourth graders perform startlingly better than might be expected, given their extremely low socioeconomic status. In fact, in 1998, the *Detroit Free Press* conducted a study of the MEAP scores, factoring in the socioeconomic makeup of the school districts (Moorlehem, Walsh-Sarnecki, & Robles, 1998). For each of the school districts in the five county metropolitan Detroit area—Livingston, Macomb, Oakland, Washtensaw, and Wayne—the actual fourth-grade combined MEAP scores for reading and math were juxtaposed to "projected" scores—the figures that would be expected on the basis of the socioeconomic composition of the student population in a school district. Although only 38.9% of Detroit students were projected to pass the

MEAP tests, in fact, 58.6% did so. The discrepancy of +19.7 percentage points for the Detroit school district exceeded that of any of the other 98 school districts in southeast Michigan!

As indicated in Table 1, beginning in middle school, the academic performance of Detroit students declines steadily, with the gap between the MEAP scores for Detroit students and the statewide average widening as students advance educationally. For example, on the 7th-grade reading test, Detroit students in 1998 placed only 29th out of 34 school districts in Wayne County (*Detroit News*, May 1999, p. B6; Hornbeck, March 1999). This progressive decline in MEAP scores and presumably educational achievement among Detroit students as they progress from elementary school to high school remains a serious concern.

Another cardinal tenet in revisionist thought is that education does not exist in isolation, as a separate component in a person's life. As impoverished inner-city youngsters, like those in Detroit, approach their teen years, external social factors related to living in poverty inhibit their physical, social, emotional, and intellectual development, resulting in low school achievement (Lipman, 1998; Henig, Hula, Orr, & Pedescleaux, 1999).

Poor health becomes evident in the lives of many low-income, inner-city youngsters during their preteen years. Constant pain produced by physical problems—bad teeth, chronic diseases like asthma, and inadequate nutrition—gradually erodes the energy and aspirations of these youngsters (Nossiter, 1995). Additional societal factors that undercut academic achievement are responsibility for siblings at home, parents unable to help with school work, and negative peer pressure that replaces the more positive socializing agents of family, school, and church (Eccles, Midgley, Wigfield, & Buchanan, 1993). According to Anyon (1997):

> The concentration effects of poverty and racial isolation in urban ghettoes—the many generations of inadequate education and employment opportunities, and a long-term lack of resources for healthy and productive living for adults—results in malnutrition, prenatal and childhood disease, emotional trauma, lack of material resources, neglect and sometimes abuse in children's lives. (p. 160)

The cumulative impact over time of the social ills of poverty and declining health steadily erodes students' determination and hope. Arguably, the resulting sense of hopelessness is a logical, rational conclusion, attending students' growing awareness of their relative deprivation and limited life chances (Fine, 1991). In *Savage Inequalities*, educator Jonathan Kozol (1991) describes how, at about age 11, some inner-city youngsters develop a keen sense of personal failure:

> Children, of course, don't understand at first that they are being cheated. They come to school with a degree of faith and optimism, and they often seem to thrive during the first few years....By fifth or sixth grade, many children demonstrate their loss of faith by staying out of school....The route from truancy to full-fledged dropout is direct and swift. (pp. 57–58)

Conclusion

Consistent with the analytical framework of revisionists, the author believes that the present movement of states to take over urban school districts is the wrong prescription based on an incorrect diagnosis. Even though Detroit is both the poorest and the third most segregated large city in the United States, the emerging blueprint for educational change in Detroit, the School Improvement Plan of 2000, does not even mention poverty or racial isolation. Jonathan Kozol's 1991 critique applies forcefully to the present Detroit school reform plan:

> None of the national reports I saw made even passing reference to inequality or segregation. Low reading scores, high dropout rates, poor motivation—symptomatic matters—seemed to dominate discussion. (p. 3)

The state takeover initiative appears to replicate both the political goals and the educational design of its predecessor drive one hundred years ago. While the target of the former crusade was the immigrant-based school board which allegedly did not keep adolescent boys in school long enough to become obedient factory workers, the current movement blames predominantly African American school boards for the high school dropout rate of inner-city students of color.

A striking resemblance between the two state takeovers movements is the leading role of the business community. The early twentieth century reformers implemented a new curriculum in which immigrant and working-class youngsters, the "hand-minded children," were tracked into courses of industrial education. Similarly, the current state takeover effort stresses a basic skills educational program.

Apparently, the overriding motivation for the corporate sector, the prime mover in the present state takeover effort, is to create a more positive public image for inner cities. Then, as this argument continues, business would be better able to recruit talented employees to fill the highly skilled positions in their companies, and current middle-class residents would stay put, allowing the city's tax base to stabilize. According to Thomas J. Bray (1999), editorial page editor for the *Detroit News*:

> But the real test for Detroit and other cities is whether they can get middle-class families, not just a few Gen X-ers and empty nesters, to move in—or at least, if they are not already Detroit residents, not to move out. And nothing could be much more important to the outcome of that test than that Detroit offer a good education in decent schools. (p. B8)

Revisionists David Berliner and Bruce Biddle (1995), authors of *The Manufactured Crisis*, persuasively argue that the current wave of school reform, based on the business model of high content and performance standards, likely will prove insufficient over the long haul, without "opportunities to learn" standards that address the core problems of poverty and racial isolation. Berliner and Biddle (1995) explain:

> How will content and performance standards raise the scores of these children when they know, in their hearts, they have been abandoned by society?...While critics find it easier to deal with content and performance demands than with poverty; hopelessness, and inequities in school funding, school improvement cannot begin without opportunity-to-learn standards. In the end, it is impoverishment of the spirit of our young people that is our real challenge. (p. 14)

The author agrees with revisionists that the corporate agenda proposed in the current movement of state takeovers of urban school districts does not constitute genuine educational reform. Instead, it falls under the rubric of what Larry Cuban (1992) nearly two decades ago labeled "the myth of a corporate formula to save the schools." Although school "reform" as promoted by Michigan's takeover of Detroit schools may furnish business with a work-ready labor supply, it gives inner-city children the "back seat on the United States society bus."

For the past half century, school conservatives have equated "liberty" with *local* school district rights in opposition to the powers of state government. Conservatives have resisted school desegregation remedies on the ground that interdistrict plans threaten local government. Similarly, for conservatives, "when equal funding is the issue...the sanctity of district borders becomes absolute" (Kozol, 1991, p. 211). It is ironic, if not downright hypocritical, for conservative Republicans, traditionally local-control advocates, to call the 1998 Michigan takeover of the local school district in Detroit a "reform."

References

Adamany, D. (1999, July 15). *Detroit schools: Preliminary school improvement plan.*

Addonizio, M.F. (1999). Public education in Michigan: An overview. *Detroit Orientation Institute: Background Materials.* Detroit: Wayne State University.

Angus, D., & Mirel, J. (1999, May 30). Changing curriculum must be focused on Detroit's reforms. *Detroit News,* p. B7.

Anyon, J. (1997). *Ghetto schooling: A political economy of urban educational reform.* New York: Teachers College Press.

Arasim, L. (1999, January/February). *States' intervention in school districts.* Report prepared by State Fiscal Agency, Michigan State Legislature.

Asher, C., Fruchter, N., & Berne, R. (1996). *Hard lessons: Public schools and privatization.* New York: The Twentieth Century Fund.

Bell, D. (1999, March 25). House, senate reach school takeover compromise, *Detroit Free Press,* p. A1.

Berliner, D.C., & Biddle, B.J. (1973). Standards amidst uncertainty and inequality, *The School Administrator,* 5, May, p. 42.

———. (1995). *The manufactured crisis: Myths, fraud, and the attack on America's public schools.* Reading, MA: Addison-Wesley.

Berube, M. (1994). *American school reform: Progressive, equity, and excellence movements, 1883–1993.* Westport, CT: Praeger.

Bowles, S., & Gintis, H. (1976). *Schooling in capitalist America: Educational reform and the contradictions of economic life.* New York: Basic Books.

Bradsher, K. (1999, March 5). Mayor is step closer to control of Detroit schools. *New York Times,* p. A10.

Brand-Williams, O., Cohen, J.S., & Puls, M. (1999, November 5). Segregation has Detroit in iron grip. *Detroit News,* p. A1.

Bray, T.J. (1999, April 11). The Milwaukee school reform model, *Detroit News*, p. B8.

Brooks, M.G., & Brooks, J.G. (1999). The courage to be constructivist. *Educational Leadership*, 57, November, pp. 18–24.

Businesses plead for overhaul. (1999, February 21). *Detroit News*, p. A14.

Christoff, C. (1999, March 3). Senate passes school plan, *Detroit Free Press*, p. A6.

Chubb, J.E., & Moe, T.M. (1990). *Politics, markets and American schools*. Washington, D.C.: Brookings Institution.

Cohen, S. (1964). *Progressives and urban school reform*. New York: Teachers College Press.

Coleman, J. (1966). *Equality of educational opportunity*. Washington, D.C.: U.S. Government Printing Office.

Counts, G.S. (1927). *The social composition of boards of education: A study in the social control of public education*. Chicago: University of Chicago Press.

Cremin, L. (1961). *The transformation of school: Progressivism in American education, 1876–1957*. New York: Vintage.

Cronin, M. (1973). *The control of urban schools: Perspectives on the power of educational reformers*. New York: Free Press.

Cuban, L. (1992). The corporate myth of reforming public schools. *Phi Delta Kappan*, 72.

Detroit public schools: A portrait of facts—dispelling the myths. (1999, January 27). Detroit Teachers Union.

Detroit system snapsho.t (1999, February 21). *Detroit News*, p. A13.

Eccles, J., Midgley, C., Wigfield, A., & Buchanan, C. (1993, February 9). Development during adolescence: Impact of stage-environment fit on young adolescents' experiences in schools and in families. *American Psychologist,* 48, pp. 90–101.

Engler: Give Detroit schools to Archer. (1999, February 9). *Oakland Press*, p. A1.

Fine, M. (1991). *Framing dropouts: Notes on the politics of urban public high school.* Albany: State University of New York Press.

Gerstner, Jr., L.V., Semerad, R.D., Doyle, D.P., and Johnston, W. (1994). *Reinventing education: Entrepreneurship in America's public schools.* New York: Dutton.

Graham, P. (1974). *Community and class in American education, 1865–1918.* New York: John Wiley.

Gray, K. (1999, March 3). Engler plan to oust school board sails through Senate, *Oakland Press*, p. A7.

Gregg, R.G. (2000, May 31). Districts fight to stay in control of schools, *Detroit News*, p. C1.

Grigg, B.G. (1999, December 1). House vote brings racism charge, *Detroit News*, p. A1.

Gross, B. & Gross, R. (Eds.). (1985). *The great school debates.* New York: Simon and Schuster.

Harmon, B. (1999, May 13). Adamany on track for CEO, *Detroit News*, p. A1.

———. (2000, January 19). Schools search starts over, *Detroit News*, p. A1.

Harmon, B., & Cohen, J.S. (2000, January 20). Feuding stalls school reform, *Detroit News*, p. A1.

Heinlein, G., Harmon, B., & French, R. (1999, March 3). Takeover heads to House, *Detroit News*, p. A1.

Henig, J.R., Hula, R.C., Orr, M., & Pedescleaux, D.S. (1999). *The color of school reform: Race, politics, and the challenge of urban education.* Princeton, NJ: Princeton University Press.

Hornbeck, M. (1999, March 26). Engler keeps grip on reform, *Detroit News*, sec. p. Al.

Hornbeck, M. (1999, June 6). Charter schools fall short of expectations, *Detroit News*, p. A11.

Hornbeck, M., & Harmon, B. (1999, March 21). Reform can work in big city schools, *Detroit News and Free Press*, p. A1.

Jencks, C. (1972). *Inequality: A reassessment of the effect of family and schooling in America.* New York: Harper and Row.

Katz, M. (1972). *Class, bureaucracy and schools.* New York: Praeger.

Kohn, A. (1999). *The schools our children deserve: Moving beyond traditional classrooms and tougher standards.* Boston: Houghton Mifflin.

Kozol, J. (1991). *Savage inequalities: Children in America's schools.* New York: Harper Perennial.

Labaree, D. (1988). *The making of an American high school: The credentials market and the central high school of Philadelphia, 1838–1939.* New Haven, CT: Yale University Press.

Last chance for reform. (1999, May 30). *Detroit News,* p. B6.

Lipman, P. (1998). *Race, class, and power in school restructuring.* Albany: State University of New York Press.

McConnell, D., & Christoff, C. (1999, March 26). School reform now needs names. *Detroit Free Press,* p. A1.

Mirel, J. (1973). *The rise and fall of an urban school system, Detroit, 1907–81* (2nd ed.) Ann Arbor: The University of Michigan Press.

Moorlehem, T.V. (1999, February 23). School takeover is no guarantee. *Detroit Free Press,* p. A1.

Moorlehem, T.V., Walsh-Sarnecki, P., & Robles, J.J. (1998, May 7) MEAP scores soar—but are they for real. *Detroit Free Press,* p. B3.

Murphy, J. (1990). *The educational reform movement of the 1980s: Perspectives and cases.* Berkeley: McCurchan.

Nasaw, D. (1979) *Schooled to order: A social history of public schooling in the United States.* Oxford: Oxford University Press.

National Commission on Excellence in Education, *A nation at risk: The imperative of educational reform.* Washington, D.C.: Government Printing Office.

Nossiter, A. (1995, September 5). Asthma common and on rise in the crowded South Bronx. *New York Times*, p. A1.

Ohanian, S. (1999). *One size fits few: The folly of educational standards*. Portsmouth, NH: Heiemann.

Oldenquist, A. (1983). The decline of American education in the '60s and '70s, *American Education,* 199 (May): pp. 12–18.

Ortiz, M. (1999, February 26). Detroit senator breaks from party ranks. *Detroit Free Press*, p. A7.

Ravitch, D. (1974). *The great school wars: New York City, 1805–1973*. New York: Basic Books.

————. (1983). *The troubled crusade: American education 1945–1980*. New York: Basic Books.

Reich, R. (1991) *The work of nations: Preparing ourselves for 21st-century capitalism*. New York: Alfred Knopf.

Spring, J. (1997). *The American school: 1642–1996*. New York: McGraw-Hill.

Traub, J. (2000, January 16). What no school can do. *New York Times Magazine,* p. 56.

Tyack, D. (1974). *The one best system: A history of American urban education*. Cambridge, MA: Harvard University Press.

Tyack, D., & Cuban, L. (1995). *Tinkering toward utopia: A century of public school reform*. Cambridge, MA: Harvard University Press.

Walsh-Sarnecki, P. (2000, January 19). Engler's man bars new schools' CEO. *Detroit Free Press*, p. A1.

Chapter Eighteen

I Speak From the Wound in My Mouth: A Critical Response to a Confrontation with Institutionalized Racism

From Catalyst, to Creation, to Conference Presentation

The Co-Performers/Respondents

Carolyne J. White, Northern Arizona University
Clarence Shelley, University of Illinois, Champaign-Urbana
George Lowery, Roosevelt University
Nona Burney, Roosevelt University
Gerae Peten, Northern Arizona University

Artist's Statement

The following intentionally "messy text" (see Denzin, 1997) is my interpretation of the catalyst for a critical collage I created in response to an incident that began with an institutionalized racist remark in a graduate level seminar. This collage began as my final project in an Aesthetics and the Curriculum Course, and was subsequently performed at the 1999 American Educational Sociological Association Conference (AESA). My purpose here is *not* to attempt to provide a factual (what does that mean anyway?) account—I acknowledge that this is a one-sided, subjective interpretation, but rather to share this process with other social activists to encourage an increase in the use of experimental forms; which I believe have a better chance at promoting social change than traditional, scholarly texts. This work is self, politically, and morally critical. It is open to multiple interpretations depending on the lived experience of each reader or co-performer.

Catalysts

Statement made by an Asian student in a graduate level seminar:

> I teach the teachers I teach that you cannot take Rembrandt into an inner city classroom where students have only been introduced to graffiti.

E-mail received from professor following my critical challenge to the Asian student's comment:

> Mary, I am thinking about what our talk yesterday, and if indeed you feel that it is difficult for you to express your thoughts and reactions in ways that are acceptable to me (and to some other class members), I would be happy to make any other arrangements so you can still get credit for the class (by writing the assignments and papers and meeting with me to talk about readings and ideas individually). I talked with [the Asian Student] and know she had no problems with your response to her.

I also received e-mails from others who indicated they feel most uncomfortable with that. Most important, I as a teacher find it inacceptable [sic] in this classroom. I also realize the caring, passion and integrity which you bring to these issues and will be happy to work with you so you don't feel you have to compromise. I will be happy to accommodate you in different ways so you don't lose the credit for the course.

Creation

Following the receipt of the above e-mail, which I interpreted as an invitation to either respond in some artificial, ambiguous professor-defined manner or remove myself from the seminar and work with the professor outside of the classroom, I wrote a memorandum articulating my concerns to the head of the professor's department. I attached the professor's e-mail and my e-mailed response. On April Fool's Day, I met with the department head, who understood my position, and said the six words which continue to inspire my work: "Why don't you write about it?"

The incident, the professor's response, and the department head's advice caused an epiphany that has affected my approach to scholarship. I realized, with the clarity of an ice-cold bucket of water on the head, that arguments expressed in traditional scholarship, touting the efforts and accomplishments of African American artists, and so-called facts would not work as a final paper in this class. I decided to use an experimental form to argue for my work as an activist artist educator for social change specifically in inner city public schools, where some of the students in this course were either already teaching, or would teach in the future. Thanks to the department head's lead, I found Albert Murray's book, *The Blue Devils of Nada*. In it he talks about the "blues statement" as something created in response to a "traumatic situation," which also brings out the best in the creator of the work. For Murray these blues statements are as spiritually reaffirming as the beat of the human heart. I realized that when Murray defined the "blues statement, " he described what I had been doing for some time: "responding to traumatic situations creatively" (1996, pp. 5–6).

I spent the next six weeks playing the blues, pouring over texts, and visual images, and creating poetry. I made my scholarly selections operating on the same creative vibe that inspired me to write the seven original poems included in the collage. I did not articulate a theoretical framework. The theory is imbedded in the collage, along with the passion and outrage I felt as the only African American voice in the class:

Freedom
is an old joke
they tell at the Comedy Club
on amateur night
and everybody laughs
until the lights go out
and they can't see the person
sitting next to them. (Weems, 1999)

The following document, included in the collage, was shared as a handout during a roundtable discussion at the 1999 American Educational Research Association Conference (AERA):

Negora Phobia: Space Issues in University Settings

Negora Phobia
1) Fear of creating open space for discourse around issues of race;
2) Fear of entering open space for discourse around issues of race;
3) Fear of bridging the open space between you and an African American.

I would like to discuss an incident which highlighted the need to address issues of race and space in university settings. It deals with what happened when a professor did not create a safe space for discourse around issues of race for students in a graduate level seminar.

- **Type of space**: "Aesthetics and the Curriculum" graduate level seminar designed to teach current and future teachers how to incorporate the arts into their curricula.
- **Overview**: Professor's focus was on aesthetic appreciation and expression and their connections to individual life experiences through in-class discussions, field trips, and reading and writing assignments.
- As the only African American artist-educator with an inner city public school, and field experence background, I brought a unique perspective to this course which I shared in what I thought was an open space for critical inquiry and reciprocal learning.
- To be brief, everything was okay until I raised my voice to critically question the following institutionalized racist statement made by a miseducated Asian student: "I teach the teachers I teach that you cannot bring Rembrandt into an inner city classroom where the students have only been exposed to graffiti."

Space will not permit a full interpretation of what followed, but I note the following:

1. The professor accused me of backing the student into a corner (which I denied), of being too quick to shout "racism," of being angry (which I denied and she insisted I WAS).

2. She informed me that my behavior was unacceptable to her as the professor of the class.

3. My immediate, conditioned "white is right" reaction as a student and an African American confronted with the effluvium of institutionalized racism was to first offer to remove myself from the class (the professor expressed the hope that I would not leave) or to sit quietly until the end of the semester. I apologized for disrespecting her space, for making the Asian student feel bad (which it turns out she did not), for making the professor think I was angry. What I did not and will not apologize for was raising my voice to critically challenge an institutionalized racist remark.

4. I left at the end of the class, believing we had both been as honest as possible—the professor had offered to accommodate me based on my decision to remain or cease attending class, and expressed her care and respect for me, which I echoed, but which rang a bit hollow under the circumstances.

5. It was only later during a discussion with several of my peers that I began to process the full impact of the incident.

6. The next morning I received an e-mail from the professor informing me that several students had e-mailed her overnight expressing their discomfort with me. In short, she stated that my behavior was "unacceptable" and that I could either respond in a manner that was acceptable to her and some of the other students or get out, complete the course work, and receive a grade.

7. The professor was unable to recognize the student's institutionalized racist remark—and remains unable to do so but she was able to conclude that I was too quick to shout "racism."

I raise the following questions:

- How can you teach future teachers how to use the arts in the curriculum without creating a safe space for discussing issues of race and cultural relevancy?
- Why was there space for the consideration of the professor's feelings, the Asian students' feelings, and the white students' feelings, but not my feelings?
- When the opportunity presented itself for dialogue around the issue of race, why did the professor prohibit the discussion, then introduce it at the beginning of the next class when I was physically invisible and unable to enter the conversation?
- Is the professor aware that one of the strategies for silencing and devaluing people of color is to accuse them of being angry when they raise their voices?
- What will happen the next time a student of color enters this unsafe, closed academic space and raises her or his voice in a critically challenging manner?

In my work I always begin by openly discussing and stressing the importance of establishing a safe space for discourse and creativity for all students. This crucial step was not taken in this course—if it had been, the outcome may have mirrored the professor's constructivist approach to aesthetics by applying it to race, which is always in the space—acknowledged or not.

The collage includes 22 pages of visual images from a number of artists including Romare Bearden, who is famous for his visual collages, but since the Asian student's remark devalued graffiti, I used the incredible work of the late Afro-Caribbean artist Jean-Michel Basquiat as the frame for the collage. The following poem, my call and response to one of his paintings, honors his work:

Needles and Pins

"Mustang Sally, I think I'm gonna slow this mustang down. . ."

Chaotic-trap-capital-dis-H-hole and cube-shit-Afro-Haitian
swimming in a bone-fish-bowl

all his skin painted on walls-slats-stretch stuff,
teeth-dick-heads, H-deposits forming bone pockets every
place white gets in

he has one H-popeye that's not a black eye
no room at the inn

you have to put your nose in to see curiosity
killed, needle centers brain covers the crown
like a cap, all the rooms behind the eyes
get full of horses. (Weems, 1999)

Jean-Michel Basquiat
Untitled (Skull), 81 ½ x 69 1/4 inches
The Eli and Edythe L. Broad Collection,
Los Angeles

The Collaboration Rehearsal: Re-constructing the Script

Setting: Me and Carolyne's Hotel Room, 1:00 p.m.
Hotel Pontchartrain, AESA Conference, October 28th, 1999

Once Carolyne suggested writing a proposal to the AESA as a possible space for the presentation of this new work, a conversation with Norm Denzin reminded me of the need to be as concise as possible. I made myself re-visit the 70-page collage to find places where sections could be cut from each page of text.

When we came together to discuss the best way to co-perform the piece, their suggestions began to reshape the work. I originally envisioned the slide presentation as providing in-between visuals to the textual pieces, but Carolyne suggested using the visual images as backdrops. Nona added two important pieces when she suggested first, that we make a copy for each co-performer/respondent rather than pass one copy around to ensure a smoother delivery, and second, when she noted that there was a crucial piece of information missing from the collage: What did I say to the Asian student which the professor found so "inaccessible?" At first I resisted her comment, because I knew I hadn't done or said anything that was not totally appropriate, but when the other co-performers echoed her concern—I realized that the audience would not know if it was not said as part of the performance.

We decided that Nona would repeat the Asian student's remark "I teach the teachers I teach that you cannot bring Rembrandt into an inner city classroom where the students have only been exposed to graffiti" and I would respond: "What exactly do you mean by that? Can you tell by looking at my Black face that I've never been to an art museum? Your knowledge of African Americans and other students of color seems to all have been derived from textbooks, maybe you need some field experience. I think that one of the main problems with public school education today is that many of these teaches give up on our students before the first lesson is taught."

At 4:30 p.m. that same day, we were ready to perform. The slides were in order, and everyone knew their part in this collaboration. All that remained was to enter the improvisational space, place poster pages of text from the collage on the walls, art-gallery style, show the first slide: an original drawing of an African American woman, her wide-open mouth framed by drops of blood, by artist Mwansa Mandella; and play the song "Mustang Sally" sung by African American singer Wilson Picket, the mood music for the performance.

The Performance: From "I Speak" to "We Speak"

We were challenged by the heat in the room. For some reason it was Hell-hot and phone calls to hotel staff did not result in relief until the performance was in process. Nevertheless, we hurriedly tacked the posters to the walls, Carolyne displayed the collage cover on the projection screen, and I pumped up the volume on "Mustang Sally" for the audience. The vibe in the room was good. After about ten minutes I welcomed the audience, then asked my co-performers/respondents to introduce themselves, and while they did I took my position standing against the wall. Once the introductions were completed I began: "I speak from the wound in my mouth: A critical response to a confrontation with institutionalized racism in an Aesthetics and the Curriculum classroom."

The audience attention and silent participation in the performance were palpable—we held them for a 40 full minutes, and when we were finished—applause! I have no words to describe how this made me feel other than "incredible." As an experienced performer, I can't remember the last time I was nervous, but later had to admit to my colleagues that I was. Maybe it was because I was putting my personal/moral/political/and professional self on the line, and unlike my previous performances prior to becoming a doctoral candidate, the stakes were raised to another level. The bottom line is I was prepared for anything—harsh criticism, challenging questions, a lack of understanding—I was not prepared for what followed.

The Response

George: "It's a travesty to have educators of teachers harboring such values. Such an attitude could be perpetuated well into the future, because of the impact future teachers have on future generations. Over the next ten years, we will hire two million new teachers, who will influence generations for at least the next half-century."

Nona: It is distressing to hear that the places where teachers are being prepared to work with our children are closed to genuine dialogue on issues of race. I left the Cleveland City Schools after 27.65 years, and came to 'the academy' because I was tired of preservice people coming to my predominantly African American, inner city magnet school, and being surprised that the children were civil, learning was going on, and the environment was peaceful, even joyful. 'Who's teaching these people?' was my question. Racism is a pernicious, insidious disease that is destroying our society. How can it be eliminated if those who teach teachers to work with our children, will not confront it head on?

Carolyne: When I first heard of this experience, I was outraged and I felt a sense of responsibility because I had encouraged Mary to attend this university and because the professor is a friend. I have known this woman for several years and believe her to be a genuinely caring and well-intentioned person. This is indeed the nature of institutionalized racism. It is perpetuated by well-meaning individuals who don't know what they don't know. This doesn't in any way excuse her behavior; rather it serves to intensify my commitment to educate people, and to understand how they—and I—have been miseducated. We are engaged in a process of massive recovery that can't begin until beneficiaries of White privilege own the problem. Through my years as a White Traitor teaching to interrupt institutional racism, I have had to learn to accept the discomfort that emerges in the classroom as inevitable. Why wouldn't people be uncomfortable learning about how their behavior has harmed others? I have also learned that I need to help students understand that real learning is often uncomfortable. This is one of the things that struck me about Mary's experience—the professor's unwillingness to be uncomfortable or to have students be uncomfortable. I have learned that a sacred space needs to be created so people can express feelings of anger, frustration, disappointment, sadness, and love. Too often I believe those of us in the academy have learned to detach our feelings from our work. Mary's work is all about calling us to feel, feel, and act to tear down the walls of institutional racism. I am honored to have been part of this panel.

Shelley: Ms. Weems's work reminds us—who often need such reminders—of the awesome power of language—to hurt and to heal—to crush and to comfort. Her experiences tell us again that we teachers must be learners and that because we share this fragile space with many, we must honor the responsibilities that attend our professional privilege.

When Shelley asked the audience for questions and/or comments, accolades, outrage, curiosity, and interest in tapping into their own creativity were expressed in response after response. One white woman commented that she felt guilty, and wanted to know if when she listened to Miles Davis she was appropriating Black Art. I respected her honest comment, but was more than a little surprised. I responded by saying that all artists are influenced by all of the art they experience; appropriation occurs when the art of African American artists is co-opted, or stolen without acknowledgment and/or compensation.

This chapter is a political act. By existing, it challenges teacher education courses that exclude discussions about cultural relevancy, institutionalized racism, and language tolerance. It critiques aesthetic and the curriculum courses that devalue the so-called "primitive" art of nonwhite cultures, and value a so-called "high art" steeped in eurocentrism. As an activist artist-educator, I see no distinction between my socially active "artist" self and my socially active "academic" self. These words are social constructs that inhibit the possibilities that occur when space is created for conversations across these artificial boundaries. I end with a poem that reminds me of why it is important to struggle against all social injustice:

Opening

Racism is so personal
if it was a carcass
the stench would block
the nose of the world
and everybody would die

One billion pages printed
to support the myth
leak death over the fingertips
of scientific bullshit artists
working themselves into sweats
to meet the emancipation deadline

White power men wear their
Black face under judicial robes
making up new games with constantly
changing rules written in invisible ink

Injustice is so personal that the woman
with the bandage over her eyes keeps
trying to take a nosedive

Way back in time today
the little white lie is a giant
wearing shit covered shoes
looking for a beanstalk
to fall down

Truth is so personal
every time it doesn't make sense
I sleep a little easier. (Weems, 1999)

References

Denzin, N. (1997). *Interpretive ethnography: Ethnographic practices for the 21ˢᵗ Century.* London: Sage.

Murray, A. (1996). *The blue devils of Nada: A contemporary American approach to aesthetic statement.* New York: Pantheon Books.

Weems, M. (1999). Unpublished series of poems created for this critical collage through word improvisation, the catalyst being the same as Albert Murray discusses in his definition of the "Blues Statement." Titles: Needles and pins, Graffiti, She Could Sing,Turning Point, Freedom, What's Wrong With This Picture?, This evolution will not be televised.

Background Readings

Angelou, M. (1990). *I shall not be moved.* New York: Random House.

Blackwell, D. *Suite Basquiat.* Unpublished poem.

Bomani, A., & Books, B. (Eds.). (1992). *Paris connections: African American artists in Paris.* San Francisco, California: Q.E.D. Press.

Bresler, L., Stake, R., & Mabry, L. (1991). *Custom and cherishing.* Urbana: Council for Research in Music Education School of Music.

DeLuca, G., & Natov,R. (Eds.) (1987). *The lion and the unicorn: A critical journal of children's literature. Vol. II, no.1.* Baltimore, Maryland: John's Hopkins University Press.

Dewey, J. (1916). *Democracy and education.* New York: The Free Press.

Driskell, D.C. (Ed.). (1995). *African American visual aesthetics.* Washington: Smithsonian Institution Press.

Eisener, E. (1998). *The kinds of schools we need.* Portsmouth: Heineman.

Feagin, J.R., Vera, H., & Imani, N. (1996). *The agony of education: Black students at white colleges and universities.* New York: Routledge.

Gablik, S. (1991). *The re-enchantment of art.* New York: Thames and Hudson.

hooks, b. (1995). *Art on my mind: Visual politics*. New York: New Press.

Kozol, J. (1991). *Savage inequalities: Children in America's schools*. New York: Crown Publishers.

Ladson-Billings, G. (1994). *The dreamkeepers*. San Francisco: Jossey-Bass

Lewis, S., & Waddy, R.G. (Eds.). (1971). *Black artists on art. vol. 1*. Los Angeles: Contemporary Crafts.

Locke, A. (1936). *Negro art. Past and present*. Washington, D.C.: Associates in Negro Folk Education.

Lord, C. (Ed.). (1993). *The theater of refusal: Black art and mainstream criticism*. Irvine, CA: Regents of the University of California Fine Arts Gallery of the University of California.

Maher, F., & Thompson Tetreault, M.K. (1997). Learning in the dark: How assumptions of whiteness shape classroom knowledge. *Harvard Educational Review*. Vol. 67. No. 2.

Turner, R. (Ed.). (1993). *Faith Ringold: Portraits of women artists for children*. Boston, MA: Little Brown and Company.

Ulmer, G. (1989). *Teletheory: Grammatology in the age of video*. New York: Routledge.

Vangelisti, P. (1995). *The selected poems of Amira Baraka/Leroi Jones (1961-1995)*. New York: Marsilio Publishers.

Chapter Nineteen

Inquiry That Incites Insight

A. Keith Carreiro

> So it is the shadow of the experience of teaching that we pursue here, hoping that as we catch a glimpse of its distortions and of the ground on which it falls, mingling the human figure with its roots, cracks, curbs, and stairwells, we shall address what is hidden...
>
> — *Madeleine R. Grumet* (1988)

Initial Statement

This article briefly discusses with, and introduces to, readers an initial philosophical approach towards implementing innovative strategies and conceptual instructional tools that can be used in helping students initiate, maintain, enrich, and weave their senses of critical thinking and creative awareness into their own research and presentation-giving skills. The freedom to explore, a collaborative spirit, inspiration, and humor are all necessary elements that help infuse such an endeavor with accompanying qualities that help deepen one's reflective efforts of study. Aimed at fulfilling the standards presented by the Council of Learned Societies in Education (CLSE) (1998), the author believes, these standards help provide invaluable analytical tools to students and to other educational practitioners. Learning and mastering the interpretive, normative, and critical perspectives becomes indispensable in understanding, on personal and professional bases, the complex realms of experience in which we dwell and from which inquiry can be steeped in true insight into our educational worlds.

As the epigraph by Grumet (1988, p. 61) alludes to the attempt to catch the essential nature of the *experience of teaching* through the study of the *shadow* cast by its practice, so this article is an initial attempt to address and discover *what is hidden* behind this shadow. The author hopes to catch not only a glimpse of the teaching experience, but to conceptually "freeze frame" the complex phenomenon of teaching in order to philosophically examine what has been found within the ground of being which this frame has found. Thus, a conceptual map of the territory glimpsed will begin to be discussed here. It is a conceptual realm in which our best selves come to fruition in creating richly diverse intellectual options and nurturing organic structures that might be able to help catch the quicksilver potential inherent within all of us in the teaching-learning relationship. Perhaps in so practicing the reflection sought and yearned for here, we may turn the light of our thought and being onto more fertile ground. To invoke the potential of our senses, beliefs, awareness, dreams and goals for living better lives, we may evoke and awaken the age-long virtue in sharing the greatness of the human spirit with one another. Perhaps, the author profoundly wishes to touch, to seek, and to fulfill his hunger for releasing what he has been told all of his life about the benefits, myths, legacies, and traditions of all those aspects of what a liberal education has to bestow upon him and his fellow colleagues and sojourners.

This chapter is not meant to be complete; it aims at proposing an introductory overview about the experience and nature of human inquiry through the eyes and vision of an educational practitioner. It casts a prototypical net of thought into the ocean of teaching in hopes of catching some fair portion of the schools of fishlike entities swimming beneath his clouded understanding and vision. With such caveats given, this article aims at provoking discussion, thought, and feedback with its readers. Key generic, yet philosophically based, terms are used in an attempt to embrace the full phenomenon toward what Fuller (1972, p. 362) describes:

> By and large, man's [our] inertias are only overcome by virtue of his [our] own personal discoveries, discernment, and understanding of what it is that is happening to him [us].

The comments found in these pages, therefore, are limited to broad brushstrokes of the artist's written attempts to find deeper insight into what can be done to enrich his craft, and to attune him further to the domain of experiences in which he has participated in his profession. The verbal painting rendered is only a sketch, at best, and only may be of interest to others, for example, in the making of curriculum, in the designing and implementing of intellectual structures into classrooms, and in the desire for policymakers to help create for their fellow teachers, students, and parents an environment in which the human spirit has opportunities to blossom into the fullness of its metaphysical destiny and intellectual fortune.

Introduction

Critical discernment and consternation about declining writing skills and research abilities of undergraduate and graduate students (Madden & Lawrence, 1994) in the author's education courses (1999a) challenged him to create an alternative approach to teaching. This challenge made itself particularly visible in seeing students struggling with elementary thinking and writing tasks, as well as the difficulty in applying content to educationally and foundationally relevant contexts. In addition, not only were students seemingly bereft of research, writing, and presentation skills; they also showed a concomitant lack of passion, vigor and spirit in their classroom participation and daily preparation activities, as well as in their choice of major study and career goals toward becoming, or being, teachers. As a result of these observations, a new instructional direction was taken by designing a variety of heuristic tools to help offset these schooling and experience deficits. These conceptual devices, alternative thinking strategies, and student-generated topics of inquiry are now being used pedagogically for facilitation and coordination of classroom, course, college, university and professional requirements. They are primarily designed to inspire, even to ignite, and to incite[1] the full range of the teaching/learning phenomenon and process.

A basic premise of teaching in this chapter is that in order to encourage a person to learn, discover, understand, evaluate performance, and

solve problems, classroom instruction and individual guidance supplied
by the teacher must be modeled and actualized upon the same guiding
principles that the instructor follows. Having the freedom to explore and
the liberty to seek emergent knowledge inherent within the dynamics of
self, course curricula and classroom dynamics must flow unimpeded between and among the experiences of the teacher and students. To flower
fully in one's abilities to express his or her own intellectual self means
that the passion to explore ideas, to critically assess an individual's state
of being, and to release the imagination into a quest for meaning, requires that a truly democratic (Dewey, 1916/1966; Taylor, 1992) learning environment be established. Incorporating the structure and processes
of a democratic community within the classroom proffers the hope of an
enlightened citizenry.

> When the school introduces and trains each child of society into membership
> within such a little community, saturating him with the spirit of service, and
> providing him with the instruments of effective self-direction, we shall have the
> deepest and best guarantee of a larger society which is worthy, lovely and har-
> monious. (Dewey, 1959, p. 49)

Hence, metacognitive (internal reviewing) processes and methods
(Lee, 1998; Flavell, 1985, 1976), guided facilitative reflection, and instructional protocols steeped in the above-stated rationale help students
produce work and participate in their studies through more thoughtful,
intentional, and deliberative ways. Intuition, emotion, and cognition are
merged into a process wherein ideas are sought, broached, investigated,
and sifted more explicitly from self-determination, interest, and knowledge with those expressions of the scholarly, professional, and technical
communities around us (Phenix, 1964; Thelen, 1960). Hence, multiple
ways of researching and completing topics of inquiry are student-
generated. The manner in which students use alternative thinking strategies to generate research ideas also extends to their selecting, compiling,
and organizing their resources. Also sought by the instructor's guidance
is their best summative attempts in comprising key ideas and concepts
from their accumulated resources and linking them to significant course
curricula goals, learning outcomes, and lesson objectives.

Philosophical Grounding

This chapter is part of a continuing investigative effort on the part of this author to delineate innovative aspects of teaching into an area referred to as *revelatory teaching* (Carreiro, 1999b, 2000). While methodology and specific teaching strategies initially have been discussed in a separate paper (Carreiro, 1998), these teaching-learning aspects are not to be isolated from their philosophical grounding. It is this conceptual foundation that is the wellspring, or the source of ideation and emanation, of the teaching ideas presented in this chapter.

While it is not the intent of this chapter to cover a rigorous discussion of the major substantive and philosophical bases upon which this chapter draws, it is nevertheless important to state the framework or the perspective taken by the author. Conceptually speaking, there are five fundamental areas that this form of teaching holds and heuristically employs in a wide variety of reflective teaching strategies: (1) existential critique; (2) phenomenological depiction; (3) hermeneutical interpretation; (4) reflective evaluation; and (5) anagogical synaesthesia. While the terms used above are not, for the most part, familiar to general reader, they do serve to depict aspects of key principles, processes, dynamics, sensitivities, and understandings of inquiry that help align a teacher's relational approach to the individuals in his or her classes. This teaching-learning approach also is viewed by the author as being a synthesis of criticocreative processes (Carreiro, 1991). Equally, this philosophical outline centers the teacher upon certain existential and phenomenological perspectives, as well as being centered in process philosophy (Oliver & Gershman, 1989; Slattery 1992a, 1992b, 1989), that encourage temporal analysis of self-awareness and one's conscious appraisal of reality, knowledge, and value notions. This appraisal is done individually and extends in a complementary fashion to one's professional concerns as well. When vigorous study of all of these facets of being, personal and professional, continuously occurs, a baseline of understanding and familiarity with these experiences and phenomena of living explicitly is revealed. Using philosophical language to describe this inquiry experience and to frame the teacher's situational orientation further, it can be stated that the teacher dwells within the phenomenon of a proleptic ontology

(Whitehead, 1929/1967, 1933). This dwelling permeates inquiry, ideation, research and discussion with an understanding of reverence. "[T]he foundation of reverence is this perception, that the present holds within itself the complete sum of existence, backwards and forwards, that whole amplitude of time which is eternity" (Whitehead, 1929, p. 14).

Existential critique, practiced and modeled by the teacher, is offered to students. This critique is based upon the work not only of the well-known existentialists of the past, such as Kierkegaard (1944, 1954), Camus (1955, 1978), and Sartre (1947, 1956, 1976), for example, but on the educational conceptions and concerns raised by those scholars such as Greene (1978, 1988, 1991), and Grumet (1990, 1992), along with those voices of the reconceptualists (Pinar, 1988, 1989, 1992; Schwab, 1978, 1983; and Eisner, 1991) and postmodernists (Apple, 1982, 1989, 1990a, 1990b; McClaren 1991a, 1991b, 1993, 1994; Noddings, 1985, 1986, 1992; Walkerdine, 1985, 1988; and Giroux, 1992). Put briefly, existential critique realizes that humanity is in a dilemma and paradox of living not only by the mere fact of existence, but through institutional and bureaucratic systems that overwhelm individual uniqueness and one's private sense of being and meaning. These systems further erode into the life world of the individual, claiming more and more of one's energies, time, thought, and sense of purpose. Self-reflection is lessened in pursuit of surviving in a world dominated by outside-imposed political, socioeconomic, and cultural values. Thus, it is existentially important, especially from an educational sense, that learning environments be constructed wherein individuals are provided with teaching-learning support that encourages, sustains, and enhances personal and professional development.

This orientation, consequently, is contextually set as a result of self–directed, supported efforts by all those participating in the teaching-learning paradigm. Innovative teaching strategies become those involved with offering opportunities in releasing the potential and actual powers of learners and teachers. This release is accomplished in such a way that the roles of learners and teachers change back and forth through a dynamic interplay with what people bring to their classes and in what emerges in the curriculum and learning culture when these existential dynamics are engaged. Hopefully, these revelations are scaffolded (Vygotsky, 1934/1962) not only within the teaching/learning area described above as existential critique, but they are fully engaged by the instructor and learners in the other four listed areas also.

Through the use of mutually engaged, philosophical speculation, the purpose of such a pedagogy is to explore some of the contributing elements of teaching that help lead students and professor together in providing an environment wherein inquiry is not only welcomed, but steeped in an enriched motivational learning and teaching climate. Such teaching is resilient in all aspects of cognitive, affective, and psychomotor domains of educational activities. This resilience allows for instructional flexibility in more fruitfully seizing those moments of grace in teaching wherein understanding dawns, potential knowledge emerges, or both. In addition, this professional suppleness, if you will, provides an intellectual ambience that honors critical thinking while simultaneously challenging normative awareness. It also welcomes all students to contribute their unique backgrounds and individual perspectives to classroom discussions in order for them to achieve greater interpretive and sensitive discernment about educational issues as well as about themselves.

Tentative Conclusion/Aspired Implication

Hopefully, as initially explored in this article above, such relationally situated instruction seeks to create a teaching-learning climate wherein greater conceptual clarity can emerge through written assignments and oral discussions as a result of individual and group activities, along with the infusion of new technologically based teaching tools. When students can help create and evaluate an intellectual environment that potentially incites professional revelation to occur, the aim of this work is to see them carry this intellectual excitement and rigor into their own classrooms and professional practice. Speculative analysis is used to examine a variety of elements that can be involved in creating classroom environments in which insightful teaching is released. Revelatory processes, epistemological dynamics and ontological approaches are also discussed. A deliberative instructional critique is evoked so that teaching in this manner will be one that is transcendent (Phenix, 1971); it is one that can be intentionally laden and imbued with metacognitive strength, with greater awareness about what one is doing, and with enhanced reflective sensitivity. Therefore, conceptual understanding about a pedagogy that invites and incites insight is formed, along with an examination of certain criteria that are attendant *upon the* success of such teaching.

The author believes that the significance of this topic rests upon its being one of the main centers of the nature of inquiry. By examining this form of inquiry-posing instruction, the practice of helping students attain greater discernment becomes not only more palpable, but it also embraces and embodies a practice involving a hunger for discernment, a passion for learning, and a great cognitive joy amidst the labor for meaning. This inquiry further centers itself amidst the heart of the foundations of education, educational studies and educational policy studies (Council of Learned Societies in Education, 1998). Such a double-edged sharpness, when wielded masterfully and clearly modeled by an instructor with students, grants one the cognitive ability and aesthetic wherewithal in making mature intellectual structures in which students can best thrive, as well as vitalizing the teaching and learning process complementary to creative awareness and imaginative thinking.

Note

1. The following definition of the word incite is taken from Gove (1986, p. 1142). The author believes that the denotative force behind the concept of incite being described below provides an excellent pedagogically symbolic field from which action can be taken to help motivate students in fully engaging the process of self–awareness/reflection and concomitant engagement with educational theories and practices.

*incite[MF *inciter*, fr. L *incitare*, fr. *in-* in- + *citare* to put in movement, summon — more at CITE]

1 to move to a course of action; stir up; spur on; urge on
    2 to bring into being; induce to exist or occur

syninstigate; foment; abet

INCITE may also indicate both an initiating, a calling into being or action, and also a degree of prompting, furthering, encouraging, or nurturing of activity

INSTIGATE implies initiating or encouraging others to initiate actions or feelings, often questionable actions initiated with dubious intention

FOMENT indicates persistent inciting, esp. of something thought of as seething or boiling

ABET is likely to indicate seconding, encouraging, or aiding some action already begun, esp. a questionable activity

References

Apple, M. (1982). *Education and power*. New York: Routledge & Kegan Paul.

————. (1989). Regulating the text: The socio/historical roots of state control. *Educational Policy*, 3, pp. 107–123.

————. (1990a). The politics of pedagogy and the building of community. *Journal of Curriculum Theorizing*, 8 (4), pp. 7–22.

———. (1990b). *Ideology and curriculum* (2nd Ed.). New York: Routledge & Kegan Paul.

Camus, A. (1955). *The myth of Sisyphus*. [Trans. J. O'Brien]. New York: Alfred A. Knopf.

———. (1978). *The rebel*. [Trans. A. Bower]. New York: Alfred A. Knopf.

Carreiro, K. (1991). A philosophical inquiry into critico–creative teaching: Toward an informed pedagogy. (Doctoral dissertation, Harvard University, 1992). University Microfilms Inc., 92–19, 106.

———. (1998). Guiding students in the research writing process. In J. A. Chambers (Ed.), *Selected papers from the 9th International Conference on College Teaching and Learning* (25–32). Jacksonville, FL: Center for the Advancement of Teaching and Learning, Florida Community College-Jacksonville.

———. (1999a). *An opportunity to reconceptualize teacher preparation programs by infusing a liberal arts and educational foundations strand into the core curriculum.* Paper presented at annual meeting of North Carolina Association of Research in Education. Greensboro, NC: University of North Carolina-Greensboro.

———. (1999b). Beyond thinking: A glimpse into revelatory teaching. *Journal of Philosophy and History of Education*, Volume 49, pp. 32–37.

———. (2000). Add one part professor, another part phenomenology, mix well into an educational pan of philosophy, *Journal of Philosophy and History of Education*, v. 50.

Council of Learned Societies in Education. (1998). *Standards for academic and professional instruction in foundations of education, educational studies, and educational policy studies.* San Francisco, CA: Caddo Gap Press.

Dewey, J. (1959). *Dewey on education: Selections.* [Edited by M. Dworkin]. New York: Teachers College Press.

———. (1916/1966). *Democracy and education.* New York: The Free Press.

Doll, W.E. (1993). *A post-modern perspective on curriculum.* New York: Teachers College Press.

Eisner, E. W. (1991). *The enlightened eye: Qualitative inquiry and the enhancement of educational practice.* New York: Macmillan.

———. (1976). Metacognitive aspects of problem solving. In L. Resnick (Ed.), *The nature of intelligence.* Hillsdale, NJ: Erlbaum.

Flavell, John. (1985). *Cognitive development* (2ⁿᵈ ed.). Engelwood Cliffs, NJ: Prentice–Hall.

Fuller, R. B. (1972). *Utopia or oblivion: The prospects for humanity.* New York: Bantam Books, Inc.

———. (1988). *Teachers as intellectuals: Toward a critical pedagogy of learning.* South Hadley, MA: Bergin & Garvey.

Giroux, H.A. (1992). *Educational leadership and the crisis of democratic culture.* University Park, PA: Pennsylvania State University, University Council of Educational Administration (UCEA).

Gove, P.B. (Ed. In Chief). (1965). *Webster's third new international dictionary of the English language unabridged.* Springfield, MA: Merriam-Webster Inc., Publishers.

Greene, M. (1978). *Landscapes of learning.* New York: Teachers College Press.

———. (1988). *The dialectic of freedom.* New York: Teachers College Press.

———. (1991). Blue guitars and the search for curriculum. In G. Willis & W. Schubert (Eds.), *Reflections from the heart of educational inquiry: Understanding curriculum and teaching through the arts* (pp. 107–122). Albany, NY: State University of New York Press.

Grumet, M. (1976). Existential and phenomenological foundations. In W. Pinar & M. Grumet, *Toward a poor curriculum* (pp. 31–50). Dubuque, IA: Kendall/Hunt.

———. (1988). *Bitter milk: Women and teaching.* Amherst, MA: University of Massachusetts Press.

———. (1990). Retrospective: Autobiography and the analysis of educational experience. *Cambridge Journal of Education,* 20 (3), pp. 321–326.

———. (1992). Existential and phenomenological foundations of autobiographical method. In W. Pinar & W. Reynolds, *Understanding curriculum as phenomenologi-*

cal and deconstructed text (pp. 28–43). New York: Teachers College Press.

Kierkegaard, Soren Aabye. (1944). *Attack on "Christendom."* Princeton, NJ: Princeton University Press.

———. (1954). *Fear and trembling, and the sickness unto death.* [Trans W. Lowrie]. Princeton, NJ: Princeton University Press.

Lee, Pei-ling Hsieh. (1998, March). *Integrating concept mapping and metacognitive methods in a hypermedia environment for learning science.* UMI Proquest Digital Dissertations, AAT 9808479.

Madden, D., & Lawrence, D. (1994). *An examination of college writing skills: Have they deteriorated?* (ERIC Document Reproduction Service No. ED 364 909)

McClaren, P. (1991a). Decentering culture: Postmodernism, resistance, and critical pedagogy. In N. Wyner (Ed.), *Current perspectives on the culture of schools* (pp. 231–257). Boston, MA: Brookline Books.

———. (1991b). Critical pedagogy: Constructing an arch of social dreaming and a doorway to hope. *Journal of Education*, 173 (1), pp. 9–34.

———. (1993). Border disputes: Multicultural narrative, identity formation, and critical pedagogy in postmodern America. In D. McLaughlin & W. Tierny (Eds.), *Naming silenced lives: Personal narratives and the process of educational change* (pp. 201–235). New York: Routledge.

———. (1994). *Life in schools: An introduction to critical pedagogy in the foundations of education.* [2nd edition]. New York: Longman.

Noddings, N. (1985). In search of the feminine. *Teachers College Record*, 87 (2), pp. 195–204.

———. (1986). Fidelity in teaching, teacher education, and research for teaching. *Harvard Educational Review*, 56 (4), pp. 496–510.

———. (1992). *The challange to care in the schools: An alternative approach to education.* New York: Teachers College Press.

Oliver, D.W., & Gershman, K. (1989). *Education, modernity and fractured meaning: Toward a process theory of teaching and learning.* Albany, New York: State University of New York Press.

Phenix, P.H. (1964). *Realms of meaning: A philosophy of the curriculum for general education*. New York: McGraw-Hill.

———. (1971). Transcendence and the curriculum. *Teachers College Record*, 73 (2), pp. 271–283.

Pinar, W.F. (1988). Autobiography and the architecture of self. *Journal of Curriculum Theorizing*, 8 (1), pp. 7–36.

———. (1989, January/February). A reconceptualization of teacher education. *Journal of Teacher Education*, pp. 9–12.

———. (1992). Cries and whispers. In W. Pinar & W. Reynolds (Eds.), *Understanding curriculum as phenomenological and deconstructed text* (pp. 92–101). New York: Teachers College Press.

Sartre, Jean-Paul. (1947). *Existentialism and human emotions*. [Trans. H. Barnes]. New York: Philosophical Library.

———. (1956). *Being and nothingness*. [Trans. H. Barnes]. New York: Philosophical Library.

———. (1976). *Critique of dialectical reason*. [Trans. A Sheridan-Smith]. New York: Schocken Books.

Schwab, J. (1978). *Science, curriculum and liberal education: Selected essays, Joseph J. Schwab*. [Edited I. Westbury & N. Wilkof]. Chicago, IL: University of Chicago Press.

———. (1983). The practical 4: Something for curriculum professors to do. *Curriculum Inquiry*, 13, pp. 239–266.

Slattery, P. (1989). *Toward an eschatological curriculum theory*. Baton Rouge, Louisana: Louisiana State University, Department of Curriculum and Instruction, unpublished Ph.D. dissertation.

———. (1992a). Toward an eschatological curriculum theory. *Journal of Curriculum Theory*, 9 (3), pp. 7–22.

———. (1992b). *Liberation theology and postmodern pedagogy: Lessons from the debate between Gustavo Gutierrez and the Vatican Congregation for the Doctrine of the Faith.* Paper presented to the Bergamo Conference on Curriculum Theory and Classroom Practice, Dayton, Ohio.

Taylor, Charles. (1992). *Multiculturalism and the politics of recognition.* Princeton, NJ: Princeton University Press.

Thelen, H. (1960). *Education and the human quest.* New York: Harper & Row.

Vygotsky, L. (1962/1934). *Thought and language.* [Edited & trans. E. Hanfamann & G. Vakar]. New York & London, England: MIT Press & John Wiley.

Walkerdine, V. (1985). Science and the female mind: The burden of proof. *PsychCritique*, 1 (1), pp. 1–20.

———. (1988). *The mastery of reason.* London, England: Routledge & Kegan Paul.

Whitehead, A.N. (1929/1967). *The aims of education.* New York: Free Press.

———. (1933). *Adventures of ideas.* New York: Macmillan.

Chapter Twenty

Where Identity Meets Knowledge: The Future of Educational Studies

George W. Noblit
Beth Hatt-Echeverria
Sherick A. Hughes

The previous chapters provided a "grounded" view of educational studies as it is practiced today. The aim of this concluding chapter is to contextualize the present work within the history and futures of educational studies, especially in the various "origins" or "moves" the field has experienced. In educational studies in the United States, change is ubiquitous, but these changes in many ways play out the dilemmas, paradoxes, contradictions, and oppositions, or combinations of these factors, that have characterized the field from its origins. The chapters in this volume are quite different from the studies that typified educational studies just some 30 years ago but there are continuities in the contradictions present in American educational studies (Pink & Noblit, 1996).

The "millennial contradiction" of identity versus knowledge was present in the origins of social foundations, the term used to characterize the field before it became an independent association of scholars. In the early history of social foundations, claims to objective disciplinary knowledge were used to legitimate education within the academy and also to bolster the status of a group of scholars who were decidedly normative. This contradiction is reproduced in the history of both social foundations and AESA. It was a key element in our claims to be a field of knowledge early in the twentieth century and in the founding of AESA in the late 1960s. Those of us who are active in the field today experience the contradiction personally. The older generation feels rejected and perceives rigor to have declined with the new focus on identity. The younger generation feels they and their work are not respected and rejects the discipline knowledge of the older generation. In oppositional language, it is a struggle for primacy of the disciplines or identities. Yet we see both as manifestations of the "millennial contradiction." Both generations have been, and are, concerned about where identity meets knowledge. While the younger generation will win (time is on their side), we think it is important to understand that the contradiction has been continuous in the field.

In this chapter, we will try to historically contextualize where identity meets knowledge in the early years of the social foundations, in the later origins of AESA, and how we are experiencing it today. This contextualization is meant to signal the inclusive nature of AESA, the multiplicity that characterizes us, and how knowledge is now personal in ways it once was not.

The Contested History of Social Foundations

> The story would be clearer, its lessons more explicit, if the history of the social foundations could be charted linearly. But the field has not moved progressively from here to there. Its steps have been more circuitous than straight, often inconsistent with plans, occasionally shortsighted, if not politically inept, and sometimes reactionary. (Warren, 1998, p. 124)

Social foundations has changed since its origins at Teachers College, Columbia University. It changed as it moved to the University of Illinois and to other institutions. The history is one in which disciplinarity appears and reappears and is connected to legitimating the scholarly identity of social foundations faculty. Our claims to be intellectuals were (and are) based in possibly contradictory claims of disciplinary rigor and educational relevance. Early social foundation scholars were pushed to be practical by teacher educators and theoretically sound by the disciplines they invoked into education. This commitment to both intellectuals and practitioners resulted in a tension about what is valuable work and how work should be conducted. This tension revolved around "what is perceived to be anti intellectualism in teacher education and very real elitism within academia" (Warren, 1998, p. 124). No consensus was forthcoming concerning whether the purpose of social foundations was to enhance practice or academic rigor within education. Thus the field shifted between a focus on separate disciplines and a more interdisciplinary approach. In its origins, the disciplines reigned.

The field can be said to have passed through several stages of development that also mark changes in teacher education in general. In the Teacher of Teachers, published in 1952, Harold Rugg divided the evolution of modern professional teacher education into two main periods, each of which was characterized by marked different types of foundational studies. What he called the "First Draft," lasting from about 1890 to 1920, was typified by course work in the separate foundational disciplines, such as philosophy of education, history of education, educational psychology, and sociology of education, among others. This instruction was suited to training teachers to take their places as preservers of the social order and was based on the work of Butler, Monroe, Strayer, Thorndike, and others. Instead of encouraging the future educator to be a critical student of civilization, foundations textbooks in these separate disciplines sought to instill—or at least did not question—conformity to conservative social and political norms (Tozer & Mcaninch, 1987, p. 13-14).

It is this reading of the disciplines that the current "identity" generation of scholars react against. They understand that in this reading of social foundations they are to be subsumed. As McClelland and Bernier (1993, p. 58) explain:

> In the "distinct institutional history" of the social foundations at Teachers College Columbia, American "culture" was taken for granted to be the culture of the dominant group; indeed, it was axiomatic that one of the central roles of schooling in the United States was to assimilate all students into the dominant culture. Similarly, the society's "educational ideas and practices" referred generally only to the formal educational systems, or schooling.

Or as Rugg (1931, p. 4) explained more critically:

> It was a social order marked by two dominant characteristics: first, the desire for things, the tendency to seek individual success through the accumulation of

money and power over men; second, a swiftly accelerating social time-beat and rhythm.

Rugg's comments also underscore that as conservative as the discipline-focused early social foundations were, there was still little consensus on what social foundations was and what it stood for. There was both an ambiguity about the term and conflicts about both ideas and political activism that has continued to today (Gallegos, 1998; Tozer, 1993; Warren, 1998). Indeed, social foundations became more interdisciplinary and critical over time.

During what Rugg calls the "Second Draft," lasting from about 1920 to 1950, scholars developed a more critical social orientation and a more creative cross disciplinary approach to the study of the social foundations of education. Rather than keep the various foundational disciplines separate, the programs of the "Second Draft" tended to combine concepts and methodological tools drawn from the social sciences and philosophy in order to form integrated studies of the origins, purposes, and functions of school in society (Tozer & Mcaninch, 1987, p. 14).

The 'second draft' of social foundations was being written in a new social context as well. As Johanningmeier (1991, p. 29) recounts:

> The foundations of social foundations were laid before World War II. Those who laid them were rightfully and understandably focusing on the transition of American society from an agrarian to an industrial society and on what some believed was the collapse of democratic capitalism.

This crisis meant that foundations scholars were no longer able to sustain their faith in the disciplines or in the social conservativism that characterized the origins of social foundations. The critical orientation that emerged was part of the social reconstructivism of the 1930s and rejected the value neutral conceptions of the academic disciplines:

> The limitations of the social sciences in the sphere of action, when divorced from all value-judgements, have been fully demonstrated. These disciplines provide neither the American people nor American statesmen with positive and definitive guidance in the realm of practical affairs. They give no direction; they make no ethical or aesthetic choices. In the presence of the perpetual battle

of conflicting interests and values, they cultivate neutrality, striving to report the social situation in terms of objective truth. (Counts, 1934, p. 3)

The cross-disciplinary and critical focus was short lived, undercut by another societal crisis: World War II. Johanningmeier (1991, p. 30) accounts for this short life: "Social reconstructionism, it may be recalled, was a response to a social-economic crisis that developed before World War II, before the emphasis on the disciplines, and before the advent of the post-industrial society." As with many wars, this critique was seen as opposed to nationalism and patriotism. This perception applied both to critiques of society and traditional knowledge bases. The postwar period was even more conservative as the country pulled women out of the workforce and struggled to create a nonwar economy. Again critique was more than out of fashion; it was actively suppressed as part of the campaign against Communism. In the language of the time, it was un-American. Social foundations again shifted its approach:

The field of foundations changed dramatically starting about the mid-1950's, a time when the major producers of foundations specialists began to emphasize the importance of the academic disciplines in the study of education. To some extent, this shift came about as a result of a growing realization that the exhortational style of the older approach to foundations was simply not very effective. To some extent, the change was a defensive reaction on the part of foundations people whose academic respectability on university campuses had always been marginal. (Lyons, 1976, p. 144)

The discourse over social foundations through midcentury was, and is, often characterized by disagreements over language, meaning, and appropriate use of social foundations as a metaphor. Social foundations has changed over time but is an idea in which disciplinarity appears and reappears. While social foundations may not be actually foundational to education (Soltis, 1990), it is remarkable that the academic disciplines have historically been foundational to social foundations. Our predecessors returned to them again and again to reestablish their position in the university and profession of education. Indeed, this was part of the reason for a new term and a new association to be created in the late 1960s;

Educational studies, it was hoped, would escape some of the history of the social foundations.

Nonetheless, our argument is that we may rethink what the meaning of the disciplines was in the social foundations. When we examine this history, the newer generation will see the disciplines as the center of foundations scholarship. However, it seems evident to us that social foundations was reactive. It changed to fit within historical circumstances rather than asserting a position and weathering the waxing and waning of historical and cultural contexts. Social foundations scholars were not asserting the disciplines regardless of circumstances. Their allegiance to the disciplines wavered over time. Foundations scholars were engaged in identity politics from the origins of the field. While they were surely concerned with developing a better understanding of education and society, they were as concerned, at a minimum, with their identities as academics and educators. Foundational scholars had to have this dual loyalty. Their fields of study were within education programs and, like educational psychology, they were part of educational programs' claim to be a legitimate part of college and university curricula.

The disciplinary focus was key to this legitimacy claim. Nevertheless, this same claim established our predecessors as outside the arts and sciences departments that were being formed during the same time period to institutionalize the disciplines. Our predecessors were betwixt and between. Their identities were challenged on both sides. Educators saw them as not being central to the training of teachers, understood as an exceedingly practical endeavor, and social scientists and humanists saw them as not being true academics, given their normative concerns with both training teachers and reconstructing the social order.

In ways difficult to understand today, these white, privileged, and largely male intellectuals were as concerned about their identities as the younger educational studies scholars of today. For them, however, identity construction moved between the polls of the disciplines and cross-disciplinary activism. Identity met knowledge in very specific ways in the field of social foundations. Their intellectual identity met academic knowledge to both claim and disclaim that they had something significant to offer from both their location within the disciplines and also peripheral to the disciplines.

Yet with all the rancor and disagreement that marked the history of social foundations, there seems to be some consensus on what held social foundations together during the late 1960s, if not from its very beginning: a concern over equality and the establishment of an independent association, the American Education Studies Association (Johanningmeier, 1991). The white males of social foundations did not experience the identity politics of women and people of color, but those who were interdisciplinary and normative were actively promoting civil rights by the 1960s.

AESA in the History of Social Foundations

While AESA did not, and does not, encompass all of what was considered social foundations or even educational studies, it does allow us to discern how the way "identity met knowledge" was, and is, changing. Thus, we use AESA primarily to ground our perspective on the history of social foundations. AESA characterizes itself:

> AESA is a society primarily comprised of college and university professors who teach and research in the field of education utilizing one or more of the liberal arts disciplines of philosophy, history, politics, sociology, anthropology, or economics as well as comparative/international studies. As with all members of academe, keeping current with research publications in one's discipline is on ongoing responsibility of critical importance to the members of AESA. AESA currently has over 600 members. (http://ericir.syr.edu/AESA/aesa.html) (9/8/2000)

AESA was founded by social foundations scholars moving away from disciplinarity and towards interdisciplinarity. The complexity of education had made the boundaries of anthropology, history, philosophy, and sociology of education more a liability than asset. The American Educational Studies Association was created to allow the boundaries to be expanded.

> You may recall that a primary purpose in founding AESA was to bring together scholars in the various academic disciplines and professional specializations which offer educational insight: anthropology, economics, history, politics, sociology, psychology, philosophy, curriculum development, and the administrative sciences. Generally, though not exclusively, AESA has appealed

to scholars affiliated with those departments in schools of education which are or once were called "foundations of education." The feeling was, in 1968 when the AESA was founded, that scholars interested in educational issues had forgotten what they had as common concerns, and indeed had stopped speaking to one another. Rather than working toward the establishment of a viable interdisciplinary study of education, scholars in education, by 1968, tended to identify with single disciplinary paradigms. (Lyons, 1976, p. 143)

AESA was a child of the 1960s, the heady days of supposed insurrection and social movements: the Youth Movement, the Women's Movement, and the Civil Rights Movement. The organization adopted the mission and vision to explore education, "as it organizes consciousness, defines and/or reflects authority and power, empowers individuals and groups, and otherwise transmits culture from one generation to the next" (Finkelstein & Jones, 1983, p. 3). AESA also provided an organizational, associative home for interdisciplinarity and multiplicity. It provided a new ground for identities as scholars—educational studies scholars could travel between and over the disciplines. The new association legitimated our "interpretive, critical, and normative approaches" (Finkelstein & Jones, 1983, p. 5). AESA's commitment to equity and social justice made it an organization of interdisciplinary white male scholars who, while committed to equity, also implicitly believed that equality would bring new people into the fold, but not change the fold all that much. The commitment to equality may have been rhetorical, but AESA soon became a scene for the struggle for equality. First, women had their impact.

On occasion, the social foundations has been unintentionally prophetic, if not downright timid. Witness the slow, hesitant welcome it extended to women's studies. Worth exploring are the reasons women and feminist scholars wanted admission to the social foundations, although there is little mystery about their basic aims. They meant to insist that attention be paid to the historic roles of women in education and to the policy environmental effects on schools of women's dominance of professional practice (e.g. on schools' budgets, salaries, and social status). Occupants of the social foundations clubhouse, almost exclusively men, tended to greet their knocks by running for cover, while the self-elected new colleagues battered down the door and then proceeded not only to

> rearrange the intellectual furniture but also to reconfigure the walls. (Warren,
> 1998, p. 128)

AESA learned that knowledge is even more political and more personal than many thought during those early years. Yet the initial meetings of AESA showed that being interdisciplinary was not sufficient. The disciplines, even put together, were unable to conceptualize the fundamental work of students and even scholars:

> It is my contention that the process of becoming somebody is relational and that the relational aspects of this production cannot be understood outside the boundaries of broader narratives regarding race, gender, and sexuality. (Weis, 1993, pp. 3–4)

First, the disciplines, individually and collectively, were exclusive, especially of women and people of color. More perspectives were needed to counteract the cultural and political limitations of the disciplines, even when spreading across their boundaries. Second, the collection of the social foundation disciplines, it soon became apparent, were all engaging in "normal science" (Kuhn, 1970). The ideas being explored were pedestrian, the implications were mundane. The challenges of race and gender equity, of qualitative methods and of postmodernism, required new paradigms, new modes of scholarship in education. AESA became one of the places where these new paradigms could be explored, in part because it was without an institutional history to defend and in part because it was a rather inclusive organization.

Scholars began to do different work at AESA. Equity became a passion, theory a chimera, identity a necessity, and disciplinary thought a limitation. These developments were wrought in struggle. As soon as equity found a united legal basis, it began to be dismantled (Orfield & Eaton, 1996). As legal segregation waned, identity born of exclusion needed new substantiation, without essentializing difference(s). Theory established the possibilities of emancipation just as education was being positioned to serve global capitalist interests (Gabbard, 1999). In all this, anthropology, history, philosophy, and sociology of education came to be seen not as traditions to be advanced but as tools to be appropriated. Qualitative research methods became the approach of choice for both local (Geertz, 1983) and transformational (Kincheloe & McLaren, 1994) knowledge. The "blurred genres" (Geertz, 1973) became multidisciplinary and then antidisciplinary as educational studies realized the limits of its subdisciplines.

In the 1990s, a backlash brought educational studies firmly into the cultural wars. An oratorical reassertion of the value of tradition included the disciplines found only a century earlier, and tried to orient educational studies once again toward the normal science of the disciplines (Kimball, 1986). The backlash had a partial success but has also spawned substantive development within educational studies.

Our early attempts at inclusion presumed an assimilation that was not. As AESA became more diverse in gender, race, sexual orientation and age we found ourselves forgetting part of our history. The older generation retreated to the disciplines when the intellectual work at AESA took a turn towards emphasizing identity. This exacerbated the misunderstandings taking place in that the language of disciplines is impersonal and thus was seen by the newer generation as an attack on themselves as well as their work. Many older members retreated from the organization, convinced that the intellectual work was no longer rigorous.

The newer generation also changed its stance vis-à-vis the organization. AESA had been an inviting place to develop their voices, positions and substance when compared to other venues (especially the American Educational Research Association), but it was now a dangerous scene, and conflict within AESA was more apparent. The irony is that the older generation was replicating the history of social foundations by retreating to the disciplines and doing so to reinscribe their identities. The younger, more diverse generation of scholars, of course, are engaging in their own identity politics, which in part sees the disciplines as agents of oppression. Taken together, the identity constructions of both generations constitute the "millennial contradiction" of educational studies.

The Millennial Contradiction

The moment poses great possibilities as well as challenges for those of us working in the field of Education. For the subaltern scholar, however, the lega-

cies of colonialism have left a crisis of location. For, at the moment of articulation, contradictory narratives that both remove and inhabit the
writer/scholar/teacher must be framed within a dominant Western academic
discourse that most often remains situated in colonial relations of power
(Prakash 1994). Locating ourselves outside of this knowledge/power field is no
easy task for we must piece together narratives from vestiges of insurgent and
sometimes even illegal memories and frame them in a discourse which we are
ultimately attempting to deconstruct. (Gallegos, 1998, p. 239)

One aspect of the "millennial contradiction" of American educational studies is that the current conflict misspecifies an opposition. As
we have argued, before social foundations and educational studies became more diverse, the disciplines were a source of identity for the white
males. Whenever the social context challenged foundations scholars,
they used the disciplines as the source of their status as well as knowledge. This is identity politics as we talk about it now, but clearly it is different from how it is currently being articulated.

Identity was conceived as dependent on disciplinary claims, but now
identity is no longer dependent in the same way. Identity has been centered. The disciplines are but suspect tools for identity construction and
politics. These suspect tools are to help the scholars who have been historically excluded from the academy (as well as their peoples) position
themselves in a place of power that does not exclude them from their
peoples. The "centering of identity" marks the transition from having
disciplinary or interdisciplinary knowledge at the center and our identities being dependent on that center to having our identities in the center
and discipline knowledge being in service to that center.[1] This shift has
only recently been possible in educational studies:

> As I look around this room tonight, I see a very different AESA from of several
> years ago when I could easily count the persons who were not of European an-
> cestry. I also recognize that there are others of you working to diversify the or-
> ganization and I both appreciate and commend your efforts, for different bodies
> bring different stories sometimes located outside of the discourses which tradi-
> tionally dominate professional organizations. (Gallegos, 1998, p. 232)

We suggest this change has marked not only a shift in the encounter
between identity and knowledge, but also a change in the construction of

the encounter itself. The "centering of identity" changes the encounter so that it escapes the origins of social foundations and now stands as a moment in itself. However, "centering identity," like all forms of centering, constructs "others."

In educational studies, we now have "othered" our origins. We have essentialized those origins and, in doing so, "forgotten" the uncertainty, the tentativeness, the contestation that has always marked social foundations, AESA, and educational studies. This "forgetting" is problematic because it reifies our new construction of where identity encounters knowledge. This encounter, we argue, is always a contradiction. When we think we have won a new position, a new conjunction, we ignore the genealogy of conceptions and claim a novelty that does not exist (Foucault, 1972).

The millennial contradiction, then, is multiple and complex. Identity and disciplinary knowledge are not opposed but related, both in the past and present. Nevertheless we experience them as an opposition and act as if the opposition is real. What has changed is the dependent entity in the relationship, but, as Gallegos notes above, even when identity is asserted it cannot escape the silencing already historically accomplished by the disciplines. Identity has constituted itself in part using disciplinary knowledge. What the older generation of scholars does not see is how demanding the centering of identity is, intellectually and personally. This work is rigorous beyond what was ever to be expected by the disciplines.

The futures of educational studies should not be thought as the natural consequences of our new understanding, but rather the play of dilemma and contradiction. As Warren has argued, we should not attempt to resolve the contradictions that are us but rather accept them as a sign of our vibrancy:

> My aim in rehearsing these familiar developments is to underscore a contextual point. The lack of consensus about the definition and purpose of the social foundations of education and its troubled relations with other teacher education faculty and programs hardly make it unusual or unhealthy. On the contrary, the conditions are both ordinary and exciting, particularly to those who find inquiry and new knowledge wondrous. They are also fragile, if the experience of faculty in other fields can be taken as instructive. Witness the weakening effects of imposed orthodoxies within sociology, political science, and philosophy de-

partments in recent years. Given the unsettling accumulation of new knowledge, the present seems to be an inappropriate time—perhaps even an educationally dangerous time—to push for consensus within the social foundations. Relative to our scholarly agenda, one could argue that we need greater diversity of methods, perspectives, and research questions, not less. (Warren, 1993, pp. 36–37)

We may not have all participated in the full history of educational studies, but it is nonetheless hard to escape. As we reject disciplinarity, we also reject a basis of legitimation for identity. That is, the centering of identity does not eliminate disciplinarity or even interdisciplinarity but rather reinscribes it. The encounter is redefined, but remains. This is the "millennial contradiction" that the authors in this book are working through. Their work is not that of the old social foundations or even the educational studies of only 10 years ago—the future is in how scholars such as the authors in this book work through the contradiction that is American educational studies for a new millennium.

Note

1. We thank Paula Groves for this conceptualization.

References

American Educational Studies Association web page (2000, September 8). Retrieved September 8, 2000, from http://ericir.syr.edu/AESA/aesa.html

Counts, G. (1934). *The social foundations of education*. New York: Scribner's.

Finkelstein, B., & Jones, A. H. (1983). The American Educational Studies Association: Guardian of the humanities in education, *Journal of Thought*, 18(1) pp. 3–5.

Foucault, M. (1972). *The archeology of knowledge*. New York: Pantheon Books.

Gabbard, D. (Ed.). (1999). *Knowledge and power in the global economy: Politics and the rhetoric of school reform*. Mahwah, NJ: Erlbaum.

Gallegos, B. (1998). Remember the Alamo: Imperialism, memory, and postcolonial educational studies, *Educational Studies*. 29(3) pp. 232–239.

Geertz, C. (1973). *The interpretation of cultures*. New York: Basic Books.

———. (1983). *Local knowledge: Further essays in interpretive anthropology*. New York: Basic Books.

Johanningmeier, E. (1991). Through the disarray of social foundations: Some notes toward a new social foundations, *Educational Foundation*, 5(4) pp. 29–30.

Kimball, B. (1986). *Orators and philosophers: A history of the idea of liberal education*. New York: Teachers College Press.

Kincheloe, J., & McLaren, P. (1994). Rethinking critical theory and qualitative research. In N. Denzin & Y. Lincoln (Eds.). *Handbook of qualitative research* (pp. 138–157). London: Sage.

Kuhn, T. (1970). *The structure of scientific revolutions*. Chicago: University of Chicago Press.

Lyons, C. (1976). Educational policy, educational expertise and the AESA, *Educational Policy*, 7, p. 144.

McClelland, A.E., & Bernier, N.R. (1993). A rejoinder to Steve Tozer's toward a new consensus among social foundations educators, *Educational Foundations*, 7.4, p. 58.

Orfield, G., & Eaton, S. (1996). *Dismantling desegregation: The quiet reversal of Brown v. Board of Education*. New York: New Press.

Pink, W., & Noblit, G. (Eds.). (1996). *Continuity and contradiction: The futures of the sociology of education*. Cresskill, NJ: Hampton Press.

Rugg, H. (1931). *Culture and education in America*. New York: Harcourt, Brace & Company.

Soltis, J. (1990). A reconceptualization of educational foundations, *Teachers College Record*, 91(3).

Tozer, S. (1993). Toward a new consensus among social foundations educators: Draft position paper of the American Educational Studies Association Committee on Academic Standards and Accreditation, *Educational Foundations*, 7(4).

Tozer, S., & Mcaninch, S. (1987). Four texts in social foundations of education in historical perspective, *Educational Studies*, 18(1), pp. 13–14.

Warren, D. (1998). From there to where: The social foundations of education in transit Again, *Educational Studies*, 29(2), pp. 124–128.

———. (1993). A wake-up call to the social foundation of education, *Educational Foundations*, 7(4) pp. 36–37.

Weis, L. (1993). At the intersection of silencing and voice: Discursive constructions in school, *Educational Studies*, 24, pp. 3–4.

Contributors

Mary Abascal-Hildebrand teaches community and organization development from a perspective that combines philosophy and anthropology, for a philosophic anthropology also known in some circles as personalism, after the influence of the French philosopher Emmanuel Mounier. Her work focuses on hermeneutic theory, especially as it is linked with critical theory, for a critical hermeneutics. Her research and publications focus on applications in workplace democracy, diversity topics, democratic economics, negotiation and conflict resolution, and urban issues. She teaches at the University of San Francisco.

Lanese Kwegyir Aggrey is a Ph.D. candidate at the University of Iowa. Her program is social foundations of education, part of the planning, policy and leadership department in the College of Education. Her primary area of interests are race, diversity and culture as it relates to higher education, particularly in the areas of multicultural education and teacher education programs. She is a Holmes Scholar.

Magnus O. Bassey is associate professor of social and philosophical foundations of education in the Department of Secondary Education and Youth Services at Queens College, The City University of New York. He has published two books and several articles in reputable academic journals, including *Educational Foundations*, *The Educational Forum*, *The Journal of Negro Education* and *The Western Journal of Black Studies*. His research interest centers on the effects of poverty on students' academic achievement.

Bryan McKinley Jones Brayboy is an assistant professor in the Department of Education, Culture, and Society and the ethnic studies program at the University of Utah. An enrolled member of the Lumbee-Cheraw tribe, his primary research interests are American Indians in higher education. He is currently involved in a longitudinal project that examines the experiences of American Indian ivy league graduates. His work incorporates anthropology of education with critical race theory.

A. Keith Carreiro is an assistant professor in the Department of Professional Studies in Education at Indiana University of Pennsylvania, Indiana, Pennsylvania. His research and teaching are concentrated in the realm of educational foundations, specifically in the philosophical and sociocultural fields of study in education. His research examines paradigmatic considerations relating to reflection, reasoning, inquiry, critical thinking, teaching effectiveness, performance, clinical teaching intervention strategies, and creativity throughout educational practice of diverse learning, research, and working environments. He is currently writing about the soul of teaching and the nature of revelatory learning.

Clinton Collins has taught philosophy of education at the University of Kentucky for 35 years. He received the Ph.D. from Indiana University, studying with the beloved Philip G. Smith. His wife retired as a professor of art education. He and his wife have three children and two recent granddaughters. His philosophical interests include ethics and the history of educational thought.

David M. Dees is an assistant professor of education at Gannon University. His scholarly presentations and publications have focused on the educational issues associated with aesthetic/artistic classroom experiences. He is currently examining the curricular and pedagogical possibilities for teacher education that arise from the teacher-as-artist perspective. Dr. Dees was recently awarded the 2000 Outstanding Teaching Award at Kent State University for his classroom efforts.

Beth Hatt-Echeverria is a doctoral candidate in the University of North Carolina at Chapel Hill's school of education. Her research focuses upon issues of social justice within education. Incarcerated youth, discipline within schools/society, and qualitative research are her primary interests. She has worked with incarcerated youth for the past three years while also working on projects relating to charter schools, school reform, and kindergarten readiness. She was a 2001–2002 AERA Spencer fellow.

Sherick A. Hughes, M.A., M.P.A, currently studies race, culture and education policy as a Ph.D. candidate at the University of North Carolina at Chapel Hill. Hughes is acknowledged for his research contributions on *Eliminating the Black/White Achievement Gap: A First in America Special Report June 2001*. He has a forthcoming article in *The High School Journal* concerning the estimated costs and benefits of a precollege program and its impact on Black high school graduates. Most recently, his research involves racial identity, agency, and perceptions of schooling during the aftermath of desegregation.

David Levine is an assistant professor of education at the University of North Carolina at Chapel Hill, where he teaches courses on American educational history and the contexts of contemporary schooling. He is an editorial associate of Rethinking Schools. His current research is on the role of radical pedagogy in the civil rights movement.

Huey-li Li is associate professor of philosophy of education at the University of Akron. Her research focuses on ethical foundations of environmental education, ecofeminism, and multicultural education. She is working on a manuscript regarding the ecological landscape of education in the age of globalization.

George W. Noblit is a professor and chair of the graduate studies division in the School of Education at the University of North Carolina at Chapel Hill. He specializes in critical race studies, the sociology of knowledge, anthropology of education, and qualitative research methods. His 1996 book, *The Social Construction of Virtue: The Moral Life of Schools* (SUNY), was selected for a Critic's Choice Award of the American Educational Studies Association, and he recently published a set of studies covering his career, *Particularities: Collected Essays on Ethnography of Education* (Peter Lang, 1999). He won the Dina Fietelson Outstanding Research award from the International Reading Association in 2000. Dr. Noblit is the editor of *The High School Journal* and co-editor of *The Urban Review* and a book series with Hampton Press, *Understanding Education and Policy*. He was the 2000–2001 president of the American Educational Studies Association.

Hye-Kyeong Pae is post-doctor associate at Georgia State University and teaches at Georgia Perimeter College. She received her Ph.D. degree from Georgia State University. Her general research interests lie in the interdisciplinary studies in education and mass communication, such as media literacy, cultural hegemony, and gender equity in the education and mass media realms. More recent interests include intercultural communication in relation to linguistic, phonological components.

Monte Piliawsky, Ph.D. from Tulane University, is an associate professor in the College of Education at Wayne State University. His more than 30 articles on race and education policy have been published in the *Review of Black Political Economy*, *Black Scholar*, *Reconstruction*, *Phylon*, and *Western Journal of Black Studies*. Piliawsky is the author of *Exit 13: Oppression and Racism in Academia* (South End Press). He has presented 50 papers at professional conferences. Presently, he directs an after school tutoring program for ninth grade students at a high school in Detroit. Piliawsky's current research involves the life cycle political socialization of sixties student activists.

Evelyn Sears, an independent scholar, is a graduate of the University of Iowa. Her research interests are Deweyan pragmatism, the philosophy of science, and school board meetings as sites of democratic citizenship. She has published works on science education, Deweyan epistemology, and democratic education, and is currently researching the teaching of evolutionary theory in American secondary schools.

Lesley Shore teaches philosophical and psychological foundations at OISE (SPELL OUT)/University of Toronto. She was gold medallist in education when she graduated from the University of Manitoba, has taught most grades from K to 13 and is the proud mother of three college students. Her research and teaching interests include: the influence of reading/culture on adolescent female development, girls' education, the life and work of Virginia Woolf, Holocaust education through literature, teacher book clubs, narrative inquiry, and integrated arts education. She is the American Educational Studies Association Book Exhibits coordinator.

Lynda Stone is a professor in philosophy of education and coordinator of the Culture, Curriculum, and Change program at the University of North Carolina at Chapel Hill. She has published internationally and nationally in the fields of philosophy of education and social and feminist theory of education. She is editor of *The Education Feminism Reader* and *Philosophy of Education: 2000* and is currently working on a project writing particular poststructuralist views against Dewey.

Steve Tozer is professor and chair of policy studies in the College of Education at the University of Illinois at Chicago. He received his B.A. degree in German at Dartmouth College, M.Ed. in elementary and early childhood education at Loyola University, and Ph.D. in philosophy of education at the University of Illinois at Urbana-Champaign. His first teaching assignments were in Chicago alternative schools, at the elementary and secondary school levels. After joining the educational policy studies faculty at the University of Illinois Urbana-Champaign in 1982, he served variously as chair of the senate committee on educational policy, chair of the vice chancellor's council on undergraduate education, and, from 1990 to 1994, head of the department of curriculum and instruction. Since moving to UIC in January 1995, Dr. Tozer has been active in school reform at the state level and in Chicago, focusing particularly on supporting the professional preparation and development of teachers. He is the author, co-author, or editor of five books, including a social foundations textbook for teachers, *School and Society*, now in its fourth edition. He has written numerous articles on the role of social foundations of education in teacher preparation programs, and recently served for two years as chair of the governor's council on teacher quality in Illinois.

Mary E. Weems, is a poet, playwright, performer, and activist artist educator committed to urban education reform. She earned her Ph.D. in education at the University of Illinois at Urbana-Champaign. An educational consultant, and widely published as a poet, her publications in education include *Cultural Studies: Critical Methodologies*, *Qualitative Inquiry*, and *xcp: Cultural Poetics*. Her book, *I Speak From the Wound in My Mouth: A Political Act*, is forthcoming from Peter Lang.

Angelique Williams is a professor of psychology at Keiser College and Everglades College in Fort Lauderdale, Florida. She is currently a graduate student, pursuing her Ph.D. degree in health psychology at the Walden University in Minneapolis, Minnesota. She specializes within the health and forensic area. She has written on the etiology of serial killers, antisocial personality disorder, sadism, and the theory of learned helplessness and its effects on society. Her current research involves the Wechsler Adult Intelligence Scale and its cultural and ethnic limitations. Angelique Williams also functions as a volunteer mentor to the children and teenagers within her community to provide guidance (i.e., homework) and mental support in an effort to keep children and adolescents in school and off the street. She was recently accepted into the Psy Chi National Honor Society in psychology and she received an award for her volunteer work at the Hospice Care of Broward County, where she participates as a bereavement counselor at their annual summer camp for children.

John A. Xanthopoulos is associate professor of education at the University of Montana-Western in Dillon, Montana. He has published and presented widely in the fields of social studies, multicultural, and global education. He is co-author of *Global Perspectives for Educators* published by Allyn and Bacon. He is currently in the process of writing a book that explores global issues and ways of solving them from a pedagogical perspective.